Hymns and Initiations

Translated by Thomas Taylor

Published by

The Prometheus Trust

Volume V

of

The Thomas Taylor Series

The Prometheus Trust

194 The Butts, Frome,
Somerset BA11 4AG, UK.

A registered charity,
number 299648.

HYMNS AND INITIATIONS,
published in 1994,
revised edition published 2003.

ISBN 1 898910 04 9

A republication of

The Mystical Hymns of Orpheus (1824)

and extracts from

Mystical Initiations (1787)
Two Orations of the Emperor Julian (1793)
Sallust on the Gods and the World (1793)
Five Books of Plotinus (1794)
The Fable of Cupid and Psyche (1794)
Miscellanies in Prose and Verse (1804)
Collectanea (1806)
and *Neoplatonic Hymns* (Philological Quarterly (1929)

British Library Cataloguing-in-Publication Data.
A catalogue record for this book is
available from the British Library.

Printed in England by Antony Rowe, Chippenham, Wiltshire.

The Prometheus Trust was founded in 1986 in order to help reintroduce to educational establishments those true First Principles which have been the basis of all the world's lasting civilisations. These Principles were given their clearest expression in the West by Plato and those great ones who either provided his grounding in Truth or continued and expanded his beautiful exposition of reality. It is for this reason that the Trust is now making available the whole of the published works of Thomas Taylor, the 'English Platonist', whose philosophical understanding of the principles enshrined in the writings of Plato, Proclus, Plotinus and others is unparalleled in recent times.

The Prometheus Trust would like to thank all those who have contributed to the work involved in the Thomas Taylor Series. We are especially indebted to members of **The Platonic Guild** and would recommend this organisation to all those who wish to make a study of this pure philosophy in order to establish the virtuous life.

The Prometheus Trust is a registered educational charity number 299648. All enquiries should be addressed to: Mr T J Addey, Chairman, The Prometheus Trust, 194 The Butts, Frome, Somerset, BA11 4AG. The Platonic Guild may also be contacted care of the same address.

For the latest information on the Trust and its publishing programme, please visit our website at:

www.prometheustrust.co.uk

CONTENTS

Preface to the Thomas Taylor Series iii

Thomas Taylor v

Introduction To Hymns and Initiations vii

Thomas Taylor's Introduction to The Hymns of Orpheus (2nd ed.) 1

The Mystical Hymns of Orpheus 23

Additional Notes to the Orphic Hymns 160

The Hymns of Thomas Taylor 193

Hymns from the authors of antiquity 257

Introduction to the 1st Edition of the Orphic Hymns (appendix I) 276

A guide to the orders of the Gods (appendix II) 314

Index to the hymns by title 318

Index to the hymns by first line 320

Preface to the Thomas Taylor Series

This series makes available all the writings of Thomas Taylor for the first time since his death in 1835. There are several general purposes for the presentation of this series; these are as follows:

Firstly, Thomas Taylor's translations and original writings represent the most comprehensive philosophical re-expression in the English language of the wisdom of European antiquity. Taylor not only understood the *philosophy* of the Platonic tradition but also revered its *religion*. His works draw upon the fragments which survive from the earliest Orphic and Pythagorean mystery schools, through Plato and Aristotle's pure philosophy, and onwards to the later Platonists who were the final flowering of the Classical civilisation. As such, Taylor's work as a whole, when studied patiently, will awaken the mind to reasonable and intuitive truth.

Secondly, it is obvious that while our educational system and institutions have grown out of the Platonic world-view, the clarity of the original vision has been gravely distorted by materialism. Therefore there is an urgent need for a purging of the damaging false opinions now so prevalent in the very institutions which should be leading enquiring minds to the intelligible beauty. The precision and purity of Thomas Taylor's writings will undoubtedly act as such a purgative.

Thirdly, that as the short-comings of the various so-called philosophies of recent centuries are exposed, a re-appraisal of the ancient philosophy prematurely rejected will need to be made. The reasons for this rejection lie in the pressures of the history of past centuries and millennia: In the fullness of time, no doubt, the exploration of empiricists, materialists and reductionists down the dead-end paths of philosophy will be seen as a dialectical testing of the negation of truth and will thus serve a better end than they themselves could imagine. Nevertheless the immediate philosophical inheritance of the twenty-first century is one that is narrow-minded and barren. A new beginning must be made: the depth and breadth of Taylor's writings (a result of a labour of truly Herculean proportions) make them an ideal foundation for a genuine philosophical education. It is to be devoutly hoped that in the not-too-distant future a system of training will be properly established on the principles expounded by the true philosophers of the ancient West, which complement and confirm the teachings of the East. Such a system will lead to a beholding of the highest truths and, ultimately, to the contemplation of Beauty itself. To those who in the future so labour, this series is especially dedicated.

Fourthly, it was almost certainly the wish of Thomas Taylor that a uniform edition of all his writings be published. After his death, his literary executor and friend, Isaac Preston Cory, arranged that his library should be auctioned by Sothebys and the final lot offered at this auction was that of the copyright of all Taylor's writings: the catalogue, which bears the marks of someone who knew Thomas Taylor well, states "The reason of the entire copy-right of all the works being offered for public competition altogether, is, to enable the purchaser to publish his works in a uniform manner....." The copyright was, unfortunately, never bought and the wish has remained, until now, unfulfilled. This series is, then, a small mark of gratitude for his selfless service to Wisdom and to those who love Wisdom.

Aside from these general purposes there are important academic reasons for the presentation of this series: it is of especial interest because Taylor's was the first complete translation into English of Plato and Aristotle along with the major part of the surviving works of the later Platonists. Taylor himself writes from within the so-called neoPlatonic tradition and this further adds to the academic value of his works. There is at present a revival of interest in the later Platonists, whose texts have become the subject of attention of certain leading authorities in the history of philosophy, to such an extent that all the available texts are being collected together, and critically examined and translated. The texts upon which Taylor worked were even more incomplete and full of errors than those which are now available. Where he came across these difficulties, Taylor rectified errors in the original Greek and filled lacunas in the text by conjecturing what, in his view, should have been there. Modern textual evidence points to the fact that he was very largely correct in these conjectures and this, in turn, bears witness to his profound understanding of the philosophy to which he devoted his life. As an aid to academic studies the series will include line and page numbering, such as Stephanus and Bekker, wherever appropriate. The wording of Taylor's books is kept except where there are obvious errors - all of which will be noted.

THOMAS TAYLOR

Born 15 May 1758, London; died 1 November 1835, London.

THOMAS TAYLOR the Platonist was certainly the most extraordinary and admirable philosophic character of modern times. He was the first English translator of the whole of Plato's works, of the whole of Aristotle, and of the majority of the works of Plotinus, Porphyry, Proclus, Iamblichus and the other later Platonists. In his own age he was the subject of the irrational and barbed criticism of pseudo-intellectual popular critics, who failed to perceive that although they may have known more Greek, Taylor knew more Plato. His intuitive appreciation of both the truth and the grandeur of Platonic thought, coupled with its living day-to-day practice, enabled him to undertake and complete a remarkable body of work. When one inspects such a collection of translations and original works, it seems extraordinary that these were the fruits of one self-taught man, labouring under the triple burdens of ill-health, financial insufficiency, and negative criticism for most of his exceptional life. His translations and commentaries were the chief source of Greek philosophy to the writers and poets of the Romantic movement, including Blake, Shelley and Wordsworth. In America his works provided the firm foundation for the Transcendentalist movement of R W Emerson and Bronson Alcott; his name was held in higher esteem here than ever it enjoyed in his native England. His living espousal of both the intellectual and religious disciplines of the ancient wisdom, coupled with his philosophical observations on the limitations of Christianity, earned him the mocking title of the "English Pagan". No doubt he would have accepted this as just praise. Taylor's motto, written by himself, was:

"No servile scribe am I, nor e'er shall be,
My sire is Mind, whose sons are always free."

His motto is at once both a dedication to the pursuit of Truth, and a rebuttal to his hireling bigoted critics, whose folly he dismisses in these vigorous verses - again, written by himself:

"Vent'rous I tread in paths untrod before,
And depths immense, and dazzling heights explore;
Anxious from Error's night to point the way
That leads to Wisdom's everlasting day;

> To check my flight in vain blind Folly tries,
> For, Heav'n my friend, I conquer as I rise."

Thomas Taylor was not only a scholar of a high order, but also an ardent philosopher in spirit and in energy. His love of wisdom dominated every last element of his life and developed an insight into the esoteric meaning of Greek philosophy that has never been equalled nor approached by any scholar of modern times. There may be 'easier' or more readily accessible translations of the sacred works of the Platonic tradition, but there are none more consistently reliable nor more replete with that profound understanding which comes from elevation of mind and inspiration alone.

Thomas Taylor was in truth "an exile straying from the orb of Light," and his epitaph, written by himself, sums up the dedication and course of his life:

> "Health, strength, and ease, and manhood's active age,
> Freely I gave to Plato's sacred page.
> With Truth's pure joys, with Fame my days were crown'd
> Tho' Fortune adverse on my labours frown'd."[†]

Thomas Taylor dedicated his works to the 'sacred majesty of Truth' - a great and noble cause for a great and noble soul.

[†] The three verses quoted can be found in Thomas Moore-Johnson's *Life of Thomas Taylor* which appeared in the journal *The Platonist*.

HYMNS AND INITIATIONS

INTRODUCTION

By The Prometheus Trust

The hymns and essays presented in this volume are collected from several publications of Thomas Taylor. In 1792 he published a book called *The Hymns of Orpheus* in which an essay on the life and theology of Orpheus was given followed by a section entitled "The Initiations of Orpheus" which presented the eighty-six hymns of Orpheus. Taylor later revised this book and published (in 1824) a second edition entitled *The Mystical Hymns of Orpheus* - the hymns were slightly altered but the introductory essay differed substantially from the earlier work. The main body of this new edition in the Thomas Taylor Series is taken from the 1824 edition. The original essay on Orpheus is also retained as an appendix.

Added to the Orphic Hymns are twenty-six hymns from Proclus, The Emperor Julian, Boethius and Thomas Taylor himself. The hymns of Proclus (To the Sun, To The Muses, To Venus, a second To Venus, and To Minerva) were originally published in *Sallust on the Gods and the World*, as were five of Taylor's own hymns - To Ceres, To Jupiter, To Minerva, To Vesta, and To Mercury ("Hermes I sing, a god supremely bright".) Four more hymns from Taylor appeared in his *Cupid and Psyche* - To Venus, To Love, To Neptune and To The Whole of Intellectual Essence. In *Collectanea* (1806) Taylor published his hymns To the Rising Sun, To the Sun attended by the Powers of the Planetary Spheres and the Four Elements, To Mercury ("Hear, Blessed Hermes, Maia's beauteous son") and the three hymns to the Monads of the Intelligible Triad. In the same work a further hymn believed to be by Proclus - A Common Hymn - was published. Julian's Hymn To The Mother of Gods was published in *Two Orations of the Emperor Julian*, as was Taylor's hymn To Apollo and the Sun. His hymns To Apollo appeared in *Five books of Plotinus* and To The Artificer of the Universe in *Miscellanies*; the Hymn of Boethius is also from here.

In this revised edition of *Hymns and Initiations* we have taken the opportunity to include seven hymns by Taylor which were published in an article by Franklin P Johnson in the Philological Quarterly (1929). The son of the great champion of Platonism in the American Midwest, Thomas Moore-Johnson, Franklin Johnson had in his possession a handwritten notebook inscribed *Hymns and Prayers by Thomas Taylor* which contained eighteen hymns published by Taylor between 1793 and 1806, all of which were in our first edition; but it also included seven unpublished hymns which are undoubtedly genuine. Johnson estimates from various other samples of his handwriting that Taylor had written the notebook around the year 1825.

The footnotes and essays of Taylor in this volume provide an invaluable guide to the choirs, or orders, of the Gods which, together with the hymns of antiquity and of the inspired Taylor, will help the earnest lover of divinity to discover their hidden depths. No greater or more beautiful task awaits the soul than the rediscovery of the Gods who, being profoundly and perfectly united with *The One*, call us ever to the perfective union with *The One and The Good*.

It is the normal condition of man to worship God both as One and as a One-manyness; as Maximus Tyrius wrote: "you will see one according law and assertion in all the earth, that there is one God, the king and father of all things, and many gods, sons of God, ruling together with him. This the Greek says, and the barbarian says, the inhabitant of the continent, and he who dwells near the sea, the wise and the unwise. And if you proceed as far as to the utmost shores of the ocean, there also there are gods, rising very near to some, and setting very near to others."† Even in the modern world, dominated materially by the monotheistic culture of the West, still the majority of mankind celebrate the manyness as well as the oneness of Divinity. And even in the monotheistic religions the natural propensity of the worshipper to discover the Gods finds expression in Trinities, in the deification of saints and in the doctrine of angelic hosts. The dangers inherent in the over-emphasis of the oneness of Divinity are just as perilous as those of the other extreme. In the philosophy and religion of the ancient Greeks, we find the balance between the paradox: and in this balance the seeker in the modern world will find the apparent conflicts of spirit and matter, life and death, masculine and feminine divinity, individuality and its merging in the One, beautifully resolved.

As an aid to those who are coming anew to the doctrine of the Gods the Prometheus Trust has added a small appendix which offers a simple framework for the *initial* consideration of the relationships of the Divinities.

---

† Maximus Tyrius, Dissertation I, TTS volume VI.

Changes to the original text

Apart from the omissions mentioned in the above introduction the only changes to Taylor's original works are as follows:

i.   Where Taylor had *the one, the one itself, the good* or *the good itself* this edition gives these names capital initials; this to distinguish them as the highest names the Platonists gave to God. Other principles have been left in lower case.

ii.   A few very obvious grammatical errors and archaic spellings have been corrected; wherever there is any doubt as to the validity of possible errors the original has been followed.

iii.   Several footnotes have had exact references added where Taylor has only made imprecise reference.

iv.   In the final paragraph of the note to hymn 83 (To Ocean) the words *physical* and *psychical* seem to have been confused in the original and they have been changed around in this edition

v.   We have followed Taylor's explicit method of printing Greek characters without accents or breathings (see his defence of his Greek at the end of his *The Fable of Cupid and Psyche* and also his reference to this in the Introduction of *Proclus Commentary on Euclid*).

The Thomas Taylor Series

Volume I - *Proclus' Elements of Theology*

Volume II - *Select Works of Porphyry*
Abstinence from Animal Food; Auxiliaries to the Perception of Intelligibles; Concerning Homer's Cave of the Nymphs; The Wanderings of Ulysses -. Taylor

Volume III - *Collected Writings of Plotinus*
Twenty-seven treatises being all the writings of Plotinus translated by Taylor.

Volume IV - *Collected Writings on the Gods & the World*
Sallust On the Gods and the World; The Sentences of Demophilus; Ocellus on the Nature of the Universe; Taurus and Proclus on the Eternity of the World; Maternus on the Thema Mundi; The Emperor Julian's Orations to the Mother of Gods and to the Sovereign Sun; Synesius on Providence; Taylor's essays on the Mythology and the Theology of the Greeks.

Volume V - *Hymns and Initiations*
The Hymns of Orpheus together with all the published hymns translated or written by Taylor; Taylor's essay on Orpheus.

Volume VI - *The Dissertations of Maximus Tyrius*
Forty-one treatises from the middle Platonist, and an essay from Taylor - The Triumph of the Wise Man over Fortune.

Volume VII - *Oracles and Mysteries*
A Collection of Chaldean Oracles; Essays on the Eleusinian and Bacchic Mysteries; The History of the Restoration of the Platonic Theology; An essay on A Platonic Demonstration of the Immortality of the Soul.

Volume VIII - *The Theology of Plato*
The six books of Proclus on the Theology of Plato; to which is added a further book (by Taylor), replacing the original seventh book by Proclus, now lost. Extensive introduction and notes are also added.

Volume IX - *The Works of Plato I*
General Introduction, Life of Plato, First Alcibiades, Republic

Volume X - *The Works of Plato II*
Laws, Epinomis, Timæus, Critias.

Volume XI - *The Works of Plato III*
Parmenides, Sophista, Phædrus, Greater Hippias, Banquet.

Volume XII - *The Works of Plato IV*
Theætetus, Politicus, Minos, Apology of Socrates, Crito, Phædo, Gorgias, Philebus, Second Alcibiades.

Volume XIII - *The Works of Plato V*
Euthyphro, Meno, Protagoras, Theages, Laches, Lysis, Charmides, Lesser Hippias, Euthydemus, Hipparchus, Rivals, Menexenus, Clitopho, Io, Cratylus, Epistles.

Volume XIV - *Apuleius' Golden Ass & Other Philosophical Writings*
The Golden Ass (or Metamorphosis), On the Dæmon of Socrates, On the Philosophy of Plato.

Volumes XV & XVI - *Proclus' Commentary on the Timæus of Plato*
The Five Books of this Commentary, with additional notes and short index.

Volume XVII - *Iamblichus on the Mysteries and Life of Pythagoras*
Iamblichus On the Mysteries of the Egyptians, Chaldeans, and Assyrians; Iamblichus' Life of Pythagoras; Fragments of the Ethical Writings of Certain Pythagoreans; Political Fragments of Archytas, Charondas, Zaleucus, and other Ancient Pythagoreans.

Volume XVIII - *Essays and Fragments of Proclus*
Providence, Fate and That Which is Within our Power; Ten Doubts concerning Providence; The Subsistence of Evil; The Life of Proclus; The Fragments of the Lost Writings of Proclus.

Volume XIX - *The Works of Aristotle I*
The Physics, together with much of Simplicius' Commentary.

Volume XX - *The Works of Aristotle II*
The Organon: The Categories (& Porphyry's Introduction); On Interpretation; Prior and Posterior Analytics; The Topics; The Sophistical Elenchus.

Volume XXI - *The Works of Aristotle III*
The Great Ethics; The Eudemian Ethics; The Politics; The Economics.

Volume XXII - *The Works of Aristotle IV*

The Rhetorics; Nichomachean Ethics; The Poetics.

Volume XXIII - *The Works of Aristotle V*

The Metaphysics (with Commentary from Alexander of Aphrodisiensis and Syrianus); Against the Dogmas of Xenophanes, Zeno and Gorgias; Mechanical Problems; On the World; On Virtues and Vices.

Volume XXIV - *The Works of Aristotle VI*

On the Soul (with Commentary from Simplicius); Sense and Sensibles; Memory and Reminiscence; Sleep and Wakefulness; On Dreams; On Divination by Sleep; The Common Motion of Animals; On the Generation of Animals; On the Length and Shortness of Life; On Youth and Old Age; On Life and Death; On Respiration.

THE

MYSTICAL HYMNS

of

ORPHEUS

The Grecian theology, which originated from Orpheus, was not only promulgated by him, but also by Pythagoras and Plato; who, for their transcendent genius, will always be ranked by the intelligent among the prodigies of the human race. By the first of these illustrious men, however, it was promulgated mystically and symbolically; by the second, enigmatically, and through images; and scientifically by the third. That this theology, indeed, was derived from Orpheus is clearly testified by those two great philosophic luminaries Iamblichus† and Proclus.‡ For by them we are informed, "that what Orpheus delivered mystically through arcane narrations, this Pythagoras learned when he celebrated orgies in the Thracian Libethra, being initiated by Aglaophemus in the mystic wisdom which Orpheus derived from his mother Calliope, in the mountain Pangæus."

This sublime theology, though it was scientifically disseminated by Plato, yet conformably to the custom of the most ancient philosophers, was delivered by him synoptically, and in such a way as to be inaccessible to the vulgar; but when, in consequence of the commencement of a degraded and barren period, this theology became corrupted through the negligence and confusion of its votaries, then such of his disciples as happened to live when it was thus degraded and deformed found it necessary to unfold it more fully, in order to prevent its becoming utterly extinct. The men by whom this arduous task was accomplished were the last of the disciples of Plato; men who, though

---

† περι θεων Πυθαγορας ο τω Μνησαρχω τουτο εξεμαθον, οργιασθεις εν Λιβηθροις τοις Θρᾳκιοις Αγλαοφαμω τελετας μεταδοντος· ως αρα Ορφευς ο Καλλιοπας κατα το Παγγαιον ορος υπο τας ματρος πινυσθεις εφα τεν αριθμω ουσιαν αϊδιον ειναι. Iamblicus de Vit. Pythag. [*Iamblichus on the Mysteries & Life of Pythagoras*, TTS vol. XVII, p. 253.]

‡ Πυθαγορειος ο Τιμαιος επεται ταις Πυθαγορειων αρχαις, αυται δε εισιν αι Ορφικαι παραδοσεις· α γαρ Ορφευς δι απορρητων λογων μυστικως παραδεδωκε, ταυτα Πυθαγορας εξεμαθεν οργιασθεις εν Διβηθροις τοις Θρακιοις, Αγλιοφαμου τελετας μεταδιδοντος, ην περι θεων σοφιαν παρα Καλλιοπης της μητρος επινυσθη. Proclus in Tim. lib. v. 291A [TTS vol. XVI, p. 875].

they lived in a base age, possessed a divine genius, and who having happily fathomed the depth of their great master's works, luminously and copiously developed their recondite meaning, and benevolently communicated it in their writings for the general good.

From this golden chain of philosophers, as they have been justly called, my elucidations of the present mystic hymns are principally derived: for I know of no other genuine sources, if it be admitted (and it must by every intelligent reader), that the theology of Orpheus is the same as that of Pythagoras and Plato. Hence I shall not take any notice of the theories of Bryant and Faber and other modern mythological writers; because these theories, however ingenious they may be, are so far from elucidating, that they darken, confound, and pollute the Grecian theology, by mingling with it other systems, to which it is as perfectly foreign and hostile as wisdom is to folly, and intellect to craft.

That the philosophic reader therefore may be convinced of the truth of this observation, the following epitome of this theology, derived from the above-mentioned sources, is subjoined. In the first place, this theology celebrates the immense principle of things as something superior even to being itself; as exempt from the whole of things, of which it is nevertheless ineffably the source; and does not therefore think fit to connumerate it with any triad, or order of beings. Indeed, it even apologizes for attempting to give an appropriate name to this principle, which is in reality ineffable, and ascribes the attempt to the imbecility of human nature, which striving intently to behold it, gives the appellation of the most simple of its conceptions to that which is beyond all knowledge and all conception. Hence Plato denominates it *The One* and *The Good*; by the former of these names indicating its transcendent simplicity, and by the latter its subsistence as the object of desire to all beings. For all things desire good. But Orpheus, as Proclus well observes,[†] "availing himself of the license of fables, manifests every thing prior to Heaven (or the intelligible and at the same time intellectual order) by names, as far as to the first cause. He also denominates the ineffable, who transcends the intelligible unities, Time." And this according to a wonderful analogy, indicating the *generation, i.e.* the ineffable evolution into light of all things, from the immense principle of all. For, as Proclus elsewhere observes, "where there is *generation* there also time has a subsistence." And in this way the celebrated *Theogony* of Orpheus and other Grecian theologists is to be understood.

[†] In Plat. Cratyl. 115 [See *Works of Plato V*, TTS vol. XIII, p. 580.]

As the first cause then is *The One*, and this is the same with *The Good*, the universality of things must form a whole, the best and the most profoundly united in all its parts which can possibly be conceived: for *The First Good* must be the cause of the greatest good, that is, the whole of things; and as goodness is union, the best production must be that which is most united. But as there is a difference in things, and some are more excellent than others, and this in proportion to their proximity to the first cause, a profound union can no otherwise take place than by the extremity of a superior order coalescing through intimate alliance with the summit of one proximately inferior. Hence the first of bodies, though they are essentially corporeal, yet κατα σχεσιν, through *habitude* or *alliance*, are most vital, or lives. The highest of souls are after this manner intellects, and the first of beings are Gods. For as *being* is the highest of things after *the first cause*, its first subsistence must be according to a superessential characteristic.

Now that which is superessential, considered as participated by the highest or *true being*, constitutes that which is called *intelligible*. So that every true being depending on the Gods is a *divine intelligible*. It is *divine* indeed, as that which is deified; but it is *intelligible*, as the object of desire to intellect, as perfective and connective of its nature, and as the plenitude of *being* itself. But in the first being life and intellect subsist according to cause: for every thing subsists either according to *cause*, or according to *hyparxis*, or according to *participation*. That is, every thing may be considered either as subsisting occultly in its cause, or openly in its own order (or according to what it is), or as participated by something else. The first of these is analogous to light when viewed subsisting in its fountain the sun; the second to the light immediately proceeding from the sun; and the third to the splendour communicated to other natures by this light.

The first procession therefore from the first cause will be the intelligible triad, consisting of *being*, *life*, and *intellect*, which are the three highest things after the first God, and of which *being* is prior to *life*, and *life* to *intellect*. For whatever partakes of life partakes also of being: but the contrary is not true, and therefore being is above life; since it is the characteristic of higher natures to extend their communications beyond such as are subordinate. But *life* is prior to *intellect*, because all intellectual natures are vital, but all vital natures are not intellectual. But in this intelligible triad, on account of its superessential characteristic, all things may be considered as subsisting according to cause: and consequently number here has not a proper subsistence, but is involved in unproceeding union, and absorbed in superessential light. Hence, when it is called a triad, we must not suppose that any *essential distinction* takes place, but must consider this appellation as expressive of its ineffable perfection. For as it is the nearest of all things to *The One*, its union must be transcendently profound and ineffably occult.

All the Gods indeed, considered according to their unities, are all in all, and are at the same time united with the first God, like rays to light, or the radii of a circle to the centre. And hence they are all established in their ineffable principle (as Proclus in Parmenid. beautifully observes), like the roots of trees in the earth; so that they are all as much as possible superessential, just as trees are eminently of an earthly nature, without at the same time being earth itself. For the nature of the earth, as being a whole, and therefore having a perpetual subsistence, is superior to the partial natures which it produces. The intelligible triad therefore, from existing wholly according to the superessential, possesses an inconceivable profundity of union both with itself and its cause; and hence it appears to the eye of intellect as one simple indivisible splendour, beaming from an unknown and inaccessible fire.

The Orphic theology, however, concerning the intelligible Gods, or the highest order of divinities, is, as we are informed by Damascius,† as follows: "*Time* [as we have already observed] is symbolically said to be the one principle of the universe; but *ether* and *chaos*‡ are celebrated as the two principles immediately posterior to this one. And *being*, simply considered, is represented under the symbol of an *egg*.§ And this is the first triad of the intelligible Gods. But for the perfection of the second triad they establish either a conceiving and a conceived egg as a God, or a white garment, or a cloud: because from these Phanes leaps forth into light. For indeed they philosophise variously concerning the middle triad. But Phanes here represents intellect. To conceive him however besides this, as father and power, contributes nothing to Orpheus. But they call the third triad Metis as *intellect*,° Ericapæus as *power*, and

---

† Vid. Wolfiii Anecdot. Græc. tom. iii. p. 252.

‡ These two principles are called by Plato, in the *Philebus* [23c], *bound* and *infinity*.

§ This Orphic *egg* is the same with the *mixture* from *bound* and *infinity*, mentioned by Plato in the *Philebus*. See the third book of my translation of Proclus on the *Theology of Plato* [TTS vol. VIII].

° ως νουν is omitted in the original.

Phanes as *father*. But sometimes† the middle triad is considered according to the three-shaped God, while conceived in the egg: for the middle always represents each of the extremes; as in this instance, where the egg and the three-shaped God subsist together. And here you may perceive that the egg is that which is united; but that the three-shaped and really multiform God is the separating and discriminating cause of that which is intelligible. Likewise the middle triad subsists according to the egg, as yet united; but the third‡ according to the God who separates and distributes the whole intelligible order. And this is the common and familiar Orphic theology. But that delivered by Hieronymus and Hellanicus is as follows. According to them *water* and *matter* were the first productions, from which earth was secretly drawn forth: so that water and earth are established as the two first principles; the latter of these having a *dispersed* subsistence; but the former conglutinating and connecting the latter. They are silent however concerning the principle prior to these two, as being ineffable: for as there are no illuminations about him, his arcane and ineffable nature is from hence sufficiently evinced. But the third principle posterior to these two, *water* and *earth*, and which is generated from them, is *a dragon*, naturally endued with the heads of a bull and a lion, but in the middle having the countenance of the God himself. They add likewise that he has wings on his shoulders, and that he is called *undecaying Time*, and *Hercules*; that *Necessity* resides with him, which is the same as *Nature*, and incorporeal *Adrastia*, which is extended throughout the universe, whose limits she binds in amicable conjunction. But as it appears to me, they denominate this third principle as established according to essence; and assert, besides this, that it subsists as male and female, for the purpose of exhibiting the generative causes of all things.

"I likewise find in the Orphic rhapsodies, that neglecting the two first principles, together with the one principle who is delivered in silence, the third principle, posterior to the two, is established by the theology as the original; because this first of all possesses something effable and commensurate to human discourse. For in the former hypothesis, the highly reverenced and undecaying *Time*, the father of æther and chaos, was the principle: but in this *Time* is neglected, and the principle becomes *a dragon*. It likewise calls triple æther, moist; and chaos, infinite; and Erebus, cloudy and dark; delivering this second triad

---

† μηποτε is erroneously printed instead of ποτε.

‡ το τριτον is I conceive erroneously omitted in the original.

analogous to the first: this being potential, as that was paternal. Hence the third procession of this triad is dark Erebus: its paternal and summit æther, not according to a simple but intellectual subsistence: but its middle infinite chaos, considered as a progeny or procession, and among these parturient, because from these the third intelligible triad proceeds. What then is the third intelligible triad? I answer, the egg; the duad of the natures of male and female which it contains, and the multitude of all-various seeds, residing in the middle of this triad: and the third among these is an incorporeal God, bearing golden wings on his shoulders; but in his inward parts naturally possessing the heads of bulls, upon which heads a mighty dragon appears, invested with the all-various forms of wild beasts. This last then must be considered as the *intellect* of the triad; but the middle progeny, which are *many* as well as *two*, correspond to *power*, and the egg itself is *the paternal principle* of the third triad: but the third God of this third triad, this theology celebrates as *Protogonus*, and calls him *Jupiter*, the disposer of all things and of the whole world; and on this account denominates him *Pan*. And such is the information which this theology affords us, concerning the genealogy of the intelligible principles of things.

But in the writings of the Peripatetic Eudemus, containing the theology of Orpheus, the whole intelligible order is passed over in silence, as being every way ineffable and unknown, and incapable of verbal enunciation. Eudemus therefore commences his genealogy from *Night*, from which also Homer begins: though Eudemus is far from making the Homeric genealogy consistent and connected, for he asserts that Homer begins from Ocean and Tethys. It is however apparent, that *Night* is according to Homer the greatest divinity, since she is reverenced even by Jupiter himself. For the poet says of Jupiter, "that he feared lest he should act in a manner displeasing to swift *Night*."† So that Homer begins his genealogy of the Gods from *Night*. But it appears to me that Hesiod, when he asserts that Chaos was first generated, signifies by Chaos the incomprehensible and perfectly united nature of that which is intelligible: but that he produces Earth‡ the first from thence, as a certain principle of the whole procession of the Gods. Unless perhaps

---

† αζετο γαρ μη νυκτι θοη αποθυμια ρεζοι. So Damascius; but instead of ρεζοι, all the printed editions of Homer read ερδοι.

‡ Την is printed instead of Γην.

Chaos is the second of the two principles: but Earth,† Tartarus, and Love form the triple intelligible. So that *Love* is to be placed for the third monad of the intelligible order, considered according to its convertive nature; for it is thus denominated by Orpheus in his rhapsodies. But *Earth* for the first, as being first established in a certain firm and essential station. But *Tartarus* for the middle, as in a certain respect exciting and moving forms into distribution. But Acusilaus appears to me to establish *Chaos* for the first principle, as entirely unknown; and after this, two principles, *Erebus* as male, and *Night* as female; placing the latter for *infinity*, but the former for *bound*. But from the mixture of these, he says‡ that *Æther*, *Love*, and *Counsel* are generated, forming three intelligible hypostases. And he places *Æther* as the summit; but *Love* in the middle, according to its naturally middle subsistence; but *Metis* or *Counsel* as the third, and the same as highly reverenced intellect. And, according to the history of Eudemus, from these he produces a great number of other Gods.

Thus far Damascius, with whose very interesting narration the doctrine of the Chaldeans concerning the intelligible order accords, as delivered by Johannes Picus in his *Conclusions according to the Opinion of the Chaldean Theologists*.§ "The intelligible coordination (says he) is not in the intellectual coordination, as Amasis the Egyptian asserts, but is above every intellectual hierarchy, imparticipably concealed in the abyss of the first unity, and under the obscurity of the first darkness." Coordinatio

---

† As the whole of the Grecian theology is the progeny of the mystic traditions of Orpheus, it is evident that the Gods which Hesiod celebrates by the epithets of *Earth*, *Heaven*, &c. cannot be the visible *Heaven* and *Earth*: for Plato in the *Cratylus*, following the Orphic doctrine concerning the Gods, as we have evinced in our notes on that dialogue, plainly shows, in explaining the name of Jupiter, that this divinity is the artificer of the sensible universe; and consequently *Saturn*, *Heaven*, *Earth*, &c. are much superior to the mundane deities. Indeed if this be not admitted, the Theogony of Hesiod must be perfectly absurd and inexplicable. For why does he call Jupiter, agreeably to Homer, (πατηρ ανδρων τε θεων τε), "*father of gods and men?*" Shall we say that he means literally that Jupiter is the father of *all* the Gods? But this is impossible; for he delivers the generation of Gods who are the parents of Jupiter. He can therefore only mean that Jupiter is the parent of all the mundane Gods: and his Theogony, when considered according to this exposition, will be found to be beautifully consistent and sublime; whereas, according to modern interpretations, the whole is a mere chaos, more wild than the delirious visions of Swedenborg, and more unconnected than any of the impious effusions of methodistical rant. I only add, that την is again erroneously printed in the Excerpta of Wolfius for γην.

‡ φημι in the original should doubtless φησι.

§ Vid. Pici. Opera, tom i. p. 54.

intelligibilis non est in intellectuali coordinatione, ut dixit Amasis Ægyptius, sed est super omnem intellectualem hierarchium, in abysso primæ unitatis, et sub caligine primarum tenebrarum imparticipaliter abscondita.

But from this triad it may be demonstrated, that all the processions of the Gods may be comprehended in six orders, *viz.* the *intelligible order*, the *intelligible and at the same time intellectual*, the *intellectual*, the *supermundane*, the *liberated*, and the *mundane*.† For the *intelligible*, as we have already observed, must hold the first rank, and must consist of *being*, *life*, and *intellect*; *i.e.* must *abide*, *proceed*, and *return*; at the same time that it is characterized, or subsists principally according to causally *permanent being*. But in the next place, that which is both *intelligible* and *intellectual* succeeds, which must likewise be triple, but must principally subsist according to *life*, or *intelligence*. And in the third place the *intellectual* order must succeed, which is *triply convertive*. But as in consequence of the existence of the sensible world, it is necessary that there should be some demiurgic cause of its existence, this cause can only be found in *intellect*, and in the last hypostasis of the *intellectual triad*. For all forms in this hypostasis subsist according to all-various and perfect divisions; and forms can only fabricate when they have a perfect intellectual separation from each other. But since *fabrication* is nothing more than *procession*, the Demiurgus will be to the posterior orders of Gods what *The One* is to the orders prior to the *Demiurgus*; and consequently he will be that secondarily which the first cause of all is primarily. Hence his first production will be an order of Gods analogous to the *intelligible* order, and which is denominated *supermundane*. After this he must produce an order of Gods similar to the *intelligible* and *intellectual* order, and which are denominated *liberated* Gods. And in the last place, a procession correspondent to the *intellectual* order, and which can be no other than the *mundane* Gods. For the Demiurgus is chiefly characterized according to diversity, and is allotted the boundary of all universal hypostases.

All these orders are unfolded by Plato in the conclusions which the second hypothesis of his *Parmenides* contains; and this in a manner so perfectly agreeable to the Orphic and Chaldaic theology, that he who can read and *understand* the incomparable work of Proclus on Plato's theology will discover how ignorantly the latter Platonists have been

---

† *i.e.* θεοι νοητοι, νοητα και νοεροι, νοεροι, υπερκοσμιοι, απολυτοι sive υπερουρανιοι, et εγκοσμιοι.

abused by the moderns, as fanatics and corrupters of the doctrine of Plato.

According to the theology of Orpheus therefore, all things originate from an immense principle, to which through the imbecility and poverty of human conception we give a name, though it is perfectly ineffable, and in the reverential language of the Egyptians, is a *thrice unknown darkness*,[†] in the contemplation of which all knowledge is refunded into ignorance. Hence, as Plato says, in the conclusion of his first hypothesis in the *Parmenides*, "it can neither be named, nor spoken of, nor conceived by opinion, nor be known or perceived by any being." The peculiarity also of this theology, and in which its transcendency consists is this, that it does not consider the highest God to be simply the principle of beings, but *the principle of principles*, i.e. of deiform processions from itself, all which are eternally rooted in the unfathomable depths of the immensely great source of their existence, and of which they may be called superessential ramifications, and superluminous blossoms.

When the ineffable transcendency of the first God, which was considered (as I have elsewhere observed) to be the grand principle in the Heathen theology, by its most ancient promulgators, Orpheus, Pythagoras, and Plato, was forgotten, this oblivion was doubtless the cause of dead men being deified by the Pagans. Had they properly disposed their attention to this transcendency, they would have perceived it to be so immense as to surpass eternity, infinity, self-subsistence, and even essence itself, and that these in reality belong to those venerable natures which are as it were first unfolded into light from the arcane recesses of the truly mystic unknown cause of all. For, as Simplicius[‡] beautifully observes, "It is requisite that he who ascends to the principle of things should investigate whether it is possible there can be any thing better than the supposed principle; and if something more excellent is found, the same inquiry should again be made respecting that, till we arrive at the highest conceptions, than which we have no longer any more venerable. Nor should we stop in our ascent till we find this to be the case. For there is no occasion to fear that our progression will be through an unsubstantial void, by conceiving

---

[†] "Of the first principle (says Damascius, in MS. περι αρχων) the Egyptians said nothing, but celebrated it as a darkness beyond all intellectual conception, a thrice unknown darkness," πρωτην αρχην ανυμνηκασων, σκοτος υπερ τασαν νοησιν, σκοτος αγνωστον, τρις τουτο επιφημιζοντες.

[‡] In Epicet.

something about the first principles which is greater than and surpasses their nature. *For it is not possible for our conceptions to take such a mighty leap as to equal, and much less to pass beyond the dignity of the first principles of things.*" He adds, "This therefore is one and the best extension [of the soul] to [the highest] God, and is as much as possible irreprehensible; *viz.* to know firmly, that by ascribing to him the most venerable excellencies we can conceive, and the most holy and primary names and things, we ascribe nothing to him which is suitable to his dignity. It is sufficient, however, to procure our pardon [for the attempt] that we can attribute to him nothing superior." If it is not possible, therefore, to form any ideas equal to the dignity of the immediate progeny of the ineffable, *i.e.* of the first principles of things, how much less can our conceptions reach the principle of these principles, who is concealed in the super-luminous darkness of occultly initiating silence? Had the Heathens therefore considered as they ought this transcendency of the supreme God and his immediate offspring, they never would have presumed to equalize the human with the divine nature, and consequently would never have worshipped men as Gods. Their theology, however, is not to he accused as the cause of this impiety, but their forgetfulness of the sublimest of its dogmas, and the confusion with which this oblivion was necessarily attended.

The following additional information also respecting the Orphic theology will greatly contribute to an elucidation of these Mystic Hymns: According to this theology, each of the Gods is in all, and all are in each, being ineffably united to each other and the highest God, because each being a superessential unity, their conjunction with each other is a union of unities. And hence it is by no means wonderful that each is celebrated as all. But another and a still more appropriate cause may be assigned of each of the celestial Gods being called by the appellations of so many other deities, which is this, that, according to the Orphic theology, each of the planets is fixed in a luminous etherial sphere called an ολοτης, or *wholeness*,† because it is a part with a *total* subsistence, and is analogous to the sphere of the fixed stars. In consequence of this analogy, each of these planetary spheres contains a multitude of Gods, who are the satellites of the leading divinity of the sphere, and subsist conformably to his characteristics. This doctrine, which, as I have elsewhere observed, is one of the grand keys to the mythology and theology of the ancients, is not clearly delivered by any

---

† Each of these spheres is called a *wholeness*, because it contains a multitude of *partial* animals coordinate with it.

other ancient writer than Proclus, and has not, I believe, been noticed by any other modern author than myself. But the following are the passages in which this theory is unfolded by Proclus, in his admirable commentaries on the *Timæus* of Plato. "In each of the celestial spheres, the whole sphere has the relation of a monad, but the cosmocrators [or planets] are the leaders of the multitude in each. For in each a number analogous to the choir of the fixed stars subsists with appropriate circulations." (See lib. ii, 256E [TTS vol. XVI], of my translation of this work.) And in another part of the same book (279A), "There are other divine animals following the circulations of the planets, the leaders of which are the seven planets; all which Plato comprehends in what is here said. For these also revolve and have a wandering of such a kind as that which he a little before mentioned of the seven planets. For they revolve in conjunction with and make their apocatastases together with their principals, just as the fixed stars are governed by the whole circulation [of the inerratic sphere]." And still more fully in p. 279D, "Each of the planets is a whole world, comprehending in itself many divine genera invisible to us. Of all these, however, the visible star has the government. And in this the fixed stars differ from those in the planetary spheres, that the former have one monad [*viz.* the inerratic sphere], which is the wholeness of them; but that in each of the latter there are invisible stars, which revolve together with their spheres; so that in each there is both the wholeness and a leader, which is allotted an exempt transcendency. For the planets, being secondary to the fixed stars, require a twofold prefecture, the one more total, but the other more partial. But that in each of these there is a multitude coordinate with each, you may infer from the extremes. For if the inerratic sphere has a multitude coordinate with itself, and earth is the wholeness of terrestrial, in the same manner as the inerratic sphere is of celestial animals, it is necessary that each intermediate wholeness should entirely possess certain partial animals coordinate with itself; through which, also, they are said to be wholenesses. The intermediate natures, however, are concealed from our sense, the extremes being manifest; one of them through its transcendently luminous essence, and the other through its alliance to us. If, likewise, partial souls [such as ours] are disseminated about them, some about the sun, others about the moon, and others about each of the rest, and prior to souls, dæmons give completion to the herds of which they are the leaders, it is evidently well said, that each of the spheres is a world; theologists also teaching us these things when they say that there are Gods in each prior to dæmons, some of which are under the government of others. Thus for instance, they assert concerning our mistress the Moon, that the Goddess Hecate is contained in her, and also Diana. Thus, too, in speaking of the sovereign Sun, and the Gods that are there, they celebrate Bacchus as being there,

> The Sun's assessor, who with watchful eye surveys
> The sacred pole.

They likewise celebrate the Jupiter who is there, Osiris, the solar Pan, and *others of which the books of theologists and theurgists* are full; from all which it is evident, that each of the planets is truly said to be the leader of many Gods, who give completion to its peculiar circulation."

From this extraordinary passage (as I have observed in a note on it in my Proclus, p. 1048, TTS vol. XVI) we may perceive at one view why the Sun in the Orphic Hymns is called Jupiter, why Apollo is called Pan, and Bacchus the Sun; why the Moon seems to be the same with Rhea, Ceres, Proserpine, Juno, Venus, &c. and, in short, why any one divinity is celebrated with the names and epithets of so many of the rest. For from this sublime theory it follows that every sphere contains a Jupiter, Neptune, Vulcan, Vesta, Minerva, Mars, Ceres, Juno, Diana, Mercury, Venus, Apollo, and in short every deity, each sphere at the same time conferring on these Gods the peculiar characteristic of its nature; so that, for instance, in the Sun they all possess a solar property, in the Moon a lunar one, and so of the rest. From this theory, too, we may perceive the truth of that divine saying of the ancients, that all things are full of Gods; for more particular orders proceed from such as are more general, the mundane from the supermundane, and the sublunary from the celestial; while earth becomes the general receptacle of the illuminations of all the Gods. "Hence," as Proclus shortly after observes [282D], "there is a terrestrial Ceres, Vesta, and Isis, as likewise a terrestrial Jupiter and a terrestrial Hermes, established about the one divinity of the earth, just as a multitude of celestial Gods proceeds about the one divinity of the heavens. For there are progressions of all the celestial Gods into the Earth: and Earth contains all things, in an earthly manner, which Heaven comprehends celestially. Hence we speak of a terrestrial Bacchus and a terrestrial Apollo, who bestows the all-various streams of water with which the earth abounds, and openings prophetic of futurity." And if to all this we only add, that all the other mundane Gods subsist in the twelve above-mentioned, and in short, all the mundane in the supermundane Gods, and that the first triad of these is *demiurgic* or *fabricative, viz.* Jupiter, Neptune, Vulcan; the second, Vesta,

Minerva, Mars, *defensive*; the third, Ceres, Juno, Diana, *vivific*; and the fourth, Mercury, Venus, Apollo, *elevating* and *harmonic*; I say, if we unite this with the preceding theory, there is nothing in the ancient theology that will not appear admirably sublime and beautifully connected, accurate in all its parts, scientific and divine.

In the next place, that the following Hymns were written by Orpheus and that they were used in the Eleusinian Mysteries, will, I think, be evident, from the following arguments, to the intelligent reader. For that hymns were written by Orpheus is testified by Plato in the eighth book of his *Laws*, and by Pausanias in his *Boeotics*, who also says that they were few and short; from whence, as Fabricius[†] justly observes, it appears that they were no other than those which are now extant.[‡] But that they were used in the Eleusinian Mysteries is evident from the testimony of Lycomedes, who says that they were sung in the sacred rites pertaining to Ceres, which honour was not paid to the Homeric hymns, though they were more elegant than those of Orpheus; and the Eleusinian were the mysteries of Ceres. And that Lycomedes alludes, in what he here says, to these hymns is manifest, first from Pausanias, who in his Attics (cap. 37) observes, "that it is not lawful to ascribe the invention of beans to Ceres." He adds, "and he who has been initiated in the Eleusinian mysteries, *or has read the poems called Orphic*, will know what I mean." Now Porphyry De Abstinentia, lib. iv, 16[§] informs us, that beans were forbidden in the Eleusinian mysteries;[◊] and in the Orphic Hymn to *Earth* the sacrificer is ordered to fumigate from every kind of seed, except *beans* and aromatics. But Earth is Vesta, and Vesta, as we are informed by Proclus,[*] is comprehended together with Juno in Ceres. Again, Suidas informs us, that τελετη signifies *a mystic sacrifice, the greatest and most venerable of all others*, (θυσια μυστηριωδης, η μεγιστη και τιμιωτατα). And Proclus, whenever he speaks of the Eleusinian mysteries, calls them the most holy *teletai*, αγιωτατοι

[†] Vid. Biblioth. Græc. tom. i. p. 114.

[‡] I omit the testimonies of Cyril contra Julian, lib. i. p. 25, and of Suidas, because their authority is of little value on this subject.

[§] TTS volume II.

[◊] Παραγγελεται γαρ και Ελευσινι απεχεσθαι και κατοικιδων ορνιθων, και ιχθυων, και κυαμων, ροιας τε και μελων. p. 353 Edit. Trajec.

[*] See the Additional Notes.

τελεται.† Agreeably to this, the Orphic Hymns are called in the Thryllitian manuscript τελεται; and Scaliger justly observes, that they contain nothing but such invocations as were used in the *mysteries*. Besides, many of the hymns are expressly thus called by the author of them. Thus the conclusion of the hymn to Protogonus invokes that deity to be present at *the holy telete*, ες τελετην αγιαν: of the hymn to the Stars, to be present *at the very learned labours of the most holy telete*:

Ελθετ᾽ επ᾽ ευιερου τελετης πολυϊστορας αθλους.

And in the conclusion of the Hymn to Latona the sacrifice is called an *all-divine telete* (βαιν᾽ επι πανθειον τελετην), as likewise in that of the Hymn to Amphietus Bacchus. And in short, the greater part of the hymns will be found to have either the word τελετη in them, or to invoke the respective divinities *to bless the mystics or initiated persons*. Thus the conclusion of the Hymn to Heaven entreats that divinity to confer a blessed life on *a recent mystic*: the conclusion of the Hymn to the Sun, *to impart by illumination a pleasant life to the mystics*:

. . . . ηδυν δε βιον μηστησι πρωφαινε.

And in a similar manner most of the other hymns.‡

Farther still, Demosthenes, in his first Oration against Aristogiton, has the following remarkable passage: και την απαραιτητον και σεμνην Δικην, ην ο τας αγιωτατας ημιν τελετας καταδειξας Ορφευς παρα τον του Διος θρονον φησι καθημενην, παντα τα των ανθρωπων εφοραν. *i.e.* "Let us reverence inexorable and venerable Justice, who is said by Orpheus, our instructor in the most holy *teletai*, to be seated by the throne of Jupiter, and to inspect all the actions of men." Here Demosthenes calls the mysteries *most holy*, as well as Proclus: and I think it may be concluded with the greatest confidence from all that has been said, that he alluded to the Hymn to Justice, which is one of the Orphic hymns, and to the following lines in that hymn:

---

† In Plat. Theol. et in Comment. in Alcibiad.

‡ For a confirmation of this I refer the reader to the conclusions of the following hymns, viz. hymn vi, xviii, xxiii, xxiv, xxv, xxxiv, xxxv, xli, xliii, xliv, xlviii, l, lii, liii, liv, lvi, lvii, lviii, lx, lxi, lxxi, lxxiv, lxxvi, lxxvii, lxxviii, lxxix, lxxxiii, and lxxxv. And what is asserted in the eighty-fourth hymn, which is to Vesta, is particularly remarkable: for in the third line the poet says:

Τους δε συ εν τελεταις οσιους μυστας αναδειξαις.

i.e. "You have appointed these holy *mystics in the teletæ*."

Ομμα Δικης μελπω πανιδεπκεος, αγλαομορφου,
Ἡ και Ζηνος ανακτος επι θρονον ιερον ιζει,
Ουρανοθεν καθορωσα βιον θνητων πολυφυλων.

i.e. "I sing the all-seeing eye of splendid Justice, who sits by the throne of king Jupiter, and from her celestial abode beholds the life of multiform mortals."

The Eleusinian mysteries also, as is well known, were celebrated at night; the principal reason of which appears to be this, that the greater mysteries pertained to Ceres, and the less to Proserpine,[†] and the latter preceded the former. But the rape of Proserpine, which was exhibited in these mysteries, signifies, as we are informed by Sallust,[‡] the descent of souls. And the descent of souls into the realms of generation is said, by Plato in the tenth book of his *Republic*, to take place at midnight, indicating by this the union of the soul with the darkness of a corporeal nature. This too, I suppose, is what Clemens Alexandrinus[§] means when he says, "that the mysteries were especially performed by night, thus signifying that the compression [*i.e.* confinement] of the soul by the body was effected at night." And that the sacrifices enjoined in the Orphic Hymns were performed by night, is evident from the hymn to Silenus, Satyrus, &c. in which Silenus, together with the Naiads, Bacchic Nymphs, and Satyrs, are implored to be present at the *nocturnal* orgies:

Οργια νυκτιφαη τελεταις αγιαις αναφαινων.

From all which I think it may be safely concluded, that these Hymns not only pertain to mysteries, but that they were used in the celebration of the Eleusinian, which by way of eminence (κατ᾽ εξοχην) were called *the mysteries*, without any other note of distinction.

In the last place, it is requisite to speak of the author of these Hymns, and in addition to the evidence already adduced of their genuine antiquity, to vindicate them against those who contend that they are spurious, and were not written by Orpheus, but either by Onomacritus, or some poet who lived in the decline and fall of the Roman empire. And first, with respect to the dialect of these Hymns, Gesner observes, "that it ought to be no objection to their antiquity. For though

---

[†] Ησαν τα μεν μεγαλα της Δημητρος· τα δε μικρα Περσεφονης της αυτης θυγατρος. Interp. Græc. ad Plut. Aristophanis.

[‡] De Diis et Mundo, cap iv. (TTS volume IV).

[§] Αι τελεται γινονται νυκτος μαλιστα, σημαινουσαι την εν νυκτι της ψυχης συστολην απο του σωματος. Clem. Alex. Stroma. lib. iv. p. 530, Sylburg.

according to Iamblichus,† the Thracian Orpheus, who is more ancient than those noble poets Homer and Hesiod, used the Doric dialect; yet the Athenian Onomacritus, who according to the general opinion of antiquity is the author of all the works now extant ascribed to Orpheus, might either, preserving the sentences and a great part of the words, only change the dialect, and teach the ancient Orpheus to speak Homerically, or as I may say Solonically; or might arbitrarily add or take away what he thought proper, which, as we are informed by Herodotus, was his practice with respect to the Oracles." Gesner adds, "that it does not appear probable to him, that Onomacritus would dare to invent all that he wrote, since Orpheus must necessarily, at that time, have been much celebrated, and a great variety of his verses must have been in circulation." And he concludes with observing, "that the objection of the Doric dialect ought to be of no more weight against the antiquity of the present works than the Pelasgic letters,‡ which Orpheus, according to Diodorous Siculus, used.

In this extract, Gesner is certainly right in asserting that Onomacritus would not dare to invent all that he wrote, and afterwards publish it as Orphic; but I add, that it is unreasonable in the extreme to suppose that he in the least interpolated or altered the genuine works of Orpheus, though he might change the dialect in which they were originally written. For is it to be supposed that the Orphic Hymns would have been used in the Eleusinian mysteries, as we have demonstrated they were, if they had been spurious productions; or that the fraud would not have been long ago discovered by some of the many learned and wise men that flourished after Onomacritus; and that the detection of this fraud would not have been transmitted so as to reach even the present times? Or indeed, is it probable that such a forgery could have existed at all, at a period when other learned men, as well as Onomacritus, had access to the genuine writings of Orpheus, and were equally capable with himself of changing them from one dialect into another? Even at a late period of antiquity, will any man who is at all familiar with the writings of Proclus, Hermias, and Olympiodorus, for a moment believe that men of such learning, profundity, and sagacity, would have transmitted to us so many verses as Orphic, though not in the Doric dialect, when at the same time they were the productions of

---

† De Vita Pythag. ch. xxxiv [TTS vol. XVII, 285].

‡ These letters are the old Etrurian or Eolian, and are perhaps more ancient than the Cadmian or Ionic.

Onomacritus? We may therefore, I think, confidently conclude, that though Onomacritus altered the dialect, he did not either add to or diminish, or in any respect adulterate the works of Orpheus; for it is impossible he should have committed such a fraud without being ultimately, if not immediately, detected.

With respect to those who contend that the works which are at present extant under the name of Orpheus were written during the decline and fall of the Roman empire, I trust every intelligent reader will deem it almost needless to say, in confutation of such an opinion, that it is an insult to the understanding of all the celebrated men of that period, by whom these writings have been quoted as genuine productions, and particularly to such among them as rank among the most learned, the most sagacious, and wisest of mankind. So infatuated, however, by this stupid opinion was Tyrwhitt, that in his edition of the Orphic poem Περι Λιθων (On Stones), he says in a note (p. 22) "there is nothing in the hymns peculiarly adapted to the person of Orpheus, except his speech to Musæus."† This speech or address to Musæus is the exordium to the Hymns. But so far is this from being true, that the author of this work expressly calls himself in two of the hymns *the son of Calliope*. Thus in the conclusion of the Hymn to the Nereids, the poet says,

> Ομεις γαρ πρωται τελετην ανεδειξατε σεμνην
> Ευιερου Βακχοιο και αγνης Φερσεφονειης,
> Καλλιοπη συν μητρι, και Απολλωνι ανακτι.

i.e.
"For you at first disclos'd the rites divine,
Of holy Bacchus, and of Proserpine,
Of fair Calliope, from whom I spring,
And of Apollo bright, the Muses' king."

And in the Hymn to the Muses, he celebrates Calliope as his mother, in the very same words as in the Hymn to the Nereids, Καλλιοπη συν μητρι. This blunder of Tyrwhitt is certainly a most egregious specimen of the folly of pervicacious adherence to an opinion which had ignorance and prejudice only for its source, and which calumniated writings far beyond the *little sphere* of its knowledge to comprehend.

As to Orpheus himself, the original author of these Hymns, scarcely a vestige of his life is to be found amongst the immense ruins of time. For who has ever been able to affirm any thing with certainty of his origin, his age, his country, and condition? This alone may be depended

---

† "In Hymnis nihil est ad personam Orphei peculiariter accommodatum, nisi allocutio ad Musæum."

on, from general assent, that there formerly lived a person named Orpheus, who was the founder of theology among the Greeks; the institutor of their life and morals; the first of prophets, and the prince of poets; himself the offspring of a Muse; who taught the Greeks their sacred rites and mysteries, and from whose wisdom, as from a perennial and abundant fountain, the divine muse of Homer and the sublime theology of Pythagoras and Plato flowed.

The following, however, is a summary of what has been transmitted to us by the ancients concerning the original Orpheus, and the great men who have at different periods flourished under this venerable name. The first and genuine Orpheus is said to have been a Thracian, and according to the opinion of many was a disciple of Linus,[†] who flourished at the time when the kingdom of the Athenians was dissolved. Some assert that he was prior to the Trojan war, and that he lived eleven, or as others say nine, generations. But the Greek word γενεα, or *generation*, signifies, according to Gyraldus,[‡] the space of seven years: for unless this is admitted, how is it possible that the period of his life can have any foundation in the nature of things? If this signification therefore of the word is adopted, Orpheus lived either seventy-seven or sixty-three years, the latter of which, if we may believe astrologers, is a fatal period, and especially to great men, as it proved to be to Aristotle and Cicero.

Our poet, according to fabulous tradition, was torn in pieces by Ciconian women; on which account Plutarch affirms the Thracians were accustomed to beat their wives, in order that they might revenge the death of Orpheus. Hence in the vision of Herus Pamphilius, in the tenth book of Plato's *Republic* [620a], the soul of Orpheus, being destined to descend into another body, is said to have chosen that of a swan, rather than to be born again of a woman; having conceived such a hatred of the sex, on account of his violent death. The cause of his destruction is variously related by authors. Some report that it arose from his being engaged in puerile loves, after the death of Eurydice. Others, that he was destroyed by women intoxicated with wine, because he was the cause of men relinquishing an association with them. Others again assert, according to Pausanias, that on the death of Eurydice, wandering to Aornus, a place in Thesprotia, where it was customary to evocate the souls of the dead, having recalled Eurydice to life, and not being able to detain her, he destroyed himself; nightingales bringing

---

[†] Vid. Suid.

[‡] Syntag. Poet. p.54.

forth their young on his tomb, whose melody exceeded every other of this species. Others again, ascribe his laceration to his having celebrated every divinity except Bacchus, which is very improbable, as among the following hymns there are nine to that deity, under different appellations. Others report that he was delivered by Venus herself into the hands of the Ciconian women, because his mother Calliope had not determined justly between Venus and Proserpine concerning the young Adonis. Many affirm, according to Pausanias, that he was struck by lightning; and Diogenes confirms this by the following verses, composed, as he asserts, by the Muses on his death:

> Here by the Muses plac'd, with golden lyre,
> Great Orpheus rests, destroy'd by heavenly fire.

Again, the sacred mysteries called Threscian derived their appellation from the Thracian bard, because he first introduced sacred rites and religion into Greece; and hence the authors of initiation into these mysteries were called Orpheotelestæ. Besides, according to Lucian, Orpheus brought astrology and the magical arts into Greece; and as to his drawing to him trees and wild beasts by the melody of his lyre, Palæphatus[†] accounts for it as follows: "The mad Bacchanalian Nymphs, says he, having violently taken away cattle and other necessaries of life, retired for some days into the mountains. But the citizens, having expected their return for a long time, and fearing the worst for their wives and daughters, called Orpheus, and entreated him to invent some method of drawing them from the mountains. Orpheus, in consequence of this, tuning his lyre conformably to the orgies of Bacchus, drew the mad nymphs from their retreats; who descended from the mountains, bearing at first ferulæ, and branches of every kind of trees. But to the men who were eyewitnesses of these wonders, they appeared to bring down the very woods, and from hence gave rise to the fable.[‡]

[†] Vid. Opusc. Mythol. p. 45.

[‡] The true meaning of the fable however, in my opinion, is this, that Orpheus by his sacred doctrines tamed men of *rustic* and *savage* dispositions. But the most careless readers must be struck with the similitude of the latter part of this fable to what took place at the wood of Birnam in Macbeth; and to which the following lines allude:
> "Macbeth shall never vanquished be, until
> Great Birnam wood to high Dunsinane hill
> Shall come against him."

This coincidence, however, has not been noticed by any of the commentators of Shakespeare.

So great indeed was the renown of Orpheus, that he was deified by the Greeks; and Philostratus relates, that his head gave oracles in Lesbos, which when separated from his body by the Thracian women, was, together with his lyre, carried down the river Hebrus into the sea. In this manner, says Lucian, singing as it were his funeral oration, to which the chords of his lyre, impelled by the winds, gave a responsive harmony, it was brought to Lesbos and buried. But his lyre was suspended in the temple of Apollo; where it remained for a considerable space of time. Afterwards, when Neanthus, the son of Pittacus the tyrant, found that the lyre drew trees and wild beasts by its harmony, he earnestly desired to possess it; and having corrupted the priest privately with money, he took the Orphic lyre, and fixed another similar to it in the temple. But Neanthus, considering that he was not safe in the city in the day, departed from it by night; having concealed the lyre in his bosom, on which he began to play. As however he was a rude and unlearned youth, he confounded the chords; yet pleasing himself with the sound, and fancying he produced a divine harmony, he thought himself to be the blessed successor of Orpheus. But in the midst of his transports, the neighbouring dogs, roused by the sound, fell on the unhappy harper and tore him in pieces.

The former part of this fable is thus admirably explained by Proclus, in his Commentaries (or rather fragments of Commentaries) on the *Republic* of Plato, "Orpheus (says he), on account of his perfect erudition, is reported to have been destroyed in various ways; because, as it appears to me, men of that age participated *partially* of the Orphic harmony: for they were incapable of receiving a universal and perfect science. But the principal part of his melody [*i.e.* of his mystic doctrine] was received by the Lesbians; and on this account, perhaps, the head of Orpheus, when separated from his body, is said to have been carried to Lesbos. Fables of this kind, therefore, are related of Orpheus no otherwise than of Bacchus, of whose mysteries he was the priest."

The second Orpheus was an Arcadian, or, according to others, a Ciconian, from the Thracian Bisaltia, and is said to be more ancient than Homer and the Trojan war. He composed fabulous figments (called μυθοποιιαι) and epigrams. The third Orpheus was of Odrysius, a city of Thrace, near the river Hebrus; but Dionysius in Suidas denies his existence. The fourth Orpheus was of Crotonia; flourished in the time of Pisistratus, about the fiftieth Olympiad, and is, I have no doubt, the same with Onomacritus, who changed the dialect of these hymns. He wrote Decennalia (δεκαετηρια), and in the opinion of Gyraldus the Argonautics, which are now extant under the name of Orpheus, with other writings called Orphical, but which according to Cicero† some ascribe to Cecrops the Pythagorean. But the last Orpheus was Camarinæus, a most excellent versifier; and the same, according to Gyraldus, whose descent into Hades is so universally known.

I shall only add to this historical detail respecting Orpheus, what Hermias excellently remarks in his Scholia on the *Phædrus* of Plato. "You may see, says he, how Orpheus appears to have applied himself to all these [*i.e.* to the four kinds of mania‡], as being in want of, and adhering to, each other. For we learn that he was most *telestic*, and most *prophetic*, and was excited by Apollo; and besides this, that he was most *poetic*, on which account he is said to have been the son of Calliope. He was likewise most *amatory*, as he himself acknowledges to Musæus, extending to him divine benefits, and rendering him perfect. Hence he appears to have been possessed by all the manias, and this by a necessary consequence. For there is an abundant union, conspiration, and alliance with each other of the Gods who preside over these manias, *viz.* of the Muses, Bacchus, Apollo, and Love."

With respect to the following translation, it is requisite to observe, that I have adopted rhyme, not because most agreeable to the general taste, but because I conceive it to be necessary to the poetry of the English language; which requires something as a substitute for the energetic cadence of the Greek and Latin hexameters. Could this be obtained by any other means, I should immediately relinquish my partiality for rhyme, which is certainly, when well executed, far more difficult than blank verse, as these Orphic Hymns must evince in an eminent degree.

Indeed, where languages differ so much as the ancient and modern, the most perfect method perhaps of transferring the poetry of the former tongue into that of the latter is by a faithful and animated paraphrase; faithful, with regard to retaining the meaning of the author; and animated, with respect to preserving the fire of the original; calling it forth when latent, and expanding it when condensed. He who is anxious to effect this will every where endeavour to diffuse the light and fathom the depth of his author; to elucidate what is obscure, and to amplify what in modern language would be unintelligibly concise.

Thus, most of the compound epithets of which the following hymns chiefly consist, though extremely beautiful in the Greek language, yet

---

† In lib. i. de Nat. Decr.

‡ *i.e.* The *telestic*, or pertaining to the mysteries, the *prophetic*, the *poetic*, and the *amatory*.

when literally translated into ours lose much of their propriety and force. In their native tongue, as in a prolific soil, they diffuse their sweets with full blown elegance; and he who would preserve their theological beauties, and exhibit them to others in a different language, must expand their elegance by the supervening and enlivening rays of a light derived from mystic lore; and, by the powerful breath of genius, scatter abroad their latent but copious sweets.

If it shall appear that the translator has possessed some portion of this light, and has diffused it in the following work, he will consider himself to be well rewarded for his laborious undertaking. The philosophy of Plato, and the theology of the Greeks, have been for the greater part of his life the only study of his retired leisure; in which he has found an inexhaustible treasure of intellectual wealth, and a perpetual fountain of wisdom and delight. Presuming, therefore, that such a pursuit must be a great advantage to the present undertaking, and feeling the most sovereign contempt for the sordid drudgery of venal composition, he desires no other reward, if he has succeeded, than the praise of the liberal; and no other defence, if he has failed, than the decision of the candid and discerning few.

The Mystical Hymns

of

Orpheus

or

Initiations

The Mystical Hymns of Orpheus

TO MUSÆUS[1]

Learn, O Musæus, from my sacred song
What rites most fit to sacrifice[2] belong.
Jove I invoke, the earth, and solar light,
The moon's pure splendour, and the stars of night.
Thee, Neptune, ruler of the sea profound,
Dark-hair'd, whose power can shake the solid ground;
Ceres abundant, and of lovely mien,
And thee, chaste Proserpine, great Pluto's queen;
The huntress Dian, and bright Phœbus' rays,
Far darting God, the theme of Delphic praise;
And Bacchus, honour'd by the heav'nly choir,
Impetuous Mars, and Vulcan, God of fire.
Th'illustrious power who sprung from foam to light,
And Pluto, potent in the realms of night;
With Hebe young, and Hercules the strong,
And you to whom the cares of births belong.
Justice and Piety august I call,
And much fam'd Nymphs, and Pan the God of all.
To Juno sacred, and to Mem'ry fair,
And the chaste Muses I address my pray'r;
The various Year, the Graces, and the Hours,
Fair-hair'd Latona, and Dione's pow'rs.
The Corybantes and Curetes armed I call,[3]
And the great Saviours, sons of Jove, the king of all:
Th'Idæan Gods, the angel of the skies,
Prophetic Themis with sagacious eyes,
With ancient Night, and Daylight I implore,

And Faith and Dice source of blameless laws adore;
Saturn and Rhea, and great Thetis too,
Hid in a veil of dark celestial blue.
I call great Ocean, and the beauteous train
Of Ocean's daughters in the boundless main:
The strength of Atlas ever in its prime,
Vig'rous Eternity, and endless Time.
The splendid Stygian pool, and placid Gods beside,
And dæmons good and bad that o'er mankind preside;
Illustrious Providence, the noble train
Of dæmon forms, who fill th'etherial plain;
Or live in air, in water, earth, or fire,
Or deep beneath the solid ground retire.
The white Leucothea of the sea I call,
And Semele, and Bacchus's associates all;
Palæmon bounteous, and Adrastia[4] great,
And sweet-tongu'd Victory, with success elate;
Great Esculapius, skill'd to cure disease,
And dread Minerva, whom fierce battles please;
Thunders, and Winds in mighty columns pent,
With dreadful roaring struggling hard for vent;
Attis, the mother of the pow'rs on high,
Mensis, and pure Adonis, never doom'd to die,
End and Beginning (greatest this to all),
These with propitious aid I suppliant call,
To this libation, and these sacred rites;
For these t'accede with joyful mind, my verse invites.

---

1 The Greek Scholiast on Aristophanes (in Ranis) observes, that Musæus was the offspring of the Moon and Eumolpus; that according to Sophocles he uttered oracles; and that he composed παραλυσεις, τελεται and καθαρμοι. Of these works, which are unfortunately lost, the παραλυσεις, or καταλυσεις, taught both individuals and cities how by religious ceremonies they might be liberated from the punishment attendant on the crimes which they had committed. His τελεται, or Mysteries, are mentioned by Plato, Lucian, and others. And the καθαρμοι contained the means of expiating and becoming *purified* from guilt.

2 For a copious development of sacrifices, and of the utility or power they possess in the universe, and also on what account they were anciently performed, see Book the Second of my translation of Porphyry's excellent

Treatise on *Abstinence from Animal Food*; and Sect. V of my translation of Iamblichus *On the Mysteries*.† Likewise, for an account of Theurgy, or the art pertaining to divine operations, see the latter of the above-mentioned works, and the accompanying notes.

3 In the translation of many of these hymns, I have been obliged to employ an Alexandrine line, as well as in this and the following line, in order to preserve the meaning of the author.

4 This divinity is one among others in this Exordium to whom there is no hymn in these Orphic Teletæ. But the following particulars respecting this Goddess, extracted from the Scholia of Hermeas on the *Phædrus* of Plato, are given on account of their great importance, and because they illustrate a part of the Orphic theology. "Adrastia is a divinity seated in the vestibules of Night, and is the offspring of Melissus and Amalthea. Melissus, therefore, is to be assumed as a power providentially attending to secondary natures; but Amalthea must be considered according to the unchanging and the uneffeminate. Hence Adrastia was generated from unchangeable Providence, and she is the sister of Ida.

> The beauteous Ida and Adrastia sprung
> From the same sire.

This Goddess, therefore, comprehends in transcendent union, and contains in herself at once the centres of all laws, *viz.* of the mundane and the supermundane, of those of Fate, and those of Jupiter: for there are Jovian and Saturnian, divine, supermundane, and mundane laws. On this account she is called Adrastia, because her legislative decrees are inevitable. Hence she is said to be seated with brazen drumsticks in her hands, before the cave of Night, and through the sound produced by her cymbals to render all things obedient to her laws. For Phanes indeed is seated within the cave, in the Adytum of Night; but Night sits in the middle of the cave, prophesying to the Gods; and Adrastia sits in the vestibules, legislatively promulgating the divine laws. She differs, however, from the justice which is there, after the same manner as the legislative differs from the judicial characteristic. And the justice which is there is said to be the daughter of the Law and Piety which are there. But Adrastia herself, who is the offspring of Melissus and Amalthea, is likewise comprehensive of Law. These, therefore, are said to have nurtured Jupiter in the cavern of Night; the theologist [Orpheus] directly asserting that which Plato says about Jupiter. For Plato represents him fabricating and promulgating laws. But divine law is imparted by Adrastia to the Gods also: for the order which is in them is derived from this Goddess. It is, however, likewise imparted to the attendants of the Gods, and in common to all, and peculiarly to each."

† TTS volumes II and XVII respectively.

I

TO HECATE

Einodian Hecate,[1] Trivia, lovely dame,
Of earthly, wat'ry, and celestial frame,
Sepulchral, in a saffron veil array'd,
Pleas'd with dark ghosts that wander thro' the shade;
Persæa,[2] solitary goddess, hail!
The world's key-bearer, never doom'd to fail;
In stags rejoicing, huntress, nightly seen,
And drawn by bulls, unconquerable queen;
Leader, nymph, nurse, on mountains wand'ring, hear
The suppliants who with holy rites thy power revere,
And to the *herdsman*[3] with a fav'ring mind draw near.[4]

---

1 Io. Diac. Allegor. ad Hesiodi Theog. p. 268, cites this line, on which, and Hymn 71. 3, he observes: Ευρισκω, τον Ορφεα και την Τυχην Αρτεμιν προσαγορευοντα, αλλα και την Σεληνην Εκατην. i.e. "I find that Orpheus calls Fortune Artemis or Diana, and also the Moon Hecate."

2 Diodorus informs us, that Diana, who is to be understood by this epithet, was very much worshipped by the Persians, and that this Goddess was called *Persæa* in his time. See more concerning this epithet in Gyrald. Syntag. ii. p. 361.

3 As Orpheus by his sacred doctrines tamed men of a *rustic and savage* disposition; which, as we have before observed, appears to be the true meaning of the fable of his drawing to him *trees and wild beasts* by the melody of his lyre; hence, alluding to this circumstance, he calls himself here, and in the hymn to the Curetes, *the herdsman*, indicating the benefit which he conferred on the vulgar part or *herd* of mankind.

4 In all the editions of these hymns, prior to that of Hermann, this hymn forms a part of the exordium to Musæus; but it is certainly better to separate it from that exordium, though I did not perceive the propriety of doing so in the former edition of this translation.

II

TO THE GODDESS PROTHYRÆA[1]

THE FUMIGATION FROM STORAX

O venerable Goddess, hear my pray'r,
For labour pains are thy peculiar care.
In thee, when stretch'd upon the bed of grief,
The sex, as in a mirror, view relief.
Guard of the race, endued with gentle mind,
To helpless youth benevolent and kind;
Benignant nourisher; great Nature's key
Belongs to no divinity but thee.
Thou dwell'st with all immanifest to sight,
And solemn festivals are thy delight.
Thine is the task to loose the virgin's zone,
And thou in ev'ry work art seen and known.
With births you sympathise, tho' pleas'd to see
The numerous offspring of fertility.
When rack'd with labour pangs, and sore distress'd,
The sex invoke thee, as the soul's sure rest;
For thou alone canst give relief to pain,
Which art attempts to ease, but tries in vain.
Assisting Goddess, venerable pow'r,
Who bring'st relief in labour's dreadful hour;
Hear, blessed Dian, and accept my pray'r,
And make the infant race thy constant care.

---

1 This is an epithet of Diana, alluding to her presiding over gates, and being as it were the gate-keeper of life. In a hymn which was first discovered by me among the Harleian MSS. in the British Museum, and which, from the manner of it, was, I have no doubt, written by Proclus, *Hecate* is called *Prothyræa*. For the second line of this hymn, which is entitled Υμνος κοινος, or a *Common Hymn*, is

    Χαιρ' Εκατη, Προθυραιε, μεγασθενες, αλλος εαυτος.

See the whole of this hymn on page 270

III

TO NIGHT

THE FUMIGATION WITH TORCHES

Night, parent Goddess, source of sweet repose,
From whom at first both Gods and men arose.¹
Hear, blessed Venus², deck'd with starry light,
In Sleep's deep silence dwelling Ebon night!
Dreams and soft ease attend thy dusky train,
Pleas'd with the length'ned gloom and feastful strain,
Dissolving anxious care, the friend of mirth,
With darkling coursers riding round the earth.
Goddess of phantoms and of shadowy play,
Whose drowsy pow'r divides the nat'ral day;
By Fate's decree you constant send the light
To deepest hell, remote from mortal sight;
For dire Necessity, which nought withstands,
Invests the world with adamantine bands.
Be present, Goddess, to thy suppliant's pray'r,
Desir'd by all, whom all alike revere,
Blessed, benevolent, with friendly aid
Dispel the fears of twilight's dreadful shade.

---

1 The first subsistence of the Goddess Night is at the summit of that divine order which is denominated by Chaldean theologists νοητος και νοερος, *i.e. intelligible and at the same time intellectual*. This order is denominated by Plato, in the *Phædrus*, the supercelestial place, and in which he says *the plain of Truth* is situated, which, as we are informed by Hermeas (in Phædr.) obscurely indicates the whole order of the series of Night. What Hermeas afterwards adds on this subject is too important to be omitted, and is as follows:- "Theologists likewise peculiarly establish *Truth* in the supercelestial place." For Orpheus, speaking about Night, says, that "she possesses the truth† of the Gods" and

> To her, prediction wholly *true* was giv'n.

---

† In the original αληθειαν is omitted in this place, but evidently ought to be inserted.

She is also said to prophesy to the Gods. Homer, too, indicates concerning this Goddess. For, speaking about Jupiter, Sleep says,

> Night, the great tamer both of Gods and men,
> To whom I fled, preserv'd me from his wrath;
> For he swift[†] Night was fearful to offend.

But Plato says he shall *dare* to speak concerning it, because he is going to assert something *affirmatively* about it. The *dread*, however, is lest we should be led to something unappropriate and vile in such like doctrinal concerns. He is also concordant in what he says about the supercelestial place, with what he asserts in [the first hypothesis of] the *Parmenides*, about the first principle of things. For he there indicates this principle by negations; except that he absolutely denies all things of the first principle: but of the supercelestial place he denies some things, and affirms others. For the Goddess Night is superior to certain orders, but inferior to others; and as the first principle of things is superessential, so Night is supercelestial [*i.e.* is above that intellectual order which is denominated Heaven]. Why, however, are souls not said to see Heaven, but to become situated in, and be conjoined with it, yet are not conjoined with the natures above Heaven, but perceive them only? In answer to this it may be said, that it is necessary contact should exist, as far as to a certain thing. Why, therefore, as far as to this? Because neither are the Gods under Jupiter said to be united to Phanes; but this is alone asserted of Jupiter, and he is said to be united through *Night* as a medium.

But how does Plato say, that the supercelestial place is without colour? Is it in the same manner as we say, that nature and soul are colourless? But what is there admirable in asserting this? And if we admit this, what[‡] will there be transcendent in the supercelestial place, since the same thing is possessed both by nature and soul? May we not say that Plato, in what is here asserted, very much follows the before-mentioned theologists [*viz.* Homer, Orpheus, Hesiod, and Musæus], and disposes what he says conformably to them? For after the order of *Nights* there are three orders of Gods, *viz.* of Heaven, the Cyclops, and the Centimani [or Gods with a hundred hands], the proper names of whom Plato denies of the supercelestial place. For of the Gods which abide within Phanes, Heaven is the first that becomes visible from him; for Heaven and Earth first proceeded out of Phanes; and Heaven is first illuminated by the divine light of Phanes; since Orpheus says that Night is united to him:

[†] As Night, from her subsistence at the summit of the intelligible and at the same time intellectual order, is absorbed in the intelligible, hence Homer divinely denominates Night *swift*. For the Chaldean Oracles call the intelligible Gods *swift*, [see fr. 66, in *Oracles and Mysteries*, TTS vol. VII, p. 23].

[‡] For τοι here, it is necessary to read τι and to make the sentence interrogatory.

> No eye but that of sacred Night alone
> Beheld Protogonus; for all the rest
> Were lost in wonder at th'unhop'd for light,
> Which glitter'd from th'immortal Phanes' skin.

But that which is visible and illuminated is coloured, since colours are certain illuminations. Hence Night and all the supercelestial place, being above Heaven, which is visible, they are very properly said to be without colour. For night also is opposed to day, because the latter is illuminated and coloured. And through *the privation of colour*, indeed, Plato manifests that the place of the Nights is above the kingdom of the Heaven; but through *the privation of figure*, that it is above the order of the Cyclops. For theology says, that figure is first unfolded into light in these, and that the divinities, the Cyclops, are the first principles and causes of the figures which subsist every where. Hence theology says, that they are *manual artificers*. For this triad[†] is perfective of figures.

> And in their forehead one round eye was fix'd.[‡]

In the *Parmenides*, likewise, Plato, when he speaks of the straight, the circular, and that which is mixed[§] [from both these], obscurely indicates this order. But these Cyclops, as being the first causes of figures, taught Minerva and Vulcan the various species of figures.

> These the first manual artists were, who taught
> Pallas and Vulcan all things:

[says Orpheus]. We must not therefore wonder on hearing that Vulcan and Minerva are the causes of figures. For Vulcan is the cause of corporeal figures, and of every mundane figure; but Minerva, of the psychical and intellectual figure; and the Cyclops of divine, and the every where existing figure. Hence it is evident, that the supercelestial place is above the order of the Cyclops.

But by *the privation of contact* Plato manifests that this place is above the *Centimani*; for these first come into contact, as it were, with all the fabrication of things. Hence theology denominates them *hundred-handed*: for through the hands we touch, make, and distinguish all things. Farther still, the touch pervades through the whole body. Theology therefore, symbolically, calls these *hundred-handed*, as *touching* all the fabrication of things, and being the causes of it. The triad,[°] however, of the Centimani is of a guardian nature. But Plato adduces negatively what he found celebrated affirmatively by the

---

[†] The triad of the cyclops consists of Brontes, Steropes, and Arges.

[‡] Hesiod Theog. 145.

[§] The words και το μικτον are omitted in the original, but ought to be inserted, as will be evident from a perusal of the first hypothesis of the Parmenides.

[°] This triad consists of Cottus, Gyges, and Briareus.

theologist. For what Orpheus calls *Night*, that Plato denominates *without colour*. And what the former says negatively is *without falsehood*,

> Prediction without falsehood was to Night
> Of all things giv'n. [says Orpheus.]

that the latter celebrates, as *having about it the genus of true science*, and *as being truly existing essence*. Plato also, having celebrated the supercelestial place by three negations, again adduces three affirmations, introducing three of them from being. For, since this order is a triadic one, Plato very properly preserves the triadic, both in the negative and affirmative conclusions. Or it may be said that, since it is both one and being, and is triadic according to each of these, he indicates the negative conclusions according to the superessential one, but the affirmative according to being. Here likewise the first number is unfolded into light.

In the next place Hermeas enumerates the different kinds of Truth, as follows: "Superior illuminate subordinate natures with the light of Truth. We must extend the eye of intellect therefore to these four; *viz. The One*, which is the first principle of things; Phanes, who is the boundary of the intelligible, but the exempt principle of the intellectual Gods (for the Nights are principles with which principle is co-ordinate); Jupiter, who is the king of the super-mundane, but the boundary of what are properly called the intellectual Gods; and the Sun, who is the king of sensible natures. But each of these illuminates the beings that are under† it with the truth, which it possesses from an order placed above that which it illuminates. Thus the Sun imparts supermundane light to sensibles; and hence the essence of it is said to be from supermundane natures. Again, Jupiter illuminates supermundane essences with intellectual light. Phanes illuminates the intellectual Gods with intelligible light; and the principle of all things fills the intelligible Gods, and all things, with the divine light proceeding from himself."‡

2 Hermann is of opinion that the line Νυξ γενεσις παντων, ην και Κυπριν καλεσωμεν, *i.e.* "Night, the source of all things, whom we also call Venus," is an interpolation. But there is no reason whatever for this supposition: for Venus in the hymn to her is called νυκτερια, and φιλοπαννυχε σεμνη.

---

† For υπερ here, it is obviously necessary to read υπο.

‡ Instead of απ' αυτων in this place, it is requisite to read απ' αυτου.

IV

TO HEAVEN

THE FUMIGATION FROM FRANKINCENSE

Great Heav'n, whose mighty frame no respite knows,
Father of all, from whom the world arose;
Hear, bounteous parent, source and end of all,
For ever whirling round this earthly ball;
Abode of Gods, whose guardian pow'r surrounds
Th'eternal world with ever during bounds;[1]
Whose ample bosom, and encircling folds
The dire necessity of nature holds.
Etherial, earthly,[2] whose all-various frame,
Azure and full of forms, no power can tame.
All-seeing, source of Saturn and of time,
For ever blessed, deity sublime,
Propitious on a novel mystic shine,
And crown his wishes with a life divine.

---

1 According to Orpheus, as we are informed by Damascius περι αρχων, "Heaven is the boundary and guardian of all things," ο του Ορφεος Ουρανος ουρος και παντων φυλαξ ειναι βουλεται.

2 The dogma that subordinate natures are causally contained in such as are supreme, and such as are supreme in the subordinate by participation, is originally Egyptian, but is also said by Proclus, in Tim. 292B [TTS vol. XVI], to be Orphical. For in enumerating the Orphic traditions concerning Phanes, Night, Heaven, Saturn, Jupiter, and Bacchus, he observes, εστι γαρ και εν Γη Ουρανος, και εν Ουρανῳ Γη (lege Γη)· και ένταυθα μεν ο Ουρανος χθονιως, εκει δὲ ουρανιως η Γη· και γαρ ουρανιαν και την (lege γην την) Σεληνην Ορφευς προσηγορευσεν. i.e. "For Heaven is in Earth, and Earth in Heaven. And here indeed [i.e. in the Earth] Heaven subsists terrestrially; but there [in the heavens] Earth subsists celestially. For Orpheus also calls the Moon *celestial earth.*"

V

TO ETHER

THE FUMIGATION FROM SAFFRON

O ever untam'd Ether, rais'd on high
In Jove's dominions, ruler of the sky;
Great portion of the Stars and lunar light,
And of the Sun, with dazzling lustre bright;
All-taming pow'r, ethereal shining fire,
Whose vivid blasts the heat of life inspire;
The world's best element, light-bearing pow'r,
With starry radiance shining, splendid flow'r;
O hear my suppliant pray'r, and may thy frame
Be ever innocent, serene, and tame.

VI

TO PROTOGONUS[1]

THE FUMIGATION FROM MYRRH

O Mighty first-begotten, hear my pray'r,
Twofold, egg-born, and wand'ring thro' the air;
Bull-roarer,[2] glorying in thy golden wings,
From whom the race of Gods and mortal springs.
Ericapæus, celebrated pow'r,
Ineffable, occult, all-shining flow'r.
'Tis thine from darksome mists to purge the sight[3],
All-spreading splendour, pure and holy light;
Hence, Phanes, call'd the glory of the sky,
On waving pinions thro' the world you fly.
Priapus, dark-eyed splendour,[4] thee I sing,
Genial, all-prudent, ever blessed king.
With joyful aspect on these rites divine
And holy Telite propitious shine.

---

1 According to Orpheus, as related by Syrianus, in Metaph. Arist. p. 114, the first principle of all things is *The One*, or *The Good Itself*; and after this, conformably to the doctrine of Pythagoras, the two principles, *ether* and *chaos*, subsist. And of these principles, the first, or *ether*, is analogous to *bound*; and the second, or *chaos*, to *infinity*. Afterwards, says Syrianus, the first and occult genera of the Gods subsist, among which the first apparent God is the king and father of the universe, who, because he is the first visible deity, is denominated Phanes. The whole of this first and occult genera of the Gods, which is called by the Chaldean theologists the intelligible triad, was represented by Orpheus under the symbol of an egg, on the exclusion of which by the Goddess Night, the God Phanes came forth, who is hence denominated Protogonus.

2 Phanes, or Protogonus, who subsists at the extremity of the intelligible triad, and is therefore νους νοητος, or *intelligible intellect*, and the exemplar of the universe, is denominated by Plato in the *Timæus* το αυτοζωον, *animal itself*, as being the primordial cause of all animal life, and was symbolically represented by Orpheus as adorned with the heads of a ram, a *bull*, a serpent, and a lion. But Jupiter, or the demiurgus of the universe, is in the intellectual what Phanes is in the intelligible order of Gods; and hence he is said by Orpheus to have

absorbed Phanes prior to his fabrication of the world; the theologist indicating by this his participation of all the primary paradigmatic causes of things which subsist in Phanes. As Porphyry, therefore, in his treatise *De Antro Nympharum*,[†] informs us, "that the Persian deity Mithra, as well as the *bull*, is the demiurgus and lord of generation," the reason is obvious why Protogonus is called in this hymn *bull-roarer*, the roaring signifying the procession of ideas to the formation of the world. And this is conformable to what is asserted respecting ideas in the Chaldæan oracles, *viz.*

Νους πατρος ερροιζησε νοησας ακμαδι βουλη
Παμμορφους ιδεας.

i.e. "The intellect of the father made a crashing noise, understanding with unwearied counsel omniform ideas." For the *crashing noise* indicates the same thing as the *roaring* of Protogonus.

3 This line in the original is,

Οσσων ος σκοτοεσσαν απημαυρωσας ομιχλην.

And Proclus, in the Fifth Book of his MS. Commentary on the *Parmenides* of Plato [1175, see *The Works of Plato III*, TTS vol. XI, p. 217], evidently, as it appears to me, alludes to this verse. For, speaking of the intelligible monad, or the summit of the intelligible order, at the extremity of which Protogonus subsists, he says, "It is by no means wonderful if this monad comprehends the whole intellectual pentad, *viz.* essence, motion, permanency, sameness, and difference, without division, and in the most profound union; since through this union all these are after a manner one. For all things are there without separation, according to a *dark mist*, as the theologist asserts." Αδιακριτων παντων οντων κατα σκοτοεσσαν ομιχλην. In which passage the two last words form a part of the above Orphic line.

But the reason why Protogonus, or Phanes, is said *to purge the sight from dark mists*, is because the primary causes of things which in the deities prior to him subsist in ineffable union, all being in all, are by him first unfolded into intelligible light.

4 Protogonus, who is *intelligible intellect*, is very properly called *dark-eyed splendour*; the intelligible, from its occult subsistence, being indicated by *darkness*, but intellect by the *eye* and *splendour*: for it is the province of intellect to *see and unfold into light*.

[†] TTS volume II, p. 156.

VII

TO THE STARS

THE FUMIGATION FROM AROMATICS

With holy voice I call the stars on high,
Pure sacred lights, and dæmons of the sky.
Celestial stars, dear progeny of Night,
In whirling circles beaming far your light;
Refulgent rays around the heav'ns ye throw,
Eternal fires, the source of all below.
With flames significant of Fate ye shine,
And aptly rule for men a path divine.
In seven bright zones ye run with wand'ring flames,
And heaven and earth[1] compose your lucid frames:
With course unwearied, pure and fiery bright,
For ever shining thro' the veil of Night.
Hail, glittering, joyful, ever wakeful fires!
Propitious shine on all my just desires,
These sacred rites regard with conscious rays,
And end our works devoted to your praise.

---

1 As Heaven, in the hymn to that divinity, is said to be both etherial and earthly, the reason of which I have explained in the note to that hymn, it is obvious why the Stars, being celestial, are here said to consist of *heaven* and *earth*.

VIII

TO THE SUN

THE FUMIGATION FROM FRANKINCENSE AND MANNA

Hear, golden Titan, whose eternal eye
With matchless sight illumines all the sky.
Native, unwearied in diffusing light,
And to all eyes the object of delight:
Lord of the Seasons, beaming light from far,
Sonorous, dancing[1] in thy four-yok'd car.
With thy right hand the source of morning light,
And with thy left the father of the night.[2]
Agile and vig'rous, venerable Sun,
Fiery and bright around the heav'ns you run,
Foe to the wicked, but the good man's guide,
O'er all his steps propitious you preside.
With various-sounding golden lyre 'tis thine
To fill the world with harmony divine.
Father of ages, guide of prosp'rous deeds,
The world's commander, borne by lucid steeds.
Immortal Jove,[3] flute-playing, bearing light,
Source of existence, pure and fiery bright;
Bearer of fruit, almighty lord of years,
Agile and warm, whom ev'ry power reveres.
Bright eye, that round the world incessant flies,
Doom'd with fair fulgid rays to set and rise;
Dispensing justice, lover of the stream,
The world's great master, and o'er all supreme.
Faithful defender[4], and the eye of right,
Of steeds the ruler, and of life the light:
With sounding whip four fiery steeds you guide,
When in the glittering car of day you ride,
Propitious on these mystic labours shine,
And bless thy suppliants with a life divine.

1 Proclus, in his most elegant hymn to the Sun, says of this divinity:

> Σης δ' απο μειλιχοδωρος αλεξικακου θιασειης
> Παιηων βλαστησεν, εην δ' επετασσεν υγειην,
> Πλησας αρμονιης παναπημονος ευρεα κοσμον.

i.e. "From thy bland *dance* repelling deadly ill,
Salubrious Pæon blossoms into light,
Health far diffusing, and th'extended world
With streams of harmony innoxious fills."

2 The hand is a symbol of power. Hence Proclus, in Theol. Plat. lib. 6, p. 380, says that those who are skilled in divine concerns attribute two hands to the Sun; denominating one the right hand, the other the left.

3 As all the celestial spheres are replete with processions from all the supermundane deities, which processions are the satellites of the leading divinities of these spheres, as we have shown in the Introduction, the reason is obvious why the sun is called Jupiter, a solar Jupiter being one of his attendants. But there is also another reason for this appellation. For what Jupiter is in the intellectual that the Sun is in the sensible order of things. Hence Proclus, in Theol. Plat. V, 20 [TTS vol. VIII, p. 346], calls the sun βασιλευς του παντος, *the king of the universe*.

4 Proclus, in Tim. lib. 5 [309A, TTS vol. XVI, p. 928], informs us, in the words of Orpheus, οτι ηλιον μεν επεστησε τοις ολοις ο δημιουργος, και φυλακα αυτον ετευξε, κελευσε τε πασιν ανασσειν. "That the Demiurgus established the Sun over the whole of the universe, and fashioned him as its *guardian*, commanding him to govern all things."

IX

TO THE MOON[1]

THE FUMIGATION FROM AROMATICS

Hear, Goddess queen, diffusing silver light,
Bull-horn'd,[2] and wand'ring thro' the gloom of Night.
With stars surrounded, and with circuit wide
Night's torch extending, through the heav'ns you ride:
Female and male,[3] with silv'ry rays you shine,
And now full-orb'd, now tending to decline.
Mother of ages, fruit-producing Moon,
Whose amber orb makes Night's reflected noon:
Lover of horses, splendid queen of night,
All-seeing pow'r, bedeck'd with starry light,
Lover of vigilance, the foe of strife,
In peace rejoicing, and a prudent life:
Fair lamp of Night, its ornament and friend,
Who giv'st to Nature's works their destin'd end.[4]
Queen of the stars,[5] all-wise Diana, hail!
Deck'd with a graceful robe and ample veil.
Come, blessed Goddess, prudent, starry, bright,
Come, moony-lamp, with chaste and splendid light,
Shine on these sacred rites with prosp'rous rays,
And pleas'd accept thy suppliants' mystic praise.

1 The Moon is called in this hymn both σεληνη and μηνη, the former of which words signify the Moon in the language of the Gods; and the latter is the appellation given to her by men, as is evident from the following Orphic fragment:

Μησατο δ' αλλην γαιαν απειριτον, ηντε Σεληνην
Αθανατοι κληζουσιν, επιχθονιοι δε τε Μηνην.
Η πολλ' ουρε εχει, πολλ' αστεα πολλα μελαθρα.

i.e. "But he (Jupiter) fabricated another boundless earth, which the Immortals call Selene, but men Mene; which has many mountains, many cities, many houses." This difference of names arises from the difference between divine and human knowledge. For, as it is well observed by the Platonic philosophers, as the knowledge of divine natures is different from that of partial souls, like ours;

so with respect to names, some are divine, exhibiting the whole essence of that which is named; but others are human, which only partially unfold their signification. On this difference of names, Proclus, in the last chapter of his first book on the *Theology of Plato*, admirably remarks as follows: "The first, most principal, and truly divine names are established in the Gods themselves. But the second names, which are imitations of the first, and which subsist intellectually, are of an allotment pertaining to dæmons. And again, we may say that those names which are the third from the truth, which are logically devised, and which receive the ultimate resemblance of divine natures, are unfolded by scientific men, at one time energizing divinely, and at another intellectually, and generating moving images of their inward spectacles. For as the demiurgic intellect establishes resemblances about matter of the first forms contained in himself, and produces temporal images of things eternal, divisible images of things indivisible, and adumbrated images as it were of true beings, after the same manner I think the science that is with us representing intellectual production fabricates resemblances of other things, and also of the Gods themselves, representing that which is void of composition in them, through composition; that which is simple, through variety; and that which is united, through multitude; and thus fashioning names ultimately exhibits images of divine natures. For it generates every where name as if it were a statue of the Gods. And as the theurgic art through certain symbols calls forth the exuberant and unenvying goodness of the Gods into the illumination of artificial statues; thus also the intellectual science of divine concerns, by the compositions and divisions of sounds, unfolds the occult essence of the Gods." See more on this subject in the additional notes to my translation of the *Cratylus* of Plato [in the *Works of Plato V*, TTS vol. XIII].

2 We are informed by Porphyry, in his treatise *De Antro Nymph*. [TTS vol. II, p. 153] that the ancient priests of Ceres, called the Moon, who is the queen of generation, *i.e.* of the sublunary regions, a bull. He adds, "And Taurus is the exaltation of the Moon." And Olympiodorus, in his MS. Commentary on the *Gorgias* of Plato [see TTS vol. XII, p 425], says that the Moon, according to ancient theologists, is drawn by two bulls; by two, on account of her increase and diminution; but by *bulls*, because as these till the ground, so the Moon governs all those parts which surround the earth.

3 Ficinus, on the *Theology of Plato* (lib. 4, p. 128), has the following remarkable passage, most probably derived from some MS. Commentary of Proclus, or some other of the latter Platonists; for unfortunately he does not acquaint us with the source of his information. "The professors (says he) of the Orphic theology consider a twofold power in souls, and in the celestial orbs; the one consisting in knowledge, the other in vivifying and governing the orb with which that power is connected. Thus, in the orb of the earth, they call the gnostic power Pluto, but the other Proserpine. In water they denominate the former power Ocean, and the latter Tethys. In air, that thundering Jove, and

this Juno. In fire, that Phanes, and this Aurora. In the soul of the lunar sphere, they call the gnostic power Liknitan Bacchus, the other Thalia. In the sphere of Mercury, that Bacchus Silenus, this Euterpe. In the orb of Venus, that Lysius Bacchus, this Erato. In the sphere of the Sun, that Trietericus Bacchus, this Melpomene. In the orb of Mars, that Bassareus Bacchus, this Clio. In the sphere of Jupiter, that Sebazius, this Terpsichore. In the orb of Saturn, that Amphietus, this Polymnia. In the eighth sphere, that Pericionius, this Urania. But in the soul of the world they call the gnostic power Bacchus Eribromus, but the animating power Calliope. From all which the Orphic theologists infer, that the particular epithets of Bacchus are compared with those of the Muses, for the purpose of informing us that the powers of the Muses are, as it were, intoxicated with the nectar of divine knowledge; and in order that we may consider the nine Muses, and nine Bacchuses, as revolving round one Apollo, that is about the splendour of one invisible Sun." The greater part of this passage is preserved by Gyraldus in his Syntagma de Musis, and by Natales Comes in his Mythology, but without mentioning the original author. As in each of the celestial spheres, therefore, the soul of the ruling deity is of the female, and the intellect is of the male characteristic, it is by no means wonderful that the Moon is called in this hymn "*female* and *male*."

4 Proclus, in Plat. Theol. VI, 22 [TTS vol. VIII, p. 455], informs us respecting Diana, who among the mundane divinities is the Moon, "That she excites all physical productive powers or forms into energy, and that she gives perfection to the imperfection of matter. Hence both Theologists and Socrates, in the *Theætetus*, call her *Lucina*, as the inspective guardian of physical progression and generation." παντασ κινουσα τους φυσικους λογους εισ ενεργειαν, και το αυτοτελες (lege το ατελες) της υλης τελειουσα· διο και Λοχιαν αυτην οιτε θεολογοι, και ο εν Θεαιτητῳ Σωκρατης καλουσιν, ως της φυσικης προοδου, και γεννησεως εφορον. The epithet in the Orphic hymn is τελεσφορος, *i.e. bringing to a perfect end.*

5 In the original αστραρχη. This appellation was first given to the Moon by the Phœnicians, as we are informed by Herodian. This Goddess likewise was called by the Africans Urania. Vide Selden. de Diis Syriis, p. 248.

X

TO NATURE[1]

THE FUMIGATION FROM AROMATICS

Nature, all-parent, ancient and divine,
O much mechanic mother, art is thine;
Heav'nly, abundant, venerable queen,
In ev'ry part of thy dominions seen.
Untam'd, all taming, ever splendid light,
All ruling, honour'd, and supremely bright.
Immortal, first-born, ever still the same,
Nocturnal, starry, shining, powerful dame.
Thy feet's still traces in a circling course,
By thee are turn'd, with unremitting force.
Pure ornament of all the Pow'rs divine,
Finite and infinite alike you shine;[2]
To all things common, and in all things known,
Yet incommunicable and alone.
Without a father of thy wondrous frame,
Thyself the father whence thy essence came;
Mingling, all-flourishing, supremely wise,
And bond connective of the earth and skies.
Leader, life-bearing queen, all various nam'd,
And for commanding grace and beauty fam'd.
Justice, supreme in might, whose general sway
The waters of the restless deep obey.
Etherial, earthly, for the pious glad,
Sweet to the good, but bitter to the bad:
All-wise, all-bounteous, provident, divine,
A rich increase of nutriment is thine;
And to maturity whate'er may spring,
You to decay and dissolution bring.
Father of all, great nurse, and mother kind,
Abundant, blessed, all-spermatic mind:
Mature, impetuous, from whose fertile seeds
And plastic hand this changing scene proceeds.
All-parent pow'r, in vital impulse seen,

Eternal, moving, all-sagacious queen.
By thee the world, whose parts in rapid flow,
Like swift descending streams, no respite know,³
On an eternal hinge, with steady course,
Is whirl'd with matchless, unremitting force.
Thron'd on a circling car, thy mighty hand
Holds and directs the reins of wide command:
Various thy essence, honour'd, and the best,
Of judgment too, the general end and test.
Intrepid, fatal, all-subduing dame,
Life everlasting, Parca, breathing flame.
Immortal Providence, the world is thine,
And thou art all things, architect divine.
O, blessed Goddess, hear thy suppliants' pray'r,
And make their future life thy constant care;
Give plenteous seasons and sufficient wealth,
And crown our days with lasting peace and health.

1 Nature, as we are informed by Proclus, in Tim. [4A, TTS vol. XV, p. 20], is the last of the demiurgic causes of this sensible world, and the boundary of the extent of incorporeal essences, and is full of productive powers and forms, through which she directs and governs mundane beings. And she is a goddess indeed in consequence of being deified; but she has not immediately the subsistence of a deity. For, says he, we call divine bodies Gods, as being the statues of Gods. He adds, "But she governs the whole world by her powers, containing the heavens in the summit of herself, but ruling over generation [or the sublunary realms] through the heavens; and every where weaving together partial natures with wholes. Being however such, she proceeds from the vivific Goddess [Rhea]. For [according to the Chaldean Oracle - TTS vol. VII, fr. 92, p. 29] "*Immense Nature is suspended from the back of the Goddess;*" from whom all life is derived, both that which is intellectual, and that which is inseparable from the subjects of its government. Hence, being suspended from thence, she pervades without impediment through, and inspires all things; so that through her the most inanimate beings participate of a certain soul, and such things as are corruptible remain perpetually in the world, being held together by the causes of forms which she contains."

Hence Nature is represented in this hymn as *turning the still traces of her feet with a swift whirling.* For since she is the last of the demiurgic causes, her operations amply symbolize with the traces of feet. But the reason why the epithets of *much-mechanic, artist, connecting, all-wise providence, &c.*, are given to Nature, which evince her agreement with Minerva, is because, as Proclus in the above extract informs us, she every where *weaves* together partial natures with wholes. Hence, according to the Orphic theology, as we also learn from Proclus, Minerva fashioned the variegated veil of Nature, from that wisdom and virtue of which she is the presiding deity. Nature therefore, from her connecting and uniting power, and from her plenitude of seminal productive powers, has an evident agreement with Minerva; whose divine arts, according to the Orphic theology, reduce whatever is discordant and different in the universe into union and consent.

Again, it is well observed by Simplicius, in his Commentary on the Second Book of Aristotle's *Physics* [Works of Aristotle, TTS vol. XIX, p. 266], "that one of the conceptions which we form of Nature is, that it is *the character of every thing*, and that in consequence of this, we employ the name of it in all things, and do not refuse to say the *nature* of soul, of intellect, and even of deity itself." Nature, therefore, as indicating the *characteristic* or hyparxis of divinity, is in perfect conformity to the symbolical theology of Orpheus, said to be without a father, and at the same time the father of her own being. For all the Gods, according to this theology, though they proceed by an αρρητος εκφανσις, or *ineffable unfolding into* light from the first principle of things, yet at the same time are αυτοτελεις υποστασεις, or self-perfect, and self-produced essences. And when Nature in this hymn is said to be *incommunicable* and *alone*, this must be considered as indicating the characteristic of the great first principle of all. For so far as *the principle of all things* he is *incommunicable*; since it is impossible that there should be more than one principle of *all things*.

2 Philolaus, as we are informed by Diogenes Laertius, published a treatise on Nature, of which this was the beginning: φυσις δε εν τω κοσμω αρμοχθη εξ απειρων τε και περαινοντων, και ολος κοσμος, και τα εν αυτω παντα, i.e. "Nature and the whole world, and whatever it contains, are aptly connected together from things *infinite* and *finite*." Hence Socrates, in the *Philebus* of Plato, says, "that all beings consist of *bound* and *infinity*, and that these two intelligible principles were produced the first of all things by the highest God." Proclus, in Plat. Theol. III, 3 [TTS vol. VIII, p. 189], cites the above passage of Philolaus.

3 As the world has an extended and composite essence, and is on this account continually separated from itself, it can alone be connected by a certain indivisible power imparted to it by divinity. Again, since from a natural appetite, it is perpetually moved in an orderly manner towards good, the nature of such an appetite and motion must originate from a divine intellect and goodness. But since, from its material imperfection, it cannot receive the whole of divine infinity at once, but in a way adapted to its temporal nature; hence it can only derive it gradually and partially, as it were by drops, in a momentary succession. So that the corporeal world is in a continual state of flowing and formation, but never possesses real being; and is like the image of a lofty tree seen in a rapid torrent, which has the appearance of a tree without the reality; and which seems to endure perpetually the same, yet is continually renewed by the continual renovation of the stream.

XI

TO PAN[1]

THE FUMIGATION FROM VARIOUS ODOURS

Strong past'ral Pan, with suppliant voice I call,
Heav'n, sea, and earth, the mighty queen of all,
Immortal fire; for all the world is thine,
And all are parts of thee, O pow'r divine.
Come, blessed Pan, whom rural haunts delight,
Come, leaping, agile, wand'ring, starry light.
Thron'd with the Seasons, Bacchanalian Pan,
Goat-footed, horn'd, from whom the world began;
Whose various parts, by thee inspir'd, combine
In endless dance and melody divine.
In thee a refuge from our fears we find,
Those fears peculiar to the humankind.
Thee, shepherds, streams of water, goats rejoice,
Thou lov'st the chase and Echo's secret voice:
The sportive Nymphs thy ev'ry step attend,
And all thy works fulfil their destin'd end.
O all-producing pow'r, much-fam'd, divine,
The world's great ruler, rich increase is thine.
All-fertile Pæan, heavenly splendour pure,
In fruits rejoicing, and in caves[2] obscure.
True serpent-horned Jove,[3] whose dreadful rage,
When rous'd, 'tis hard for mortals to assuage.
By thee the earth wide-bosom'd, deep and long,
Stands on a basis permanent and strong.
Th'unwearied waters of the rolling sea,
Profoundly spreading, yield to thy decree.
Old Ocean, too, reveres thy high command,
Whose liquid arms begird the solid land.
The spacious air, whose nutrimental fire
And vivid blasts the heat of life inspire;
The lighter frame of fire, whose sparkling eye
Shines on the summit of the azure sky,
Submit alike to thee, whose gen'ral sway
All parts of matter, various form'd, obey.

All natures change thro' thy protecting care,
And all mankind thy lib'ral bounties share;
For these, where'er dispers'd thro' boundless space,
Still find thy providence support their race.
Come, Bacchanalian, blessed pow'r, draw near,
Enthusiastic Pan, thy suppliants hear,
Propitious to these holy rites attend,
And grant our lives may meet a prosp'rous end;
Drive panic fury too, wherever found,
From humankind to earth's remotest bound.

1 Pan, as we are informed by Damascius, first subsists at the extremity of the *intelligible* order, being there no other than the celebrated Protogonus or Phanes; but, according to his mundane subsistence, he is the monad or summit of all the local Gods and dæmons. In the statues of him his upper parts resemble those of a man, but his lower parts those of a brute [*viz.* of a goat] indicating by this, that in the universe rationality has dominion over irrationality. As, therefore, according to his first subsistence, he is the primary exemplar of the universe; the reason is obvious why in this hymn he is celebrated as *all things*.

2 A cave, as we are informed by Porphyry *De Antr. Nymph.*† is an apt symbol of the material world; since it is agreeable at its first entrance on account of its participation of form, but is involved in the deepest obscurity to the intellectual eye, which endeavours to discern its dark foundation. Hence, like a cave, its exterior and superficial parts are pleasant, but its interior parts are obscure; and its very bottom darkness itself.

3 Pan, as we have already observed, first subsists at the extremity of the intelligible order, and is the same with Protogonus or Phanes. This being the case, in the intellectual order he is analogous to Jupiter the Demiurgus, by whom, according to Orpheus, Phanes was absorbed. Hence, as Jupiter is said to be the mingler of all things by Orpheus, as we learn from Io. Diac. Allegor. in Hesiod, p. 305, horns are an occult symbol of the mingling power of the Demiurgus of the world. For the literal meaning of the word κεραστης, used in this hymn, is horned serpent; and one of the heads of Protogonus is that of a serpent. And the word κεραστης is, as Gesner observes, derived from the verb κεραννυμι, *to mingle*.

---

† See *The Select Works of Porphyry*, TTS vol. II, p. 148.

XII

TO HERCULES

Hear, strenuous Hercules, untam'd and strong,
To whom grand works and powerful hands belong,
Titan untam'd, rejoicing and benign,
Of various forms, eternal and divine.
Father of Time, the theme of gen'ral praise,
Ineffable, adored in various ways,
Magnanimous, in divination skill'd,
And in th'athletic labours of the field.
'Tis thine, strong archer, all things to devour,
Supreme, all-helping, all-producing pow'r.
To thee mankind as their deliv'rer pray,
Whose arm can chase the savage tribes away.
Unweary'd, earth's best blossom,[1] offspring fair,
To whom calm peace and peaceful works are dear.
Self-born, with primogenial fires[2] you shine,
And various names, and strength of heart are thine:
Thy mighty head supports the morning light,
And bears, untam'd, the silent gloomy night;
From east to west, endu'd with strength divine,
Twelve glorious labours to absolve is thine;
Supremely skill'd, thou reign'st in heav'n's abodes,
Thyself a God, amidst th'immortal Gods.
With arms unshaken, infinite, divine,
Come, blessed pow'r, and to our rites incline;
The mitigations of disease convey,
And drive disastrous maladies away.
Come, shake the branch with thy almighty arm,
Dismiss thy darts, and noxious fate disarm.

---

1 Since, according to Orpheus, there is an intellectual which is the source of the sensible world; the former containing in a primary and causal manner what the latter comprehends secondarily and sensibly; hence the former contains an intellectual heaven and earth, not like the material existing in place, and conversant with the circulations of time; but subsisting immaterially in the stable essence of eternity. In this divine world another sun and moon and stars

shine with intellectual light; for every thing there is perfectly lucid, light continually mingling with light. From this heaven and earth resident in the *intellectual* Phanes, Orpheus, according to Proclus, derives the sublunary orders of the Gods; and among these [vid. Procl. in Tim. p. 295D, TTS vol. XVI, p. 888], he enumerates the following progeny of the intellectual earth. "She produced seven beautiful pure virgins with voluble eyes, and seven sons, all of them kings, and covered with downy hair. The daughters are Themis and prudent Tethys, and fair-haired Mnemosyne and blessed Thea; together with Dione, having an illustrious form, and Phœbe, and Rhea the mother of king Jupiter. Moreover, this illustrious earth generated celestial sons, which are also surnamed Titans, because they took revenge on the great starry Heaven; and these are Cæus, and great Cræus, and robust Phorcys, and Saturn, and Ocean, and Hyperion, and Jupiter." Now as Hercules is celebrated in this hymn as the Sun, and the Sun is the same with Hyperion, the reason is obvious why Hercules is called "Earth's best blossom." And we shall find that Saturn, in the following hymn, is called "blossom of Earth;" and Themis, in hymn 79, "Young blossom of Earth;" and the Titans, in hymn 37, "The illustrious progeny of Heaven and Earth." Again, Phanes, as we are informed by Athenagoras, is denominated by Orpheus Hercules and Time. Hence, we see the reason why Hercules in this hymn is said "to shine with primogenial fires;" since he is no other than *Protogonus* in the intelligible and intellectual worlds, and the Sun in the sensible world. Or in conformity to the Orphic theory mentioned in the Introduction, it may be said that he is celebrated with solar epithets, as being one of the satellites of the Sun.

2 In the editions of Gesner and Hermann we have in this place βολισιν, and in the edition of Eschenbach φολισι; but the true reading is, I have no doubt, φλογισι, conformably to the above translation. Scaliger also in his version has "*Ignibu'* primigenis florens."

XIII

TO SATURN

THE FUMIGATION FROM STORAX

Etherial father, mighty Titan,[1] hear,
Great sire of Gods and men, whom all revere;
Endu'd with various counsel, pure and strong,
To whom increase and decrement belong.
Hence matter's flowing forms thro' thee that die,
By thee restor'd, their former place supply.
The world immense in everlasting chains,
Strong and ineffable thy pow'r contains;
Father of vast eternity, divine,
O mighty Saturn, various speech is thine;
Blossom of earth and of the starry skies,
Husband of Rhea, and Prometheus wise.
Obsteteric pow'r and venerable root,
From which the various forms of being shoot;
No parts peculiar can thy pow'r enclose,
Diffus'd thro' all, from which the world arose.
O best of beings, of a subtle mind,
Propitious hear, to suppliant pray'rs inclin'd;
The sacred rites benevolent attend,
And grant a blameless life, a blessed end.

---

1 Saturn is one of the Titans produced by the intellectual Earth, as is evident from note 1, on the hymn to Hercules.

XIV

TO RHEA[1]

THE FUMIGATION FROM AROMATICS

Illustrious Rhea, to my pray'r incline,
Daughter of various-form'd Protogonus[2] divine,
Who driv'st thy sacred car with speed along,
Drawn by fierce lions, terrible and strong.
Mother of Jove, whose mighty arm can wield
Th'avenging bolt and shake the dreadful shield.
Brass-sounding,[3] honour'd, Saturn's blessed queen,
Drum-beating, fury-loving, of a splendid mien.
Thou joy'st in mountains and tumultuous fight,
And mankind's horrid howlings thee delight.
War's parent, mighty, of majestic frame,
Deceitful saviour,[4] liberating dame.
Mother of Gods and men, from whom the earth
And spacious heav'ns derive their glorious birth.
Th'etherial gales, the deeply spreading sea,
Goddess, aerial-form'd, proceed from thee.
Come, pleas'd with wand'rings, blessed and divine,
With peace attended on our labours shine;
Bring rich abundance; and, wherever found,
Drive dire disease to earth's remotest bound.

1 Rhea, according to the Orphic and Platonic theology, is one of the zoogonic or vivific principles of the universe, having a maternal rank among the paternal orders, *i.e.* between Saturn, who subsists at the summit, and Jupiter, who subsists at the extremity of the intellectual order. Hence, she calls forth the causes latent in Saturn to the procreation of the universe; and definitely unfolds all the genera of the Gods. So that she is filled from Saturn, with an intelligible and prolific power, which she imparts to Jupiter, the Demiurgus of the universe; filling his essence with a vivific abundance. Since this Goddess then is a medium between the two intellectual parents of the universe, Saturn and Jupiter, the former of which collects intellectual multitude into one, but the latter scatters and divides it; - hence, says Proclus (in Plat. Theol. V, 11, TTS vol. VIII, p. 322), this Goddess produces in herself the demiurgic causes of the

universe; but imparts her diffusive power abundantly to secondary natures. On this account Plato assimilates her prolific abundance to the flowing of waters; signifying nothing more by the word *flowing* than that fontal power by which she contains in transcendent union the divisible rivers of life. Proclus likewise in [TTS vol. VIII] p. 323 of the same work informs us, that this Goddess, according to Orpheus, when considered as united to Saturn by the most exalted part of her essence, is called Rhea; but considered as producing Jupiter, and together with Jupiter unfolding the total and partial orders of the Gods, she is called Ceres.

2 Phanes or Protogonus, as we are informed by Proclus in Tim. [291B, TTS vol. XVI, p. 876] not only subsists among the intelligible, but also among the intellectual Gods; in the demiurgic order, and among the supermundane and mundane Gods. And in a similar manner Night and Heaven: for the peculiarities of these are received through all the middle orders. Hence, as Rhea is one of the progeny of the intellectual Earth resident in Phanes, as we have before observed, the reason is obvious why she is said in this hymn to be the daughter of Protogonus. The Phanes, however, and Earth, from which Rhea proceeds, subsist in that divine order which is denominated by the Chaldean theologists νοητος και νοερος, *intelligible and at the same time intellectual*, and is celebrated by Plato in the *Phædrus* under the appellation of *Heaven*. This order, as subsisting between the intelligible and intellectual orders, participates of the former, and is κατα σχεσιν through proximity and alliance, the latter. Hence it is *primarily* intellectual.

3 The reason why Rhea is here called *brass-sounding*, and in the next line *drum-beating*, is in consequence of the enthusiastic energy of which she is the source. Hence, says Porphyry, in his Epistle to Anebo [14, TTS vol. XVII, p.14]: "Some of those who suffer a mental alienation energize enthusiastically on hearing certain cymbals or drums, or a certain modulated sound, such as those who are Corybantically inspired, those who are possessed by Sabazius, and those who are inspired by the mother of the Gods." On this passage, Iamblichus (De Myst. III, 9, 118, TTS vol. XVII, p. 71) beautifully observes as follows: "That music is of a motive nature, and is adapted to excite the affections, and that the melody of pipes produces or heals the disordered passions of the soul, changes the temperaments or dispositions of the body, and by some melodies causes a Bacchic fury, but by others occasions this fury to cease; and likewise how the differences of these accord with the several dispositions of the soul, and that unstable and variable melody is adapted to ecstasies, such as are the melodies of Olympus, and others of the like kind; all these appear to me to be adduced in a way foreign to enthusiasm. For they are physical and human, and the work of our art; but nothing whatever of a divine nature in them presents itself to the view.

"We must rather, therefore, say that sounds and melodies are appropriately consecrated to the Gods. There is also an alliance in these sounds and melodies to the proper orders and powers of the several Gods, to the motions in the universe itself, and to the harmonious sounds which proceed from the motions. Conformably therefore to such like adaptations of melodies to the Gods, the Gods themselves become present. For there is not any thing which intercepts; *so that whatever has but a casual similitude to directly participates of them.* A perfect possession likewise immediately takes place, and a plenitude of a more excellent essence and power." In Cap.10, also he observes, "that since the power of the Corybantes is in a certain respect of a guardian and efficacious nature, and that of Sabazius appropriately pertains to Bacchic inspiration, the purifications of souls, and the solutions of ancient divine anger, on this account the inspirations of them entirely differ from each other. With respect, however, to the Mother of the Gods, those who are precedaneously inspired by her are women; but the males that are thus inspired are very few in number, and such as are more effeminate. This enthusiasm, however has a *vivific* and replenishing power, on which account also it in a remarkable degree differs from all other mania." In this extract the reason why Iamblichus says that the enthusiasm of the Mother of the Gods has a *vivific* power is because she is a vivific Goddess, or the source of life to all things, being the same with Rhea. See more on this most interesting subject in my translation of this work of Iamblichus *On the Mysteries* [TTS vol. XVII].

4 When Jupiter was born (says the fable), his mother Rhea, in order to deceive Saturn, gave him a stone wrapped in swaddling bands, in the place of Jupiter, at the same time informing Saturn that what she gave him was her offspring. Saturn immediately devoured the stone; and Jupiter, who was *secretly* educated, at length obtained the government of the world. Such is the fable, as narrated by Phurnutus. (Vid. Opusc. Mythol. p. 147.) According to Phurnutus also, this fable adumbrates the creation of the world. "For at that time (says he) Nature [*i.e.* Jupiter according to him] was then nourished in the world, and at length prevailed. But the stone devoured by Saturn is the earth, alluding to its firmly occupying the middle place: for beings could not be permanent, without such a foundation for their support. From this all things are produced, and derive their proper aliment." This explanation of the, fable by Phurnutus, who was a Stoic philosopher, is very foreign from its true meaning. But the Stoics, though they greatly excelled in ethics, were very deficient in theology. The true solution of the fable, therefore, is only to be derived from Platonic, which are the same with the Orphic dogmas; and conformably to these, the development of the fable is as follows: Rhea is the fontal cause of all life, and is the middle deity of the intellectual triad, which consists of Saturn, Rhea, and Jupiter. But the peculiarities of the vivific order are (as Proclus demonstrates in MS. Comment. in Parmenidem, 1153 [see The Works of Plato III, TTS vol. XI, p. 211]) motion and permanency, the former unfolding into light the fountains of life, and the latter firmly establishing this life exempt from its proper rivers. The same thing is also demonstrated by him in Plat. Theol. lib. v. Damascius also, περι αρχων, observes, Τη Ρεα η ογδοας προσηκει, ως επι

παν κινηθειση κατα τασ διαιρεσεις, και ουδεν ηττον εστωση παγιως και κυβικως. *i.e.* "The ogdoad, or number eight, pertains to Rhea, as being moved to every thing, according to divisions or distributions of her essence, and nevertheless at the same time she remains firmly and cubically established." Damascius uses the word *cubically*, because eight is a cubic number. Rhea, therefore, considered as firmly establishing her offspring Jupiter, in Saturn, who exists in unproceeding union, is fabulously said to have given Saturn a stone instead of Jupiter, the stone indicating the *firm* establishment of Jupiter in Saturn. For all divine progeny, at the same time that they proceed from, abide in their causes. And the *secret* education of Jupiter indicates his being nurtured in the intelligible order: for this order is denominated by ancient theologists *occult*.

XV

TO JUPITER[1]

THE FUMIGATION FROM STORAX

O Jove, much-honour'd, Jove supremely great,
To thee our holy rites we consecrate,
Our pray'rs and expiations, king divine,
For all things to produce with ease thro' mind[2] is thine.
Hence mother Earth and mountains swelling high
Proceed from thee, the deep and all within the sky.
Saturnian king, descending from above,
Magnanimous, commanding, sceptred Jove;
All-parent, principle and end of all,[3]
Whose pow'r almighty shakes this earthly ball;
Ev'n Nature trembles at thy mighty nod,
Loud-sounding, arm'd with light'ning, thund'ring God.
Source of abundance, purifying king,
O various-form'd, from whom all natures spring;
Propitious hear my pray'r, give blameless health,
With peace divine, and necessary wealth.

---

1 For a copious development of the nature of this divinity, see the additional notes.

2 What I have here translated *thro' mind*, is in the original διὰ συν κεφαλήν, as it appeared to me to be obvious, that by the head *mind* must be indicated, of which the head is the receptacle.

3 Jupiter is *the principle* of all things in the universe, so far as he is the Demiurgus, but so far as be is the final cause, he is *the end of all*. Hence, too, Jupiter as the principle of the universe contains it in himself: for all things flow from their principle. In conformity to this, the following Orphic verses are cited by Proclus, in Tim. [95E, TTS vol. XV, p. 290]

> Hence with the universe great Jove contains
> Extended ether, heav'n's exalted plains;
> The barren sea, wide-bosom'd earth renown'd,
> Ocean immense, and Tartarus profound;

> Fountains and rivers, and the boundless main,
> With all that Nature's ample realms contain,
> And Gods and Goddesses of each degree;
> All that is past, and all that e'er shall be,
> Occultly, and in fair connection lies
> In Jove's vast belly, ruler of the skies.

In the last line of these verses, *the belly* of Jupiter is indicative of all that subsists as a *middle* in the universe; the belly being the middle part of the body. So that the poet, by asserting that all things are contained in the belly of Jupiter, occultly signifies to us, that this deity is not only the beginning and end, but also the *middle* of all things, as comprehending all *middles* in himself. A certain modern, not having the smallest conception of what the Greek theologist meant by the belly of Jupiter, says, somewhere in his voluminous mythological treatise, in answer to one who rightly conceived that the latter part of the above Orphic lines contained a grand image of the maker of the universe, "that it excited no other idea of Jupiter than that of an enormous glutton."

In the same place also, Proclus cites other Orphic verses, which are likewise to be found in the Treatise de Mundo (ascribed to Aristotle [TTS vol. XXIV]); previous to which he observes, that the Demiurgus, being full of ideas, comprehended through these all things in himself, as the theologist Orpheus says. With these verses I have connected others, conformably to the order of Stephens, Eschenbach, and Gesner, as follows:

> Jove is the first and last, high thund'ring king,
> Middle and head, from Jove all beings spring.
> In Jove the male and female forms combine,
> For Jove's a man, and yet a maid divine.
> Jove the strong basis of the earth contains,
> And the deep splendour of the starry plains.
> Jove is the breath of all; Jove's wondrous frame
> Lives in the rage of ever-restless flame.
> Jove is the sea's strong root, the solar light;
> And Jove's the moon, fair regent of the night.
> Jove is a king, by no restraint confin'd;
> And all things flow from Jove's prolific mind:
> One is the power divine, in all things known,
> And one the ruler absolute, alone.
> For in Jove's royal body all things lie,
> Fire, night and day, earth, water, and the sky;
> The first begetter's pleasing Love and Mind;
> These in his mighty body Jove confin'd.
> See how his beauteous head and aspect bright
> Illumine heav'n, and scatter boundless light!
> Round which his pendent golden tresses shine,
> Form'd from the starry beams, with light divine,

> On either side two radiant horns behold,
> Shap'd like a bull's, and bright with glitt'ring gold;
> And East and West in opposition lie,
> The lucid paths of all the Gods on high.
> His eyes the Sun and Moon with borrow'd ray:
> His mind is truth, unconscious of decay,
> Royal, etherial; and his ear refin'd
> Hears ev'ry voice and sounds of ev'ry kind.
> Thus are his head and mind immortal bright,
> His body boundless, stable, full of light.
> Strong are his members, with a force endu'd,
> Pow'rful to tame, but ne'er to be subdu'd.
> Th'extended region of surrounding air
> Forms his broad shoulders' back, and bosom fair;
> And thro' the world the ruler of the skies,
> Upborne on natal rapid pinions, flies.
> His sacred belly earth with fertile plains
> And mountains swelling to the clouds contains.
> His middle zone's the spreading sea profound,
> Whose roaring waves the solid globe surround.
> The distant realms of Tartarus obscure,
> Within Earth's roots, his holy feet secure;
> For these, Earth's utmost bounds, to Jove belong,
> And form his basis permanent and strong.
> Thus all things Jove within his breast conceal'd,
> And into beauteous light from thence reveal'd.

Jupiter, therefore, or the Demiurgus, is, according to Orpheus, all things, as containing in the unfathomable depths of his essence the causes of every thing which the sensible universe contains, these causes infinitely transcending the effects which they produce. Hence, by a causal priority, he is every thing which is contained in the sensible world. Pherecydes Syrus, also, conformably to this doctrine, says of Jupiter, as we learn from Kircher (in Œdip. Egypt. tom. ii. p. 89),

> Ο θεοσ εστι κυκλος, τετραγωνος, και δε τριγωνος
> Κεινος δ' η γραμμη, κεντρον, και παντα προ παντων.

i.e.
> "Jove is a circle, trigon, and a square,
> Centre and line, and all things before all."

Thus too, the ineffable principle of things is said to be *all things prior to all*, not as containing all things multitudinously in itself, but as that from which all things are ineffably unfolded into light.

XVI

TO JUNO[1]

THE FUMIGATION FROM AROMATICS

O royal Juno, of majestic mien,
Aerial-form'd, divine, Jove's blessed queen,
Thron'd in the bosom of cerulean air,
The race of mortals is thy constant care.
The cooling gales thy pow'r alone inspires,
Which nourish life, which ev'ry life desires.
Mother of show'rs and winds, from thee alone,
Producing all things, mortal life is known:
All natures share thy temp'rament divine,
And universal sway alone is thine,
With sounding blasts of wind, the swelling sea
And rolling rivers roar when shook by thee.
Come, blessed Goddess, fam'd almighty queen,
With aspect kind, rejoicing and serene.

---

1 Juno is called by the Orphic theologians, as we are informed by Proclus, ζωογονος θεα, *the vivific Goddess*; an epithet perfectly agreeing with the attributes ascribed to her in this hymn. Proclus also in Plat. Theol. VI, 22, [TTS vol. VIII, p. 455] says, "that Juno is the source of the procreation of the soul." See more concerning this divinity in the additional notes.

XVII

TO NEPTUNE[1]

THE FUMIGATION FROM MYRRH

Hear, Neptune, ruler of the sea profound,
Whose liquid grasp begirds the solid ground;
Who, at the bottom of the stormy main,
Dark and deep-bosom'd hold'st thy wat'ry reign.
Thy awful hand the brazen trident bears,
And Ocean's utmost bound thy will reveres.
Thee I invoke, whose steeds the foam divide,
From whose dark locks the briny waters glide;
Whose voice, loud sounding thro' the roaring deep,
Drives all its billows in a raging heap;
When fiercely riding thro' the boiling sea,
Thy hoarse command the trembling waves obey.
Earth-shaking, dark-hair'd God, the liquid plains
(The third division) Fate to thee ordains.
'Tis thine, cerulean dæmon, to survey,
Well-pleas'd, the monsters of the ocean play.
Confirm earth's basis, and with prosp'rous gales
Waft ships along, and swell the spacious sails;
Add gentle Peace, and fair-hair'd Health beside,
And pour abundance in a blameless tide.

1 See the nature of this divinity unfolded in the additional notes.

XVIII

TO PLUTO

A HYMN

Pluto, magnanimous, whose realms profound
Are fix'd beneath the firm and solid ground,
In the Tartarean plains remote from sight,
And wrapt for ever in the depths of night.
Terrestrial Jove,[1] thy sacred ear incline,
And pleas'd accept these sacred rites divine.
Earth's keys[2] to thee, illustrious king, belong,
Its secret gates unlocking, deep and strong.
'Tis thine abundant annual fruits to bear,
For needy mortals are thy constant care.
To thee, great king, all-sov'reign Earth's assign'd,
The seat of Gods and basis of mankind.
Thy throne is fix'd in Hades' dismal plains,
Distant, unknown to rest, where darkness reigns;
Where, destitute of breath, pale spectres dwell,
In endless, dire, inexorable hell;
And in dread Acheron, whose depths obscure,
Earth's stable roots eternally secure.
O mighty dæmon, whose decision dread,
The future fate determines of the dead,
With captive Proserpine, thro' grassy plains,
Drawn in a four-yok'd car with loosen'd reins,
Rapt o'er the deep, impell'd by love, you flew
Till Eleusina's city rose to view:
There, in a wondrous cave obscure and deep,
The sacred maid secure from search you keep,
The cave of Atthis, whose wide gates display
An entrance to the kingdoms void of day.
Of works unseen and seen thy power alone
To be the great dispensing source is known.
All-ruling, holy God, with glory bright,
Thee sacred poets and their hymns delight,
Propitious to thy mystics' works incline,
Rejoicing come, for holy rites are thine.

1 Pluto, says Proclus, in Plat. Theol. VI, 10 [TTS vol. VIII p. 421], is called *terrestrial Jupiter*, because he governs by his providence the earth and all it contains.

2 Proclus, in the Excerpta from his Commentary on the *Cratylus* of Plato [56, see *The Works of Plato V*, TTS vol. XIII, p. 555], informs us that initiators into the Mysteries, in order that sensibles might sympathize with the Gods, employed the shuttle as a signature of *separating*, a cup of *vivific*, a sceptre of *ruling*, and a KEY of *guardian power*. Hence Pluto, as the guardian of the earth, is here said to be the keeper of the earth's keys.

XIX

TO THUNDERING JUPITER

THE FUMIGATION FROM STORAX

O Father Jove, who shak'st with fiery light
The world, deep-sounding from thy lofty height.
From thee proceeds th'etherial lightning's blaze,
Flashing around intolerable rays.
Thy sacred thunders shake the blest abodes,
The shining regions of th'immortal Gods.
Thy pow'r divine the flaming lightning shrouds
With dark investiture in fluid clouds.
'Tis thine to brandish thunders strong and dire,
To scatter storms, and dreadful darts of fire;
With roaring flames involving all around,
And bolts of thunder of tremendous sound.
Thy rapid dart can raise the hair upright,
And shake the heart of man with wild affright.
Sudden, unconquer'd, holy, thund'ring God,
With noise unbounded flying all abroad;
With all-devouring force, entire and strong,
Horrid, untam'd, thou roll'st the flames along.
Rapid, etherial bolt, descending fire,
The earth, all-parent, trembles at thine ire;
The sea all-shining, and each beast, that hears
The sound terrific, with dread horror fears:
When Nature's face is bright with flashing fire,
And in the heav'ns resound thy thunders dire.
Thy thunders white the azure garments tear,
And burst the veil of all-surrounding air.
O Jove, all-blessed, may thy wrath severe,
Hurl'd in the bosom of the deep appear,
And on the tops of mountains be reveal'd,
For thy strong arm is not from us conceal'd.
Propitious to these sacred rites incline,
And to thy suppliants grant a life divine,
Add royal health, and gentle peace beside,
With upright reas'ning for a constant guide.

XX

TO JUPITER

As the Primary Cause of Lightning

THE FUMIGATION FROM FRANKINCENSE AND MANNA

I call the mighty, holy, splendid, light,
Aerial, dreadful-sounding, fiery-bright,
Flaming, etherial light, with angry voice,
Lightning thro' lucid clouds with crashing noise.
Untam'd, to whom resentments dire belong,
Pure, holy pow'r, all-parent, great and strong:
Come, and benevolent these rites attend,
And grant the mortal life a pleasing end.

XXI

TO THE CLOUDS

THE FUMIGATION FROM MYRRH

Aerial Clouds, thro' heav'ns resplendent plains
Who wander, parents of prolific rains;
Who nourish fruits, whose wat'ry frames are hurl'd,
By winds impetuous, round the mighty world.
Loud-sounding, lion-roaring, flashing fire,
In Air's wide bosom bearing thunders dire:
Impell'd by each sonorous stormy gale,
With rapid course along the skies ye sail.
With gentle gales your wat'ry frames I call,
On mother Earth with fruitful show'rs to fall.

XXII

TO TETHYS[1]

THE FUMIGATION FROM FRANKINCENSE AND MANNA

Tethys I call, with eyes cerulean bright,
Hid in a veil obscure from human sight:
Great Ocean's empress, wand'ring thro' the deep,
And pleas'd, with gentle gales, the earth to sweep;
Whose ample waves in swift succession go,
And lash the rocky shore with endless flow:
Delighting in the sea serene to play,
In ships exulting, and the wat'ry way.
Mother of Venus, and of clouds obscure,
Great nurse of beasts, and source of fountains pure.
O venerable Goddess, hear my pray'r,
And make benevolent my life thy care;
Send, blessed queen, to ships a prosp'rous breeze,
And waft them safely o'er the stormy seas.

1 See the nature of this divinity unfolded in the additional notes.

XXIII

TO NEREUS

THE FUMIGATION FROM MYRRH

O Thou who dost the roots of Ocean keep
In seats cerulean, dæmon of the deep,
With fifty nymphs (attending in thy train,
Fair virgin artists) glorying thro' the main:
The dark foundation of the rolling sea,
And Earth's wide bounds belong, much-fam'd, to thee.
Great dæmon, source of all, whose pow'r can make
The sacred basis of blest Ceres shake,
When blust'ring winds in secret caverns pent,
By thee excited, struggle hard for vent.
Come, blessed Nereus, listen to my pray'r,
And cease to shake the earth with wrath severe;
Send to thy mystics necessary wealth,
With gentle peace, and ever tranquil health.

XXIV

TO THE NEREIDS

THE FUMIGATION FROM AROMATICS

Daughters of Nereus, resident in caves
Merg'd deep in ocean, sporting thro' the waves;
Fifty inspir'd Nymphs, who thro' the main
Delight to follow in the Triton's train,
Rejoicing close behind their cars to keep;
Whose forms half wild are nourish'd by the deep,
With other Nymphs of different degree,
Leaping and wand'ring thro' the liquid sea.
Bright, wat'ry dolphins, sonorous and gay,
Well-pleas'd to sport with bacchanalian play;
Nymphs beauteous-ey'd, whom sacrifice delights,
Give plenteous wealth, and *bless our mystic rites*;
For you at first disclosed the rites divine,
Of holy Bacchus and of Proserpine,
Of fair Calliope, from whom I spring,
And of Apollo bright, the Muses' king.

XXV

TO PROTEUS[1]

Proteus I call, whom Fate decrees to keep
The keys which lock the chambers of the deep;
First-born, by whose illustrious pow'r alone
All Nature's principles were clearly shown.
Pure sacred matter to transmute is thine,
And decorate with forms all-various and divine.
All-honour'd, prudent, whose sagacious mind
Knows all that was and is of ev'ry kind,
With all that shall be in succeeding time,
So vast thy wisdom, wondrous and sublime:
For all things Nature first to thee consign'd,
And in thy essence omniform confin'd.
O father, to thy mystics' rites attend,
And grant a blessed life a prosp'rous end.

---

1 Proteus, says Proclus, in Plat. Repub. [see *The Works of Plato I*, TTS vol. IX, p. 273-4], though inferior to the primary Gods, is immortal; and though not a deity, is a certain angelic intellect of the order of Neptune, comprehending in himself all the forms of things generated in the universe.

XXVI

TO EARTH[1]

THE FUMIGATION FROM EVERY KIND OF SEED,
EXCEPT BEANS AND AROMATICS

O Mother Earth, of Gods and men the source,
Endu'd with fertile, all-destroying force;
All-parent, bounding, whose prolific pow'rs
Produce a store of beauteous fruits and flow'rs.
All-various maid, th'immortal world's strong base,
Eternal, blessed, crown'd with ev'ry grace;
From whose wide womb as from an endless root,
Fruits many-form'd, mature, and grateful shoot.
Deep-bosom'd, blessed, pleas'd with grassy plains,
Sweet to the smell, and with prolific rains.
All-flow'ry dæmon, centre of the world,
Around thy orb the beauteous stars are hurl'd
With rapid whirl, eternal and divine,
Whose frames with matchless skill and wisdom shine.
Come, blessed Goddess, listen to my pray'r,
And make increase of fruits thy constant care;
With fertile Seasons in thy train draw near,
And with propitious mind thy suppliants hear.

---

1 According to the Orphic theology, Earth is the mother of every thing of which Heaven is the father. See the additional notes.

XXVII

TO THE MOTHER OF THE GODS

THE FUMIGATION FROM A VARIETY OF ODORIFEROUS SUBSTANCES

Mother of Gods, great nurse of all, draw near,
Divinely honour'd, and regard my pray'r.
Thron'd on a car, by lions drawn along,
By bull-destroying lions, swift and strong,
Thou sway'st the sceptre of the pole divine,[1]
And the world's middle seat, much fam'd, is thine.
Hence earth is thine, and needy mortals share
Their constant food, from thy protecting care.
From thee at first both Gods and men arose;
From thee the sea and ev'ry river flows.
Vesta and source of wealth thy name we find
To mortal men rejoicing to be kind;
For ev'ry good to give thy soul delights.
Come, mighty pow'r, propitious to our rites,
All-taming, blessed, Phrygian Saviour, come,
Saturn's great queen, rejoicing in the drum.
Celestial, ancient, life-supporting maid,
Inspiring fury; give thy supplaint aid;
With joyful aspect on our incense shine,
And pleas'd, accept the sacrifice divine.

---

1 The Mother of the Gods is the same with Rhea; and Proclus, in the second book of his Commentary on Euclid, informs us, *that the pole of the world is called by the Pythagoreans the seal of Rhea.*

XXVIII

TO MERCURY[1]

THE FUMIGATION FROM FRANKINCENSE

Hermes, draw near, and to my pray'r incline,
Angel of Jove, and Maia's son divine;
Prefect of contests, ruler of mankind,
With heart almighty, and a prudent mind.
Celestial messenger of various skill,
Whose pow'rful arts could watchful Argus kill.
With winged feet 'tis thine thro' air to course,
O friend of man, and prophet of discourse:
Great life-supporter, to rejoice is thine
In arts gymnastic, and in fraud divine.
With pow'r endu'd all language to explain,
Of care the loos'ner, and the source of gain.
Whose hand contains of blameless peace the rod,
Corucian, blessed, profitable God.
Of various speech, whose aid in works we find,
And in necessities to mortals kind.
Dire weapon of the tongue, which men revere,
Be present, Hermes, and thy suppliant hear;
Assist my works, conclude my life with peace,
Give graceful speech, and memory's increase.

---

[1] Proclus, in his admirable Commentary on the *First Alcibiades*, of which two excellent editions have been recently published by Cousin and Creuzer, gives us the following information respecting Mercury, which as the reader will easily perceive greatly elucidates some parts of this hymn. "Mercury is *the source of invention*; and hence he is said to be the son of Maia; because *search*, which is implied by *Maia*, leads invention into light. He bestows too *mathesis* on souls, by unfolding the will of his father Jupiter; and this he accomplishes, as the angel or messenger of Jupiter. He is likewise the inspective guardian of *gymnastic exercises*; and hence *hermæ*, or carved statues of Mercury, were placed in the Palæstræ; of *music*, and hence he is honoured as λυραιος, the *lyrist* among the celestial constellations; and of *disciplines*, because the invention of geometry, reasoning, and language is referred to this God. He presides,

therefore, over every species of erudition, leading us to an intelligible essence from this mortal abode, governing the different herds of souls, and dispersing the sleep and oblivion with which they are oppressed. He is likewise the supplier of recollection, the end of which is a genuine intellectual apprehension of divine natures." [Comm. Alc. I, 188, see *The Works of Plato I*, TTS vol. IX, p. 278.]

XXIX

TO PROSERPINE

A HYMN

Daughter of Jove, Persephone divine,
Come, blessed queen, and to these rites incline:
Only-begotten,[1] Pluto's honour'd wife,
O venerable Goddess, source of life:
'Tis thine in earth's profundities to dwell,
Fast by the wide and dismal gates of hell.
Jove's holy offspring, of a beauteous mien,
Avenging Goddess, subterranean queen.
The Furies' source, fair-hair'd, whose frame proceeds
From Jove's ineffable and secret seeds.
Mother of Bacchus, sonorous, divine,
And many-form'd, the parent of the vine.
Associate of the Seasons, essence bright,
All-ruling virgin, bearing heav'nly light.
With fruits abounding, of a bounteous mind,
Horn'd, and alone desir'd by those of mortal kind.
O vernal queen, whom grassy plains delight,
Sweet to the smell, and pleasing to the sight:
Whose holy form in budding fruits we view,
Earth's vig'rous offspring of a various hue:
Espous'd in autumn,[2] life and death alone
To wretched mortals from thy pow'r is known:
For thine the task, according to thy will,
Life to produce, and all that lives to kill.[3]
Hear, blessed Goddess, send a rich increase
Of various fruits from earth, with lovely Peace:
Send Health with gentle hand, and crown my life
With blest abundance, free from noisy strife;
Last in extreme old age the prey of Death,
Dismiss me willing to the realms beneath,
To thy fair palace and the blissful plains
Where happy spirits dwell, and Pluto reigns.

1 Proclus, in Tim. lib II, 139B [TTS vol. XV, p. 418], says, "that the theologist [Orpheus] is accustomed to call Proserpine *only-begotten*." Και γαρ ο Θεολογος την Κορην μουνογενειαν ειωθε προσαγορευειν. See the additional notes.

2 "The rape of Proserpine, says Sallust (De Diis et Mundo, cap. 4[†]) is fabled to have taken place about the opposite equinox; and this rape signifies the descent of souls." περι γουν την εναντιαν ισημεριαν η της Κορης αρπαγη μυθολογειται ηενεσθαι, ο δη καθοδος εστι των ψυχων. According to Lydus De Mensibus, the festival of Proserpine was celebrated on the sixth of the Nones of October. Hence the reason is obvious why Proserpine is said in this hymn to have been espoused in autumn.

3 Proclus, in Plat. Theol. VI, 11 [TTS vol. VIII, p. 423], informs us, that according to the Eleusinian mysteries, Proserpine, together with Pluto, governs terrestrial concerns, and the recesses of the earth; and that she supplies the extreme parts of the universe with life, and imparts soul to those who by her power are rendered inanimate and dead. This is perfectly conformable to what is said in the above hymn.

[†] TTS volume IV.

XXX

TO BACCHUS[1]

THE FUMIGATION FROM STORAX

Bacchus I call loud-sounding and divine,
Inspiring God, a twofold shape is thine:
Thy various names and attributes I sing,
O firstborn, thrice begotten, Bacchic king.
Rural, ineffable, two-form'd, obscure,
Two-horn'd, with ivy crown'd, and Euion[2] pure:
Bull-fac'd and martial, bearer of the vine,
Endu'd with counsel prudent and divine:
Omadius, whom the leaves of vines adorn,
Of Jove and Proserpine occultly born
In beds ineffable; all-blessed pow'r,
Whom with triennial off'rings men adore.
Immortal dæmon, hear my suppliant voice,
Give me in blameless plenty to rejoice;
And listen gracious to my mystic pray'r,
Surrounded with thy choir of nurses fair.

1 See the additional notes.

2 So called from the voice of the Bacchants.

XXXI

TO THE CURETES

A HYMN

Leaping Curetes, who with dancing feet
And circling measures armed footsteps beat:
Whose bosoms Bacchanalian furies fire,
Who move in rhythm to the sounding lyre:
Who traces deaf when lightly leaping tread,
Arm-bearers, strong defenders, rulers dread:
Fam'd Deities the guards of Proserpine,[1]
Preserving rites mysterious and divine:
Come, and benevolent this hymn attend,
And with glad mind the *herdsman's* life defend.

---

1 The Corybantes, who in the *supermundane* are the same as the Curetes in the *intellectual* order, are said by Proclus, in Plat. Theol. VI, 13 [TTS vol. VIII, p. 433], "to be the guards of Proserpine." And in hymn xxxviii, the Curetes are celebrated as being also the Corybantes; in consequence of both these triads being of a guardian characteristic, and subsisting in profound union with each other.

XXXII

TO PALLAS[1]

A HYMN

Only-begotten, noble race of Jove,
Blessed and fierce, who joy'st in caves to rove:
O warlike Pallas, whose illustrious kind,
Ineffable, and effable we find:
Magnanimous and fam'd, the rocky height,
And groves, and shady mountains thee delight:
In arms rejoicing, who with furies dire
And wild the souls of mortals dost inspire.
Gymnastic virgin of terrific mind,
Dire Gorgon's bane, unmarried, blessed, kind:
Mother of arts, impetuous; understood
As fury by the bad, but wisdom by the good.
Female and male, the arts of war are thine,
O much-form'd, dragoness,[2] inspir'd, divine:
O'er the Phlegrean giants,[3] rous'd to ire,
Thy coursers driving with destruction dire.
Sprung from the head of Jove, of splendid mien,
Purger of evils, all-victorious queen.
Hear me, O Goddess, when to thee I pray,
With supplicating voice both night and day,
And in my latest hour give peace and health,
Propitious times, and necessary wealth,
And ever present be thy vot'ries aid,
O much implor'd, art's parent, blue-ey'd maid.

---

1 The supermundane vivific triad consists (as we are informed by Proclus in Plat. Theol. VI, 11 [TTS vol. VIII, p. 423]) of three *zoogonic* monads; and these are Diana, Proserpine, and Minerva. "And of these (says he) the highest or first is arranged according to *hyparxis* [*i.e.* the summit of essence]; the second according to *power*, which is definitive of life; and the third according to *vivific intellect*. Theologists, also, are accustomed to call the first *Coric Diana*; the second *Proserpine*; and the third *Coric Minerva*. I mean that they are thus denominated by the primary leaders of the Grecian theology. For by the

Barbarians, likewise [*i.e.* the Chaldean theologists], the same things are manifested through other names. For they call the first monad *Hecate*; the middle monad *Soul*; and the third *Virtue*." Conformably to this, Psellus, in his Exposition of the Chaldaic Dogmas, says:[†] των δε ζωογονων αρχων, η μεν ακροτης Εκατη καλειται· η δε μεσοτης, ψηχη αρχικη· η δε περατωσις, αρετη αρχικη. *i.e.* "Of the zoogonic principles, the summit is called *Hecate*; the middle, *ruling Soul*; and the extremity, *ruling Virtue*." The supermundane order is also called by Proclus αρχικη, because the divinities of which it consists are *principles* and *rulers*.

The reason, therefore, is obvious why Minerva in this hymn is said *to delight in caves, rocks, groves, and shady mountains*; for this arises from her union with Diana. And hence it appears, that Runkenius was mistaken in asserting that these epithets were misplaced. We may likewise hence see the reason why, in line thirteen, Minerva is called, "*female* and *male*," as well as the Moon; and why the Moon in the hymn to her is called πανσοφε κουρη, "*all-wise virgin*."

2 It is easy to perceive the agreement between Minerva, who is characterized by divine wisdom and providence, and a dragon; since, according to Phurnutus, a dragon is of a vigilant and guardian nature.

3 As the fable of the giants is well known, but its real meaning is known only to a few, the following explanation of the battles of the Gods is inserted from the Fragments of the Commentary of Proclus on the *Republic* of Plato:[‡] "The divided progressions of all things and their essential separations supernally originate from that division of first operating causes [*i.e.* from bound and infinity], which is perfectly arcane; and subsisting according to those principles which are expanded above wholes, they dissent from each other; some being suspended from the unifying monad *bound*, and about this determining their subsistence, but others receiving in themselves a never failing power from that *infinity* which is generative of wholes, and is a cause productive of multitude and progression, and about this establishing their proper essence. Just, therefore, as the first principles of things are separated from each other, all the divine genera and true beings are divided from each other, according to an orderly progression. Hence some of them are the leaders of *union* to secondary natures, but others impart the power of *separation*; some are the causes of *conversion*, convolving the multitude of progressions to their proper principles; but others *bound the progressions*, and the subordinate *generation* from the principles. Again, some supply a *generative abundance* to inferior natures, but

---

[†] See *Oracles and Mysteries*, TTS vol. VII, p. 4.

[‡] See *The Works of Plato I* (TTS vol. IX) in which a large part of this extant commentary is included as an introduction to the second and third books of the *Republic*; this passage is to be found on p. 256 ff.

others impart an *immutable* and *undefiled purity*; some bind to themselves the cause of *separate* good, but others of the good which is *consubsistent* with the beings that receive it. And thus in all the orders of being is such a contrariety of genera diversified. Hence *permanency*, which establishes things in themselves, is opposed to *efficacious powers*, and which are full of *life* and *motion*. Hence, too, the kindred communion of *sameness* receives a division according to species opposite to the separations of *difference*; but the genus of *similitude* is allotted an order contrary to *dissimilitude*; and that of *equality* to *inequality*, according to the same analogy. Is it, therefore, any longer wonderful, if the authors of fables, perceiving such contrariety in the Gods themselves and the first of beings, obscurely signified this to their pupils through battles? the divine genera, indeed, being perpetually united to each other, but at the same time containing in themselves the causes of the union and separation of all things.

"We may also, I think, adduce another mode of solution; *viz.* that the Gods themselves are impartibly connascent with each other, and subsist uniformly in each other, but that their progressions into the universe, and their communications are separated in their participants, become divisible, and are thus filled with contrariety; the objects of their providential exertions not being able to receive in an unmingled manner the powers proceeding from thence, and without confusion their multiform illuminations. We may likewise say, that the last orders which are suspended from divine natures, as being generated remote from first causes, and as being proximate to the subjects of their government, which are involved in matter, participate themselves of all-various contrariety and separation, and partibly preside over material natures, minutely dividing those powers which presubsist uniformly and impartibly in their first operating causes. Such, then, and so many, being the modes according to which the mystic rumours of theologists refer war to the Gods themselves: - other poets, and those who have explained divine concerns through a divinely inspired energy, have ascribed wars and battles to the Gods according to the first of those modes we related, in which the divine genera are divided conformably to the first principles of wholes. For those powers which *elevate to causes* are, after a manner, opposed to those that are *the sources of generation*, and the *connective* to the *separating*; those that *unite* to those that *multiply* the progression of things; *total* genera to such as fabricate *partibly*; and those which are *expanded above* to those that *preside over* partial natures: and hence fables, concealing the truth, assert that such powers fight and war with each other. On this account, as it appears to me, they assert that the Titans were the antagonists of Bacchus, and the Giants of Jupiter. For union, indivisible energy, and a wholeness prior to parts[†] are adapted to those fabricators that have a subsistence prior to the world. But the Titans and Giants produce the

---

[†] *Whole* has a triple subsistence; for it is either prior to parts, *i.e.* is the *cause* of the parts which it contains; or it is the aggregate of parts; or it subsists in a part. See my translation of Proclus' *Elements of Theology* (TTS Volume I).

demiurgic powers into multitude, divisibly administer the affairs of the universe, and are the proximate fathers of material natures."

Proclus, in his elegant hymn to Minerva, says of this victory of Minerva over the Giants:

>Η σοφιης πετασασα θεοστιβεασ πυλεωνας,
>Και χθονιων δαμασασα θεωμαχα φυλα γιγαντων.

i.e.
"The God-trod gates of wisdom by thy hand
Are wide unfolded, and the daring band
Of earth-born giants, that in impious fight,
Strove with thy sire, were vanquish'd by thy might."

XXXIII

TO VICTORY

THE FUMIGATION FROM MANNA

O Powerful Victory, by men desir'd,
With adverse breasts to dreadful fury fir'd,
Thee I invoke, whose might alone can quell
Contending rage and molestation fell.
'Tis thine in battle to confer the crown,
The victor's prize, the mark of sweet renown;
For thou rul'st all things, Victory divine!
And glorious strife, and joyful shouts are thine.
Come, mighty Goddess, and thy suppliant bless,
With sparkling eyes, elated with success;
May deeds illustrious thy protection claim,
And find, led on by thee, immortal fame.

XXXIV

TO APOLLO

THE FUMIGATION FROM MANNA

Blest Pæan, come, propitious to my pray'r,
Illustrious pow'r, whom Memphian tribes revere,
Slayer of Tityus, and the God of health,
Lycorian Phœbus, fruitful source of wealth:
Spermatic, golden-lyr'd, the field from thee
Receives its constant rich fertility.
Titanic, Grunian,[1] Smynthian, thee I sing,
Python-destroying,[2] hallow'd, Delphian king:
Rural, light-bearer, and the Muses' head,
Noble and lovely, arm'd with arrows dread:
Far-darting, Bacchian, twofold, and divine,
Pow'r far diffus'd, and course oblique is thine.
O Delian king, whose light-producing eye
Views all within, and all beneath the sky;
Whose locks are gold, whose oracles are sure,
Who omens good reveal'st, and precepts pure;
Hear me entreating for the human kind,
Hear, and be present with benignant mind;
For thou survey'st this boundless ether all,
And ev'ry part of this terrestrial ball
Abundant, blessed; and thy piercing sight
Extends beneath the gloomy, silent night;
Beyond the darkness, starry-ey'd,[3] profound,
The stable roots, deep-fix'd by thee, are found.
The world's wide bounds, all-flourishing, are thine,
Thyself of all the source and end divine.
'Tis thine all Nature's music to inspire
With various-sounding, harmonizing lyre:[4]
Now the last string thou tun'st to sweet accord,[5]
Divinely warbling, now the highest chord;
Th'immortal golden lyre, now touch'd by thee,
Responsive yields a Dorian melody.
All Nature's tribes to thee their diff'rence owe,

And changing seasons from thy music flow:
Hence, mix'd by thee in equal parts, advance
Summer and Winter in alternate dance;
This claims the highest, that the lowest string,
The Dorian measure tunes the lovely spring:
Hence by mankind Pan royal, two-horn'd nam'd,
Shrill winds emitting thro' the syrinx fam'd;[6]
Since to thy care the figur'd seal's consign'd,[7]
Which stamps the world with forms of ev'ry kind.
Hear me, blest pow'r, and in these rites rejoice,
And save thy mystics with a suppliant voice.

1 Grynæus, according to Strabo, lib. 13, is a town of Myrinæus, and is likewise a temple of Apollo, and a most ancient oracle and temple, sumptuously built of white stone.

2 "Typhon, Echidna, and Python being the progeny of Tartarus and Earth, which is conjoined with Heaven, (says Olympiodorus in MS. Comment. in Phædon. [142, *The Works of Plato IV*, TTS vol XII, p. 321) form, as it were, a certain Chaldaic triad, which is the inspective guardian of the whole of a disordered fabrication [*i.e.* of the fabrication of the last of things]." Οτι Ταρταρου και Γης της συζυγουσης τω Ουρανω, ο Τηφων, η Εχιδα, ο Πυθων, οιον Χαλδαικη τις τριας εφοπος της ατακτους πασης δημιουργιας. And in another part of the same Commentary he says, "that Typhon is the cause of the all-various subterranean winds and waters, and of the violent motion of the other elements. But Echidna is a cause revenging and punishing rational and irrational souls; and hence the upper parts of her are those of a virgin, but the lower those of a serpent. And *Python* is the guardian of the whole of prophetic production. Though it will be better to say, that he is the cause of the disorder and obstruction pertaining to things of this kind. Hence, also, Apollo destroyed Python, in consequence of the latter being adverse [to the prophetic energy of the former]. Ο μεν Τυφων της παντοιας των υπογειων πνευματων και υδατων, και των αλλων στοιχειων βιαιου κινησεως αιτιος· η δε Αιχιδνα τιμωρος αιτια και κολαστικη λογικων τε και αλογων ψυχων· διο τα μεν ανω παρθενος· τα δε κατω εστιν οφεωδης· ο δε Πυθων φρουρος της μαντικης ολης αναδοσεως· αμεινον δε της περι ταυτα αταξιας τε και αντιφραξεως αιτιον λεγειν· διο και Απολλων αυτον αναιρει εναντιουμενον.

3 *The starry-eyed darkness*, beyond which Apollo is here said to fix his roots, is the sphere of the fixed stars, the region immediately beyond which consists of the etherial worlds, which according to the Chaldeans are three. For they assert that there are seven corporeal worlds, one empyrean and the first; after this, three etherial, and then three material worlds, which last consist of the inerratic sphere, the seven planetary spheres, and the sublunary region. But that,

according to the Orphic theology, there is an etherial world beyond the sphere of the fixed stars is evident from the following mystic particulars respecting the Oracle of Night, which are transmitted to us by Proclus in his admirable Commentary on the *Timæus*, p. 63E and p. 96A [TTS vol XV, p. 194 & 291]. "The artificer of the universe (says he), prior to his whole fabrication, is said to have betaken himself to the Oracle of Night, to have been there filled with divine conceptions, to have received the principles of fabrication, and, if it be lawful so to speak, to have solved all his doubts. Night, too, calls upon the father Jupiter to undertake the fabrication of the universe; and Jupiter is said by the theologist [Orpheus] to have thus addressed Night:

        Μαια θεων υπατη, Νυξ αμβροτε, πως ταδε φρασεις;
        Πως δει μ' αθανατων αρχην κρατεροφρονα θεσθαι;
        Πως δε μοι εν τι τα παντ' εσται, και χωρις εκαστον;

i.e.   O Nurse supreme of all the pow'rs divine,
        Immortal Night! how with unconquer'd mind
        Must I the source of the Immortals fix?
        And how will all things but as one subsist,
        Yet each its nature separate preserve?

To which interrogations the Goddess thus replies:

        Αιθερι παντα περιξ αφατῳ λαβε· τῳ δ' ενι μεσσω
        Ουρανον, εν δε τε γαιαν απειριτον, εν δε θαλασσαν,
        Εν δε τε τειπεα παντα, τα τ' ουρανος εστεφανωτο.

i.e.   All things receive enclos'd on ev'ry side,
        In Ether's wide, ineffable embrace;
        Then in the midst of Ether place the Heav'n,
        In which let Earth of infinite extent,
        The Sea, and Stars the crown of Heav'n be fixt.

We also learn from Psellus, that according to the Chaldeans there are two solar worlds; *one which is subservient* to the etherial profundity; the other zonaic, being one of the seven spheres. (See his concise Exposition of Chaldaic Dogmas [TTS vol. VII, p. 3 ff].) And Proclus, in Tim. p. 264D, informs us, "that according to the most mystic assertions, the *wholeness* of the Sun is in the supermundane order. For there a solar world and a total light subsist, as the Oracles of the Chaldeans affirm." Οι γε μυστικωτατοι των λογων, και την ολοτητα αυτου (solis) την εν τοις υπερκοσμιοις παραδεδωκασιν· εκει γαρ ο ηλιακος κοσμος, και το ολον φως, ως αι τε Χαλδαιων φημοι λεγουσι. These etherial worlds pertain to the supermundane order of Gods, in which the *wholeness* of the Sun subsists. But by the *wholeness* (ολοτης) Proclus means the sphere in which the visible orb of the Sun is fixed, and which is called a *wholeness*, because it has a perpetual subsistence, and comprehends in itself all the multitude of which it is the cause. Conformably to this, the Emperor

Julian (in Orat. v.) says: "The orb of the Sun revolves in the starless, much above the inerratic sphere. Hence he is not the middle of the planets, but of the three worlds [*i.e.* of the three etherial worlds], according to the telestic hypothesis." Ο δισκος επι της αναστρου φερεται, πολυ της απλανους υψηλοτερας, και ουτω δε των μεν πλανωμενων ουκ εξει το μεσον, τριων δε των κοσμων κατα τας τελεστικας υποθεσεις. From all this, therefore, it is evident why Apollo in this hymn is said to fix his roots beyond the starry-eyed darkness; for this signifies that Gods are inserted by him in the etherial worlds; *roots* being indicative of *summits* (ακροτητες) and such, according to the Orphic and Chaldaic theologists, are the Gods. Hence Proclus (in MS. Comment. in Parmenid. [1050, *The Works of Plato III*, TTS vol. XI, p. 184]) beautifully observes, "As trees by their summits are firmly established in the earth, and all that pertains to them is through this earthly; after the same manner divine natures are by their summits *rooted in The One*, and each of them is a unity and one, through an unconfused union with *The One Itself.*" καθαπερ γαρ τα δενδρα ταις εαυτων κορυφαις ενιδρυνται τη γη, και εστι γηινα τα κατ' εκεινας, τον αυτον τροπον και τα θεια, ταις εαυτων ακροτησιν ενερριζωται τω ενι, και εκαστον αυτων ενας εστι και εν, δια την προς το εν ασυγχυτον ενωσιν.

4 Gesner well observes, in his notes on this hymn, that the comparison and conjunction of the musical and astronomical elements are most ancient; being derived from Orpheus and Pythagoras to Plato. The lyre of Apollo, however, is not only indicative of the harmony of the universe, of which this divinity is the source, but particularly adumbrates according to the Orphic and Pythagoric doctrine, the celestial harmony, or the melody caused by the revolutions of the celestial spheres. This harmony of the spheres is admirably unfolded by Simplicius in his Commentary on the second book of Aristotle's *Treatise on the Heavens*, as follows:[†] "The Pythagoreans said, that an harmonic sound is produced from the motion of the celestial bodies; and they scientifically collected this from the analogy of their intervals; since not only the ratios of the intervals of the sun and moon, and Venus and Mercury, but also of the other stars, were discovered by them." Simplicius adds, "Perhaps the objection of Aristotle to this assertion of the Pythagoreans may be solved as follows, according to the philosophy of those men: all things are not commensurate with each other, nor is every thing sensible commensurate to every thing, even in the sublunary region. This is evident from dogs, who scent animals at a great distance, and which are not smelt by men. How much more, therefore, in things which are separated by so great an interval as those which are incorruptible from the corruptible, and celestial from terrestrial natures, is it true to say that the sound of divine bodies is not audible by terrestrial ears? But if any one, like Pythagoras, who is reported to have heard this harmony,

---

[†] See *The Works of Aristotle VII*, TTS vol. XXV, note (no. 37) to the text of Aristotle 290b10.

should have his terrestrial body exempt from him, and his luminous and celestial vehicle, and the senses which it contains, purified, either through a good allotment, or through probity of life, or through a perfection arising from sacred operations, such a one will perceive things invisible to others, and will hear things inaudible by others. With respect to divine and immaterial bodies, however, if any sound is produced by them, it is neither percussive nor destructive, but it excites the powers and energies of sublunary sounds, and perfects the sense which is coordinate with them. It has also a certain analogy to the sound which concurs with the motion of terrestrial bodies. But the sound which is with us, in consequence of the sonorific nature of the air, is a certain energy of the motion of their impassive sound. If then, air is not passive there, it is evident that neither will the sound which is there be passive. Pythagoras, however, seems to have said that he heard the celestial harmony, as understanding the harmonic proportions in numbers, of the heavenly bodies, and that which is audible in them. Some one, however, may very properly doubt why the stars are seen by our visive sense, but the sound of them is not heard by our ears? To this we reply, that neither do we see the stars themselves; for we do not see their magnitudes, or their figures, or their surpassing beauty. Neither do we see the motion through which the sound is produced; but we see, as it were, such an illumination of them as that of the light of the sun about the earth, the sun himself not being seen by us. Perhaps too, neither will it be wonderful, that the visive sense, as being more immaterial, subsisting rather according to energy than according to passion, and very much transcending the other senses, should be thought worthy to receive the splendour and illumination of the celestial bodies, but that the other senses should not be adapted for this purpose."

5 The following quotations from Nicomachus (Harm. lib. i. p. 6) illustrates the meaning of the hypate and nete, or the highest and lowest string, in the lyre of Apollo: "From the motion of Saturn (says he) the most remote of the planets, the appellation of the gravest sound, hypate, is derived; but from the lunar motion, which is the lowest of all, the most acute sound is called nete, or the lowest." But Gesner observes, that a more ancient, and as it were archetypal, appellation is derived from the ancient triangular lyre, a copy of which was found among the pictures lately dug out of the ruins of Herculaneum; in which the highest chord next to the chin of the musician is the longest, and consequently (says he) the sound is the most grave. Gesner proceeds in observing, that three seasons of the year are so compared together in a musical ratio, that hypate signifies the Winter, nete the Summer, and the Dorian measure represents the intermediate seasons, Spring and Autumn. Now the reason why the Dorian melody is assigned to the Spring, is because that measure wholly consists in temperament and moderation, as we learn from Plutarch in his Treatise De Musica. Hence it is with great propriety attributed to the Spring, considered as placed between Winter and Summer; and gratefully tempering the fervent heat of the one, and the intense cold of the other.

6 According to the Pythagoric and Platonic theology, which is perfectly conformable to that of Orpheus, Apollo is in the supermundane what Jupiter is in the intellectual order. For as the former illuminates mundane natures with supermundane light, so the latter illuminates the supermundane order with intellectual light. Indeed, there is such a wonderful agreement between these two divinities, that the Cyprian priests, as we are informed by the Emperor Julian, in his most excellent *Oration to the Sovereign Sun*,† raised common altars to Jupiter and the Sun. Hence we cannot wonder that the same thing is here asserted of Apollo which Orpheus elsewhere asserts of Jupiter. For Johan. Diaco. in Hesiod. Theog. quotes the following lines from Orpheus:

Ζευς δε τε παντων εστι θεος, παντων τε κεραστης,
Πνευμασι συριζων, φοναισι τε αερομικτοις.

i.e. "Jupiter is the God of all, and the mingler of all things, *emitting shrill sounds* from winds and air-mingled voices."

7 In the preceding note we have mentioned the profound union which subsists between Apollo and Jupiter. As Jupiter, therefore, considered as the Demiurgus, comprehends in himself the archetypal ideas of all sensible forms, and what these forms are *intellectually* in the Demiurgus they are according to a *supermundane* characteristic in Apollo; hence the latter divinity, as well as the former, may be said to possess the figured seal, of which every visible species is nothing more than an impression.

---

† TTS volume IV.

XXXV

TO LATONA[1]

THE FUMIGATION FROM MYRRH

Dark-veil'd Latona, much invoked queen,
Twin-bearing Goddess, of a noble mien;
Cæantis great, a mighty mind is thine,
Offspring prolific, blest, of Jove divine:
Phœbus proceeds from thee, the God of light,
And Dian fair, whom winged darts delight;
She in Ortygia's honour'd regions born,
In Delos he, which lofty mounts adorn.
Hear me, O queen, and fav'rably attend,
And to this *Telete divine afford a pleasing end.*

1 See the additional notes.

XXXVI

TO DIANA

THE FUMIGATION FROM MANNA

Hear me, Jove's daughter, celebrated queen,
Bacchian and Titan, of a noble mien:
In darts rejoicing, and on all to shine,
Torch-bearing Goddess, Dictynna divine.
O'er births presiding,[1] and thyself a maid,
To labour pangs imparting ready aid:
Dissolver of the zone, and wrinkled care,
Fierce huntress, glorying in the silvan war:
Swift in the course, in dreadful arrows skill'd,
Wand'ring by night, rejoicing in the field:
Of manly form, erect, of bounteous mind,
Illustrious dæmon, nurse of humankind:
Immortal, earthly, bane of monsters fell,
'Tis thine, blest maid, on woody mounts to dwell:
Foe of the stag, whom woods and dogs delight,
In endless youth you flourish fair and bright.
O universal queen, august, divine,
A various form, Cydonian pow'r, is thine.
Dread guardian Goddess, with benignant mind,
Auspicious come, to mystic rites inclin'd;
Give earth a store of beauteous fruits to bear,
Send gentle Peace, and Health with lovely hair,
And to the mountains drive Disease and Care.

---

1 In the original λοχεια; and Proclus, in Plat. Theol. VI, 22 [TTS vol. VIII, p. 455], informs us that this epithet is given by theologists to Diana, because she is the inspective guardian of natural progression and generation. See more concerning this divinity in the additional notes.

XXXVII

TO THE TITANS

THE FUMIGATION FROM FRANKINCENSE

O mighty Titans, who from Heav'n and Earth
Derive your noble and illustrious birth,
Our fathers' sires, in Tartarus[1] profound
Who dwell, deep merg'd beneath the solid ground:
Fountains and principles from whom began
Th'afflicted miserable race of man:[2]
Who not alone in earth's retreats abide,
But in the ocean and the air reside;
Since ev'ry species from your nature flows,
Which, all-prolific, nothing barren knows.
Avert your rage, if from th'infernal seats
One of your tribe should visit our retreats.

---

1 "Tartarus (says Olympiodorus in MS. in Comment. on Phædon.) is a Deity who is the inspective guardian of the extremities of the world, just as Pontus [the sea] is the guardian of the middle, and Olympus of the summits of the universe. And these three are to be found not only in the sensible world, but also in the demiurgic intellect, in the supermundane, and the celestial order." Οτι ο ταρταρος εστι τας εσχατιας του κοσμου επισκοπων, ως ο Ποντος τας μεσοτητας, ως ο Ολυμπος τας ακροτητας· εστιν ουν τρεις ευρειν ουκ εν τω αισθητω μονω τω δε κοσμω, αλλα και εν τω δημιουργικω νω, και εν τω κοσμιω (lege υπερκοσμιω) διακοσμω, και εν τω ουρανιω.

2 The reasons why the Titans are said in this hymn to be the fountains and principles of mankind depends on the following arcane narration, for the sources of which I refer the reader to my Treatise on the *Eleusinian and Bacchic Mysteries* [in Oracles and Mysteries, TTS vol VII, p. 111]: Dionysius, or Bacchus, while he was yet a boy, was engaged by the Titans, through the stratagems of Juno, in a variety of sports, with which that period of life is so vehemently allured; and among the rest, he was particularly captivated with beholding his image in a mirror; during his admiration of which he was miserably torn in pieces by the Titans; who, not content with this cruelty, first boiled his members in water, and afterwards roasted them by the fire. But while they were tasting his flesh thus dressed, Jupiter, excited by the steam, and perceiving

the cruelty of the deed, hurled his thunder at the Titans; but committed his members to Apollo, the brother of Bacchus, that they might be properly interred. And this being performed, Dionysius (whose heart during his laceration was snatched away by Minerva and preserved), by a new regeneration, again emerged, and he, being restored to his pristine life and integrity, afterwards filled up the number of the Gods. But in the mean time, from the exhalations formed from the ashes of the burning bodies of the Titans mankind were produced. The reader who is desirous of having a complete development of this fable will find it in my above-mentioned Treatise on the Mysteries. Suffice it to say at present, in elucidation of this Orphic hymn, that (as Olympiodorus beautifully observes in MS. Comment. in Phædon.) we are composed from *fragments*, because through falling into generation, *i.e.* into the sublunary region, our life has proceeded into the most distant and extreme division; but from *Titannic fragments*, because the Titans are the ultimate artificers of things, and the most proximate to their fabrications. Of these Titans, Bacchus, or the mundane intellect, is the *monad*, or proximately exempt producing cause.

XXXVIII

TO THE CURETES[1]

THE FUMIGATION FROM FRANKINCENSE

Brass-beating Salians, ministers of Mars,
Who wear his arms the instruments of wars;
Whose blessed frames, heav'n, earth, and sea compose,
And from whose breath all animals arose:
Who dwell in Samothracia's sacred ground,
Defending mortals through the sea profound.
Deathless Curetes, by your pow'r alone,
The greatest mystic rites to men at first were shown.
Who shake old Ocean thund'ring to the sky,
And stubborn oaks with branches waving high.
'Tis yours in glittering arms the earth to beat,
With lightly leaping, rapid, sounding feet;
Then ev'ry beast the noise terrific flies,
And the loud tumult wanders thro' the skies.
The dust your feet excites, with matchless force
Flies to the clouds amidst their whirling course;
And ev'ry flower of variegated hue
Grows in the dancing motion form'd by you;
Immortal dæmons, to your pow'rs consign'd,
The task to nourish and destroy mankind,
When rushing furious with loud tumult dire,
O'erwhelm'd, they perish in your dreadful ire;
And live replenish'd with the balmy air,
The food of life, committed to your care.
When shook by you, the seas with wild uproar,
Wide-spreading, and profoundly whirling, roar.
The concave heav'ns with echo's voice resound,
When leaves with rustling noise bestrew the ground.
Curetes, Corybantes, ruling kings,
Whose praise the land of Samothracia sings;
Great Jove's assessors; whose immortal breath
Sustains the soul, and wafts her back from death;
Aerial-form'd, who in Olympus shine

The heavenly Twins[2] all-lucid and divine:
Blowing, serene, from whom abundance springs,
Nurses of seasons, fruit-producing kings.

1 The first subsistence of the Curetes is in the *intellectual* order, as we have before observed, in which they form a triad characterized by *purity*. They are also the guards of that order. But in the *supermundane* order, they are the Corybantes. Hence they are celebrated in this hymn as the Corybantes as well as the Curetes. As they are likewise celebrated as *Winds* in this hymn, it follows that in the sublunary region they are the divinities of such winds as are of a purifying nature.

2 I have before observed that the Curetes and Corybantes are celebrated in this hymn as one and the same, on account of the profound union subsisting between the two. Hence the progression of these two orders into the heavens forms the constellation called the *Twins*.

XXXIX

TO CORYBAS[1]

THE FUMIGATION FROM FRANKINCENSE

The mighty ruler of this earthly ball
For ever flowing, to these rites I call;
Martial and blest, unseen by mortal sight,
Preventing fears, and pleas'd with gloomy night:
Hence fancy's terrors are by thee allay'd,
All-various king, who lov'st the desert shade.
Each of thy brothers killing, blood is thine,
Twofold Curete, many-form'd, divine.
By thee transmuted, Ceres' body pure
Became a dragon's savage and obscure:
Avert thy anger, hear me when I pray,
And, by fix'd fate, drive fancy's fears away.

---

1 Corybas is celebrated in this hymn as one of the Curetes; for he is called *Curete*. Perhaps, therefore, he is the last monad of the Curetic triad, and the extremity of every divine order being of a convertive nature, he is said to have killed each of his brothers. For slaughter, when applied to the Gods, signifies a segregation from secondary and a conversion to primary natures. Hence Corybas slaughters, *i.e.* converts his brothers to a superior order of Gods.

XL

TO CERES

THE FUMIGATION FROM STORAX

O universal mother, Ceres fam'd,
August, the source of wealth,[1] and various nam'd:
Great nurse, all-bounteous, blessed and divine,
Who joy'st in peace; to nourish corn is thine.
Goddess of seed, of fruits abundant, fair,
Harvest and threshing are thy constant care.
Lovely delightful queen, by all desir'd,
Who dwell'st in Eleusina's holy vales retir'd.
Nurse of all mortals, whose benignant mind
First ploughing oxen to the yoke confin'd;
And gave to men what nature's wants require,
With plenteous means of bliss, which all desire.
In verdure flourishing, in glory bright,
Assessor of great Bacchus, bearing light:
Rejoicing in the reapers' sickles, kind,
Whose nature lucid, earthly, pure, we find.
Prolific, venerable, nurse divine,
Thy daughter loving, holy Proserpine.
A car with dragons yok'd 'tis thine to guide,
And, orgies singing, round thy throne to ride.
Only-begotten, much-producing queen,
All flowers are thine, and fruits of lovely green.
Bright Goddess, come, with summer's rich increase
Swelling and pregnant, leading smiling Peace;
Come with fair Concord and imperial Health,
And join with these a needful store of wealth.

---

1 The following Orphic verse, which is to be found in Diodorus Siculus, i. 12, perfectly accords with what is said in this and the first line,

$$\Gamma\eta \ \mu\eta\tau\eta\rho \ \pi\alpha\nu\tau\omega\nu, \ \Delta\eta\mu\eta\tau\eta\rho \ \pi\lambda o \upsilon\tau o \delta o\tau\epsilon\iota\rho\alpha.$$

i.e.   "Earth, mother of all things, Ceres, source of wealth."

It must be observed that, according to the Orphic theology, Ceres is the same with Rhea, the vivific Goddess, who is the centre of the *intellectual* triad. See the additional notes.

XLI

TO THE CERALIAN MOTHER

THE FUMIGATION FROM AROMATICS

Ceralian queen, of celebrated name,
From whom both men and Gods immortal came;
Who widely wand'ring once, oppress'd with grief,
In Eleusina's valleys found'st relief,
Discovering Proserpine thy daughter pure
In dread Avernus, dismal and obscure;
A sacred youth while thro' the earth you stray,
Bacchus, attending leader of the way;
The holy marriage of terrestrial Jove
Relating, while oppress'd with grief you rove.
Come, much invok'd, and to these rites inclin'd,
Thy mystic suppliant bless, with fav'ring mind.

XLII

TO MISA

THE FUMIGATION FROM STORAX

I call Thesmophorus[1], spermatic God,
Of various names, who bears the leafy rod:
Misa, ineffable, pure, sacred queen,
Twofold Iacchus,[2] male and female seen.
Illustrious, whether to rejoice is thine
In incense offer'd in the fane divine;[3]
Or if in Phrygia most thy soul delights,
Performing with thy mother sacred rites;
Or if the land of Cyprus is thy care,
Pleas'd with the well crown'd Cytheria fair;
Or if exulting in the fertile plains
With thy dark mother Isis, where she reigns,
With nurses pure attended, near the flood
Of sacred Egypt, thy divine abode:
Wherever resident, benevolent attend,
And in perfection these our labours end.

---

1 *i.e.* The legislator.

2 It is well known that Iacchus is a mystic appellation of Bacchus, so that Misa is Bacchus. Misa is also said to be both male and female, because this divinity comprehends in himself stable power and sameness, which are of a masculine characteristic, and the measures of life and prolific powers, which are feminine peculiarities. This mixture of the male and female in one and the same divinity is no unusual thing in the Orphic theology.

3 *i.e.* The temple of Ceres Eleusina.

XLIII

TO THE SEASONS[1]

THE FUMIGATION FROM AROMATICS

Daughters of Jove and Themis, Seasons bright,
Justice, and blessed Peace, and lawful Right,
Vernal and grassy, vivid, holy pow'rs,
Whose balmy breath exhales in lovely flow'rs;
All-colour'd Seasons, rich increase your care,
Circling, for ever flourishing and fair:
Invested with a veil of shining dew,
A flow'ry veil delightful to the view:
Attending Proserpine, when back from night
The fates and graces lead her up to light;
When in a band harmonious they advance,
And joyful round her form the solemn dance.
With Ceres triumphing, and Jove divine,
Propitious come, and on our incense shine;
Give earth a store of blameless fruits to bear,
And make these novel mystics' life your care.

---

1 Sacred rumour (says Procl. in Tim. [266C, TTS vol. XVI, p. 804], of my translation of that work) venerates the invisible periods [subsisting under one first time], and which are the causes of those that are visible; delivering the divine names of Day and Night, and also the causes that constitute, and the invocations and self manifestations of Month and Year. Hence they are not to be surveyed superficially, but in divine essences, which the laws of sacred institutions and the oracles of Apollo order us to worship and honour, by statues and sacrifices, as histories inform us. When these also are reverenced, mankind are also supplied with the benefits arising from the periods of the *Seasons*, and of the other divinities in a similar manner; but a preternatural disposition of every thing about the earth is the consequence of the worship of these being neglected. Plato, likewise, in the Laws proclaims that all these are Gods, *viz.* the Seasons, Years, and Months, in the same manner as the Stars and the Sun; and we do not introduce any thing new by thinking it proper to direct our attention to the invisible powers of these prior to those that are visible."

Conformably to what Proclus here says, *viz.* "that a preternatural disposition of every thing about the earth is the consequence of the worship of these powers being neglected." The inhabitants of Patros, in Egypt, said to the prophet Jeremiah, "But we will certainly do whatsoever thing goeth out of our mouth, to burn incense to the Queen of Heaven, and to pour out drink-offerings unto her, as we have done, we, and our fathers, our kings, and our princes, in the cities of Judah, and in the streets of Jerusalem: for *then had we plenty of victuals and were well, and saw no evil.* But since we left off to burn incense to the Queen of Heaven, and to pour out drink-offerings unto her, *we have wanted all things*, and have been consumed by the sword and by famine." Jeremiah, chap. 44, v. 17, 18.

XLIV

TO SEMELE

THE FUMIGATION FROM STORAX

Cadmean Goddess, universal queen,
Thee, Semele, I call, of beauteous mien;
Deep-bosom'd, lovely flowing locks are thine,
Mother of Bacchus, joyful and divine,
The mighty offspring, whom Jove's thunder bright
Forc'd immature, and fright'ned into light.
Born from the deathless counsels, secret, high,
Of Jove Saturnian, regent of the sky;
Whom Proserpine permits to view the light,
And visit mortals from the realms of night.
Constant attending on the sacred rites,
And feast triennial, which thy soul delights;
When thy son's wondrous birth mankind relate,
And secrets pure and holy celebrate.
Now I invoke thee, great Cadmean queen,
To bless thy mystics, lenient and serene.

XLV

TO DIONYSIUS BASSAREUS TRIENNALIS[1]

A HYMN

Come, blessed Dionysius, various-nam'd,
Bull-fac'd, begot from thunder, Bacchus fam'd.
Bassarian God, of universal might,
Whom swords and blood and sacred rage delight:
In heaven rejoicing, mad, loud-sounding God,
Furious inspirer, bearer of the rod:
By Gods rever'd, who dwell'st with humankind,
Propitious come, with much rejoicing mind.

1 So called because his rites were performed every third year.

XLVI

TO LICKNITUS BACCHUS[1]

THE FUMIGATION FROM MANNA

Licknitan Bacchus, bearer of the vine,
Thee I invoke to bless these rites divine:
Florid and gay, of Nymphs the blossom bright,
And of fair Venus, Goddess of delight.
'Tis thine mad footsteps with mad Nymphs to beat,
Dancing thro' groves with lightly leaping feet:
From Jove's high counsels nurst by Proserpine,
And born the dread of all the pow'rs divine.
Come, blessed God, regard thy suppliant's voice,
Propitious come, and in these rites rejoice.

---

1 *i.e.* The Fan-bearer. Concerning Liknitus, and the following Bacchuses, see note 3, on the Moon.

XLVII

TO BACCHUS PERICIONIUS[1]

THE FUMIGATION FROM AROMATICS

Bacchus Pericionius, hear my pray'r,
Who mad'st the house of Cadmus once thy care,
With matchless force his pillars twining round,
When burning thunders shook the solid ground,
In flaming, sounding torrents borne along,
Propt by thy grasp indissolubly strong.
Come, mighty Bacchus, to these rites inclin'd,
And bless thy suppliants with rejoicing mind.

1 So called from περι, and κιονις, *a little pillar.*

XLVIII

TO SABAZIUS[1]

THE FUMIGATION FROM AROMATICS

Hear me, illustrious father, dæmon fam'd,
Great Saturn's offspring, and Sabazius nam'd;
Inserting Bacchus, bearer of the vine,
And sounding God, within thy thigh divine,
That when mature, the Dionysian God
Might burst the bands of his conceal'd abode,
And come to sacred Tmolus, his delight,
Where Ippa[2] dwells, all beautiful and bright.
Blest Phrygian God, the most august of all,
Come aid thy mystics, when on thee they call.

---

1 "Many (says Plutarch, Symp. 4, 5 p. 671) even now call the Bacchuses *Sabbi*, and they utter this word when they celebrate the orgies of the God" [Bacchus]. Σαββους και νυν ετι πολλοι τους βακχους καλουσι, και ταυτην αφιασι την φωνην, οταν οργιαζουσι τῳ τεῳ. "But the power of Sabazius (says Iamblichus de Myst. sect. iii. cap. x.) appropriately pertains to Bacchic inspiration, the purifications of souls, and the solutions of ancient divine anger." See the note on this passage in my translation of that work.

2 Ippa (says Proclus in Tim. [124C, TTS vol. XV, p. 374]), who is the soul of the universe, and is thus called by the theologist [Orpheus], perhaps because her intellectual conceptions are essentialized in the most vigorous motions, or perhaps on account of the most rapid lation of the universe, of which she is the cause, - placing a testaceous vessel on her head, and encircling the fig leaves that bind her temples with a dragon, receives Dionysius [or Bacchus]. For with the most divine part of herself, she becomes the receptacle of an intellectual essence, and receives *the mundane intellect*, which proceeds into her from the thigh of Jupiter. For there it was united with Jupiter; but proceeding from thence, and becoming participable by her, it elevates her to the intelligible, and to the fountain of her nature. For she hastens to the mother of the Gods, and to mount Ida [*i.e.* to the region of ideas, and an intelligible nature], from which all the series of souls is derived. Hence, also, Ippa is said to have received Dionysius when he was brought forth from Jupiter." Η μεν γαρ Ιππα του παντος ουσα ψυχη, και ουτω κεκλημενη παρα τῳ θεολογῳ, ταχα μεν οτι και εν

ακμαιοταταις κινησεσιν εννοησεις αυτης ουσιωνται, ταχα δε και δια την αξυτατην του παντος φοραν ης εστιν η αιτια, λεκιον (lege λικινον) επι της κεφαλης θεμενη, και δρακοντι αυτω περιστρεψασα, το κραδιαιον υποδεχεται Διονυσον· τω γαρ εαυτης θειοτατω, γινεται της νοερας ουσιας υποδοχη, και δεχεται τον εγκοσμιον νουν, ο δε απο του μηρου του Διος προεισιν εις αυτην· ην γαρ εκει συνηνωμενος, και προελθων, και μεθεκτος αυτη γενομενος, επι το νοητον αυτην αναγει, και την εαυτης πηγην· επειγεται γαρ προς την μητερα των θεον, και την Ιδην, αφ' ης πασα των ψυχων η σειρα· διο και συλλαμβανεσθαι και Ιππα λεγεται τικτοντι τω Δυ.

XLIX

TO IPPA

THE FUMIGATION FROM STORAX

Great nurse of Bacchus, to my pray'r incline,
For holy Sabus' secret rites are thine,
The mystic rites of Bacchus' nightly choirs,
Compos'd of sacred, loud-resounding fires.
Hear me, terrestrial mother, mighty queen,
Whether on Ida's holy mountain seen,
Or if to dwell in Tmolus thee delights,
With holy aspect come, and bless these rites.

L

TO LYSIUS LENÆUS

A HYMN

Hear me, Jove's son, blest Bacchus, God of wine,
Born of two mothers, honour'd and divine;
Lysian Euion Bacchus, various-nam'd,
Of Gods the offspring, secret, holy, fam'd.
Fertile and nourishing, whose liberal care
Augments the fruit that banishes despair.
Sounding, magnanimous, Lenæan pow'r,
O various-form'd, medicinal, holy flow'r:
Mortals in thee repose from labour find,
Delightful charm, desir'd by all mankind.
Fair-hair'd Euion, Bromian, joyful God,
Lysian, insanely raging with the leafy rod.
To these our rites, benignant pow'r, incline,
When fav'ring men, or when on Gods you shine;
Be present to thy mystics' suppliant pray'r,
Rejoicing come, and fruits abundant bear.

LI

TO THE NYMPHS[1]

THE FUMIGATION FROM AROMATICS

Nymphs, who from Ocean fam'd derive your birth,
Who dwell in liquid caverns of the earth;
Nurses of Bacchus, secret-coursing pow'rs,
Fructiferous Goddesses, who nourish flow'rs:
Earthly, rejoicing, who in meadows dwell,
And caves and dens, whose depths extend to hell.
Holy, oblique, who swiftly soar thro' air,
Fountains, and dews, and winding streams your care,
Seen and unseen, who joy with wand'rings wide,
And gentle course thro' flow'ry vales to glide;
With Pan exulting on the mountains' height,
Inspir'd, and stridulous, whom woods delight:
Nymphs od'rous, rob'd in white, whose streams exhale
The breeze refreshing, and the balmy gale;
With goats and pastures pleas'd, and beasts of prey,
Nurses of fruits, unconscious of decay.
In cold rejoicing, and to cattle kind,
Sportive, thro' ocean wand'ring unconfin'd.
O Nysian nymphs, insane, whom oaks delight,
Lovers of spring, Pæonian virgins bright;
With Bacchus and with Ceres hear my pray'r,
And to mankind abundant favour bear;
Propitious listen to your suppliant's voice,
Come, and benignant in these rites rejoice;
Give plenteous seasons and sufficient wealth,
And pour in lasting streams, continued health.

---

1 "Nymphs (says Hermeas, in Schol. in Phædrum. [*Works of Plato III*, TTS vol. XI, p. 399]) are Goddesses who preside over regeneration, and are ministrant to Bacchus, the offspring of Semele. Hence they dwell near water, *i.e.* they ascend into generation [or the sublunary realms]. But this Bacchus [of whom they are the offspring] supplies the regeneration of the whole sensible world." Νυμφαι δε εισιν εθοροι θεαι της παλιγγενεσιας, υπουργοι του εκ Σεμελης Διονυσου· διο

και παρα τω υδατι εισι, τουτεστι τη γενεσει επιβεβηκασιν· ουτος δε ο Διονησος της παλιγγενεσιας υπαρχει παντος του αισθητου. He adds, "that some of them excite the irrational nature, others nature herself, and others preside over bodies."

LII

TO TRIETERICUS[1]

THE FUMIGATION FROM AROMATICS

Bacchus phrenetic,[2] much nam'd, blest, divine,
Bull-horn'd, Lenæan, bearer of the vine;
From fire descended, raging, Nysian king,
From whom initial ceremonies spring.
Liknitan Bacchus, pure and fiery bright,
Prudent, crown-bearer, wand'ring in the night;
Nurst in Mount Mero, all-mysterious pow'r,
Triple, ineffable, Jove's secret flow'r:
Ericapæus, first-begotten nam'd,
Of Gods the father and the offspring fam'd.
Bearing a sceptre, leader of the choir,
Whose dancing feet phrenetic furies fire,
When the triennial band thou dost inspire,
Omadian, captor, of a fiery light,
Born of two mothers, Amphietus bright;
Love, mountain-wand'ring,[3] cloth'd with skins of deer,
Apollo golden-ray'd,[4] whom all revere.
Great annual God of grapes, with ivy crown'd,
Bassarian, lovely, virginlike, renown'd.
Come, blessed pow'r, regard thy mystics' voice,
Propitious come, and in these rites rejoice.

---

1 According to the fragment preserved by Ficinus, which we have before cited, Trietericus Bacchus is the gnostic power, or intellect of the Sun. Hence as the Sun is to the sensible world what Protogonus, or Phanes, is to the intellectual orders; for the latter illuminates those orders with intelligible, and the former the sensible world with supermundane light; in consequence of this analogy, the reason is obvious why Trietericus is called in this hymn Ericapæus, *i.e.* Protogonus; and also why he is said to be both the father and the offspring of Gods. For Protogonus is *intelligible intellect* (νους νοητος), and is the father of the Gods; and Trietericus, or the *solar intellect*, subsists causally in Protogonus, and proceeds from him and the intellectual orders of Gods. From his causal subsistence, therefore, in Protogonus, he is the father of the Gods; but as proceeding from them, he is their offspring.

2 This word, and others of a similar kind, which literally signify insanity, are to be considered according to their recondite meaning, as indicative of a divinely inspired energy.

3 The reason why Trietericus Bacchus is called "*Love*" in this hymn is from the profound union subsisting between Phanes, or Protogonus, Jupiter, and Bacchus. For the first subsistence of Love, according to the Orphic theology, is in Phanes; and Phanes is *intelligible intellect*. But the intelligible order to which Phanes belongs being absorbed in the *superessential*, contains in itself intellect *causally*, and consequently is superior to *essential* intellect and intellectual vision. Hence Love, according to his first subsistence, is said to be *blind*, as having a superintellectual energy. This being premised, it is no longer wonderful that Trietericus should be called Love. "For the theologist [Orpheus], says Proclus, in Tim. [102D, TTS vol. XV, p. 311], long before us, celebrates the demiurgic cause in Phanes. *For there, as he says, the great Bromius, or all-seeing Jupiter, was, and antecedently existed*; in order that he might have as it were the fountains of the twofold fabrication of things. He also celebrates the paradigmatic cause [*i.e.* Phanes] in Jupiter. For again, he likewise is, as he says, *Metis the first generator, and much pleasing Love.* He is also continually denominated by him Dionysius, and Phanes, and Ericapæus. All the causes, therefore, participate of, and are in each other. παλαι γαρ ο θεολογος εν γε τῳ φανητι την δημιουργικην αιτιαν ανυμνησεν· εκει γαρ ην τε και προην ωσπερ εφη και αυτος, βρομιος τε μεγας και ζευς ο πανοπτης· και εν τῳ δι την παραδειγματικην· μητις γαρ αυ και ουτις εστιν ως φησι.

Και Μητις πρωτος γενετωρ, και Ερως πολυτερπης·

αυτος τε ο Διονυσος και φανης και ηρικεπαιος, συνεχως ονομαζεται· παντα αρα μετειληχην αλληλων τα αιτια, και εν αλληλοις εστιν

4 As according to the Orphic theology Trietericus is *the intellect of the Sun*, this divinity is with great propriety celebrated in this hymn as *Apollo golden-ray'd* (παιαν χρυσεγχης). But Hermann, not knowing who Trietericus is in the Orphic theology, substitutes θυρσεγχης for χρυσεγχης; conceiving that Trietericus is the same with Bacchus, or the *mundane intellect*. His words are, "Vocabulum παιαν postulat, ut nomen addatur, quo ab Apolline distinguatur Bacchus. Itaque pro χρυσεγχης reposui θυρσεγχης." Vid. Orphic. Hermann. p. 317.

LIII

TO AMPHIETUS BACCHUS

THE FUMIGATION FROM EVERY AROMATIC EXCEPT FRANKINCENSE

Terrestrial Dionysius, hear my pray'r,
Rise vigilant with Nymphs of lovely hair:
Great Amphietus Bacchus, annual God,
Who laid asleep in Proserpine's abode,
Her sacred seat, didst lull to drowsy rest
The rites triennial and the sacred feast;
Which rous'd again by thee, in graceful ring,
Thy nurses round thee mystic anthems sing;
When briskly dancing with rejoicing pow'rs,
Thou mov'st in concert with the circling hours.
Come blessed, fruitful, horned, and divine,
And on this sacred Telete propitious shine;
Accept the pious incense and the pray'r,
And make prolific holy fruits thy care.

LIV

TO SILENUS, SATYRUS,

AND THE PRIESTESSES OF BACCHUS

THE FUMIGATION FROM MANNA

Great nurse of Bacchus, to my pray'r incline,
Silenus, honour'd by the pow'rs divine;
And by mankind at the triennial feast
Illustrious dæmon, reverenc'd as the best:
Holy, august, the source of lawful rites,
Phrenetic pow'r, whom vigilance delights;
Surrounded by thy nurses young and fair,
Naiads and Bacchic Nymphs who ivy bear,
With all thy Satyrs on our incense shine,
Dæmons wild-form'd, and bless the rites divine.
Come, rouse to sacred joy thy pupil king,[1]
And Brumal Nymphs with rites Lenæan bring;
Our orgies shining thro' the night inspire,
And bless, triumphant pow'r, the sacred choir.

---

1 Silenus is so called because he was the foster father or nurse of Bacchus.

LV

TO VENUS

A HYMN

Heav'nly, illustrious, laughter-loving queen,
Sea-born, night-loving, of an awful mien;
Crafty, from whom necessity first came,
Producing, nightly, all-connecting dame.
'Tis thine the world with harmony to join,[1]
For all things spring from thee, O pow'r divine.
The triple Fates are ruled by thy decree,
And all productions yield alike to thee:
Whate'er the heav'ns, encircling all, contain,
Earth fruit-producing, and the stormy main,
Thy sway confesses, and obeys thy nod,
Awful attendant of the Brumal God.
Goddess of marriage, charming to the sight,
Mother of Loves, whom banquetings delight;
Source of persuasion, secret, fav'ring queen,
Illustrious born, apparent and unseen;
Spousal, Lupercal, and to men inclin'd,
Prolific, most-desir'd, life-giving, kind.
Great sceptre-bearer of the Gods, 'tis thine
Mortals in necessary bands to join;
And ev'ry tribe of savage monsters dire
In magic chains to bind thro' mad desire.
Come, Cyprus-born, and to my pray'r incline,
Whether exalted in the heav'ns you shine,
Or pleas'd in od'rous Syria to preside,
Or o'er th'Egyptian plains thy car to guide,
Fashion'd of gold; and near its sacred flood,
Fertile and fam'd, to fix thy blest abode;
Or if rejoicing in the azure shores,
Near where the sea with foaming billows roars,
The circling choirs of mortals thy delight,
Or beauteous Nymphs with eyes cerulean bright,
Pleas'd by the sandy banks renown'd of old,

To drive thy rapid two-yok'd car of gold;
Or if in Cyprus thy fam'd mother fair,
Where nymphs unmarried praise thee ev'ry year,
The loveliest nymphs, who in the chorus join,
Adonis pure to sing, and thee divine.
Come, all-attractive, to my pray'r inclin'd,
For thee I call, with holy, reverent mind.

1 Venus, according to her first subsistence, ranks among the supermundane divinities. But she is the cause of all the harmony and analogy in the universe, and of the union of form with matter, connecting and comprehending the powers of all the mundane elements. See the additional notes.

LVI

TO ADONIS

THE FUMIGATION FROM AROMATICS

Much nam'd, and best of dæmons, hear my pray'r,
The desert loving, deck'd with tender hair;
Joy to diffuse, by all desir'd, is thine,
Much form'd, Eubulus, aliment divine.
Female and male, all-charming to the sight,
Adonis, ever flourishing and bright;
At stated periods doom'd to set and rise
With splendid lamp, the glory of the skies.[1]
Two horn'd and lovely, reverenc'd with tears,
Of splendid form, adorn'd with copious hairs.
Rejoicing in the chase, all-graceful pow'r,
Sweet plant of Venus, Love's delightful flow'r:
Descended from the secret bed divine
Of Pluto's queen, the fair-hair'd Proserpine.
'Tis thine to sink in Tartarus profound,
And shine again thro' heav'ns illustrious round;
Come, timely pow'r, with providential care,
And to thy mystics earth's productions bear.[2]

---

1 Proclus, in his very elegant hymn to the Sun, celebrates him as frequently called Adonis; and this perfectly agrees with what is said in this and the preceding verse, and with many other parts of the hymn.

2 "Adonis (says Hermeas, in his Scholia on the *Phædrus* of Plato) presides over every thing that grows and perishes in the earth." επειδη των εν γη φυομενων και αποβιωσκομενων ο δεσποτης Αδωνις εφεστησε. p 202.

LVII

TO THE TERRESTRIAL HERMES

THE FUMIGATION FROM STORAX

Hermes, I call, whom Fate decrees to dwell
Near to Cocytos, the fam'd stream of hell,
And in Necessity's dread path, whose bourn
To none that reach it e'er permits return.
O Bacchic Hermes, progeny divine
Of Dionysius, parent of the vine,
And of celestial Venus, Paphian queen,
Dark-eyelash'd Goddess, of a lovely mien:
Who constant wand'rest thro' the sacred seats
Where Hell's dread empress, Proserpine, retreats;
To wretched souls the leader of the way,
When Fate decrees, to regions void of day.
Thine is the wand which causes sleep to fly,
Or lulls to slumb'rous rest the weary eye;
For Proserpine, thro' Tart'rus dark and wide,
Gave thee for ever flowing souls to guide.
Come, blessed pow'r, the sacrifice attend,
And grant thy mystics' works a happy end.

LVIII

TO LOVE[1]

THE FUMIGATION FROM AROMATICS

I call, great Love, the source of sweet delight,
Holy and pure, and charming to the sight;
Darting, and wing'd, impetuous fierce desire,
With Gods and mortals playing, wand'ring fire:
Agile and twofold, keeper of the keys
Of heav'n and earth, the air, and spreading seas;
Of all that Ceres' fertile realms contains,
By which th'all parent Goddess life sustains,
Or dismal Tartarus is doom'd to keep,
Widely extended, or the sounding deep;
For thee all Nature's various realms obey,
Who rul'st alone, with universal sway.
Come, blessed pow'r, *regard these mystic fires*,
And far avert unlawful mad desires.

---

1 The following development of the nature of the Divinity Love is extracted from the admirable Commentary of Proclus on the *First Alcibiades* of Plato, as illustrative of the Orphic dogmas respecting this God. "Love is neither to be placed in the first nor among the last of beings. Not in the first, because the object of Love is superior to Love; nor yet among the last, because the lover participates of Love. It is requisite, therefore, that Love should be established between the object of love and the lover, and that it should be posterior to the beautiful, but prior to every nature endued with love. Where then does it first subsist? How does it extend itself through the universe, and with what monads does it leap forth?

"There are three hypostases among the intelligible and occult Gods; and the first, indeed, is characterized by *The Good*, understanding *The Good Itself*, and residing in that place where, according to the [Chaldean] Oracle, the paternal monad abides; but the second is characterized by *wisdom*, where the first intelligence flourishes; and the third by *the beautiful*, where, as Timæus says, the most beautiful of intelligibles abides. But there are three monads according to these intelligible causes, subsisting uniformly according to cause in intelligibles, but first unfolding themselves into light in the ineffable order of the Gods, [*i.e.* in the summit of that order which is called intelligible, and at the same time intellectual,] I mean *faith, truth,* and *love*. And *faith*, indeed, establishes all things in good; but *truth* unfolds all the knowledge in beings; and lastly, *love* converts all things, and congregates them into the nature of the beautiful. This triad thence proceeds through all the orders of the Gods, and imparts to all things by its light a union with the intelligible itself. It also unfolds itself differently in different orders, every where combining its powers with the peculiarities of the Gods. And among some it subsists ineffably, incomprehensibly, and with transcendent union; but among others, as the cause of connecting and binding; and among others, as endued with a perfective and forming power. Here again, it subsists intellectually and paternally; there, in a manner entirely motive, vivific, and effective: here, as governing and assimilating; there, in a liberated and undefiled manner; and elsewhere, according to a multiplied and divided mode. Love, therefore, supernally descends from intelligibles to mundane concerns, calling all things upwards to divine beauty. Truth, also, proceeds through all things, illuminating all things with knowledge. And lastly, faith proceeds through the universe, establishing all things with transcendent union in good. Hence the [Chaldean] Oracles assert, "that all things are governed by and abide in these." And, on this account, they order Theurgists to conjoin themselves to divinity through this triad. Intelligibles themselves, indeed, do not require the amatory medium, on account of their ineffable union. But where there is a union and separation of beings, there also Love abides. For it is the binder and conciliator of natures posterior and prior to itself; but the converter of subsequent to prior, and the elevating and perfecting cause of imperfect natures.

"The [Chaldean] Oracles, therefore, speak of Love as binding, and residing in all things; and hence, if it connects all things, it also copulates us with the governments of dæmons. But Diotima calls Love *a great dæmon*, because it every where fills up the medium between desiring and desirable natures. And, indeed, that which is the object of Love vindicates to itself the first order; but that which loves is in the third order from the beloved object. Lastly, Love usurps a middle situation between each, congregating and collecting together that which desires and that which is desired, and filling subordinate from superior natures. But among the intelligible and occult Gods, it unites intelligible intellect to the first and secret beauty, by a certain life better than intelligence. Hence [Orpheus] the theologian of the Greeks calls this Love *blind*; for he says of intelligible intellect,

$$\Pi οιμαινων \; πραπεδεσσιν \; ανομματον \; ωκυν \; ερωτα.$$

i.e. In his breast feeding *eyeless* rapid Love.

But in natures posterior to intelligibles, it imparts by illumination an indissoluble bond to all things perfected by itself: for a bond is a certain union, but accompanied by much separation. On this account the [Chaldean] Oracles are accustomed to call the fire of this Love *a copulator*: for proceeding from intelligible intellect, it binds all following natures with each other, and with itself. Hence it conjoins all the Gods with intelligible beauty, and dæmons with Gods; but it conjoins us with both Gods and dæmons. In the Gods, indeed, it has a primary subsistence; in dæmons a secondary one; and in partial souls a subsistence through a certain third procession from principles. Again, in the Gods it subsists above essence: for every genus of Gods is superessential. But in dæmons it subsists according to essence: and in souls according to illumination. And this triple order appears similar to the triple power of intellect. For one intellect subsists as imparticipable, being exempt from all partial genera; but another as participated, of which also the souls of the Gods participate as of a better nature; and another is from this ingenerated in souls, and which is, indeed, their perfection." See more concerning this Divinity in the notes on the speech of Diotima in the *Banquet* of Plato. [*The Works of Plato IV*, TTS vol. XII].

LIX

TO THE FATES

THE FUMIGATION FROM AROMATICS

Daughters of darkling Night, much nam'd, draw near,
Infinite Fates, and listen to my pray'r;
Who in the heavenly lake[1] (where waters white
Burst from a fountain hid in depths of night,
And thro' a dark and stony cavern glide,
A cave profound, invisible) abide;
From whence, wide coursing round the boundless earth,
Your pow'r extends to those of mortal birth;
To men with hope elated, trifling, gay,
A race presumptuous, born but to decay.
To these acceding, in a purple veil
To sense impervious, you yourselves conceal,
When in the plain of Fate you joyful ride
In one great car, with Glory for your guide;
Till all-complete your heav'n appointed round,
At Justice, Hope, and Care's concluding bound,
The terms absolv'd, prescrib'd by ancient law,
Of pow'r immense, and just without a flaw.
For Fate alone with vision unconfin'd
Surveys the conduct of the mortal kind.
Fate is Jove's perfect and eternal eye,
For Jove and Fate our ev'ry deed descry.
Come, gentle pow'rs, well born, benignant, fam'd,
Atropos, Lachesis, and Clotho nam'd;
Unchang'd, aerial, wand'ring in the night,
Untam'd, invisible to mortal sight;
Fates all-producing, all-destroying, hear,
Regard the incense and the holy pray'r;
Propitious listen to these rites inclin'd,
And far avert distress, with placid mind.

1 Gesner confesses he is ignorant what the poet means by the λιμνη ουρανια, or *heavenly lake*; as likewise of the *dark cavern* in which Orpheus places the Fates. At first sight, indeed, the whole seems impenetrably obscure; but on comparing this hymn with the sixty-ninth, which is to the Furies, we shall find that the poet expressly calls them the Fates; and places them in an obscure cavern by the holy water of Styx. And from hence it appears, that *the heavenly lake* is the same with *the Stygian pool*; which is called *heavenly*, perhaps because the Gods swear by it. But it is not wonderful that the water is called white; since Hesiod, in Theog. v. 791, speaks of the Stygian waters as falling into the sea with *silvery* whirls. And what strengthens the illustration still more, Fulgentius asserts that the Fates dwell with Pluto.

LX

TO THE GRACES[1]

THE FUMIGATION FROM STORAX

Hear me, illustrious Graces, mighty nam'd,
From Jove descended, and Eunomia fam'd,
Thalia and Aglaia fair and bright,
And blest Euphrosyne, whom joys delight:
Mothers of mirth; all lovely to the view,
Pleasure abundant, pure, belongs to you:
Various, for ever flourishing and fair,
Desir'd by mortals, much invok'd in pray'r;
Circling, dark-ey'd, delightful to mankind,
Come, and your mystics bless with bounteous mind.

---

1 In the same manner as Bacchus subsists in Jupiter, and Esculapius in Apollo, so the Graces subsist in Venus, as we are informed by the philosopher Sallust, in his golden Treatise *On the Gods and the World*.[†]

[†] TTS volume IV.

LXI

TO NEMESIS

A HYMN

Thee, Nemesis, I call, almighty queen,
By whom the deeds of mortal life are seen:
Eternal, much rever'd, of boundless sight,
Alone rejoicing in the just and right:
Changing the counsels of the human breast
For ever various, rolling without rest.
To ev'ry mortal is thy influence known,
And men beneath thy righteous bondage groan;
For ev'ry thought within the mind conceal'd
Is to thy sight perspicuously reveal'd.
The soul unwilling reason to obey,
By lawless passion rul'd, thine eyes survey.
All to see, hear, and rule, O pow'r divine,
Whose nature equity contains, is thine.
Come, blessed, holy Goddess, hear my pray'r,
And make thy mystics' life thy constant care:
Give aid benignant in the needful hour,
And strength abundant to the reas'ning pow'r;
And far avert the dire, unfriendly race
Of counsels impious, arrogant, and base.

LXII

TO JUSTICE

THE FUMIGATION FROM FRANKINCENSE

The piercing eye of Justice bright I sing,
Plac'd by the sacred throne of Jove the king,
Perceiving thence, with vision unconfin'd,
The life and conduct of the human kind.[1]
To thee revenge and punishment belong,
Chastising ev'ry deed unjust and wrong.
Whose pow'r alone dissimilars can join,
And from th'equality of truth combine:
For all the ill persuasion can inspire,
When urging bad designs with counsel dire,
'Tis thine alone to punish; with the race
Of lawless passions, and incentives base;
For thou art ever to the good inclin'd,
And hostile to the men of evil mind.
Come, all-propitious, and thy suppliant hear,
Till fates' predestin'd fatal hour draws near.

---

1 The first four lines of this hymn are, as I have observed in the Introduction, cited by Demosthenes in his first Oration against Aristogiton.

LXIII

TO EQUITY

THE FUMIGATION FROM FRANKINCENSE

O blessed Equity, mankind's delight,
Th'eternal friend of conduct just and right:
Abundant, venerable, honour'd maid,
To judgments pure dispensing constant aid,
And conscience stable, and an upright mind;
For men unjust by thee are undermin'd,
Whose souls perverse thy bondage ne'er desire,
But more untam'd decline thy scourges dire.
Harmonious, friendly pow'r, averse to strife,
In peace rejoicing, and a stable life:
Lovely, convivial, of a gentle mind,
Hating excess, to equal deeds inclin'd:
Wisdom and virtue, of whate'er degree,
Receive their proper bound alone in thee.
Hear, Goddess Equity, the deeds destroy
Of evil men, which human life annoy;
That all may yield to thee of mortal birth,
Whether supported by the fruits of earth,
Or in her kindly fertile bosom found,
Or in the realms of marine Jove profound.

LXIV

TO LAW

A HYMN

The holy king of Gods and men I call,
Celestial Law, the righteous seal of all:
The seal which stamps whate'er the earth contains,
And all conceal'd within the liquid plains:
Stable, and starry, of harmonious frame,
Preserving laws eternally the same.
Thy all-composing pow'r in heav'n appears,
Connects its frame, and props the starry spheres;
And unjust Envy shakes with dreadful sound,
Toss'd by thy arm in giddy whirls around.
'Tis thine the life of mortals to defend,
And crown existence with a blessed end;
For thy command alone, of all that lives,
Order and rule to ev'ry dwelling gives.
Ever observant of the upright mind,
And of just actions the companion kind.
Foe to the lawless, with avenging ire,
Their steps involving in destruction dire.
Come, blest, abundant pow'r, whom all revere,
By all desir'd, with fav'ring mind draw near;
Give me thro' life on thee to fix my sight,
And ne'er forsake the equal paths of right.

LXV

TO MARS[1]

THE FUMIGATION FROM FRANKINCENSE

Magnanimous, unconquer'd, boist'rous Mars,
In darts rejoicing, and in bloody wars;
Fierce and untam'd, whose mighty pow'r can make
The strongest walls from their foundations shake:
Mortal-destroying king, defil'd with gore,
Pleas'd with war's dreadful and tumultuous roar.
Thee human blood,[2] and swords, and spears delight,
And the dire ruin of mad savage fight.
Stay furious contests, and avenging strife,
Whose works with woe embitter human life;
To lovely Venus and to Bacchus yield,
For arms exchange the labours of the field;
Encourage peace, to gentle works inclin'd,
And give abundance, with benignant mind.

---

1 Mars, as we are informed by Proclus, in Plat. Repub. [*The Works of Plato I*, TTS vol. IX, p. 294], is the source of division and motion, separating the contrarieties of the universe, which he also perpetually excites, and immutably preserves in order that the world may be perfect and filled with forms of every kind. Hence, also, he presides over war. But he requires the assistance of Venus, that he may insert order and harmony into things contrary and discordant.

2 "The *slaughter* which is ascribed to Mars (says Hermias, in Plat. Phædr. [see *The Works of Plato III*, TTS vol. XI, p. 416]) signifies a divulsion from matter through rapidly turning from it, and no longer energizing physically, but intellectually. For slaughter, when applied to the Gods, may be said to be an apostacy from secondary natures, just as slaughter in this terrestrial region signifies a privation of the present life."

LXVI

TO VULCAN[1]

THE FUMIGATION FROM FRANKINCENSE AND MANNA

Strong, mighty Vulcan, bearing splendid light,
Unweary'd fire, with flaming torrents bright:
Strong-handed, deathless, and of art divine,
Pure element, a portion of the world is thine:
All-taming artist, all-diffusive pow'r,
'Tis thine, supreme, all substance to devour:
Ether, Sun, Moon, and Stars, light pure and clear,
For these thy lucid parts to men appear.
To thee all dwellings, cities, tribes belong,
Diffus'd thro' mortal bodies, rich and strong.
Hear, blessed pow'r, to holy rites incline,
And all propitious on the incense shine:
Suppress the rage of fire's unweary'd frame,
And still preserve our nature's vital flame.

---

1 Vulcan is that divine power which presides over the spermatic and physical productive powers which the universe contains: for whatever Nature accomplishes by verging to bodies, that Vulcan effects in a divine and exempt manner, by moving Nature, and using her as an instrument in his own proper fabrication. For natural heat has a Vulcanian characteristic, and was produced by Vulcan for the purpose of fashioning a corporeal nature. Vulcan, therefore, is that power which perpetually presides over the fluctuating nature of bodies; and hence, says Olympiodorus, he operates with *bellows*, (εν φυσαις) which occultly signifies his operating in natures (αντι του εν ταις φυσεσι). This deity, also, as well as Mars, as Proclus observes, in Plat. Repub. p. 388, requires the assistance of Venus, in order that he may invest sensible effects with beauty, and thus cause the pulchritude of the world.

LXVII

TO ESCULAPIUS[1]

THE FUMIGATION FROM MANNA

Great Esculapius, skill'd to heal mankind,
All-ruling Pæan, and physician kind;
Whose arts medic'nal can alone assuage
Diseases dire, and stop their dreadful rage.
Strong, lenient God, regard my suppliant pray'r,
Bring gentle Health, adorn'd with lovely hair;
Convey the means of mitigating pain,
And raging deadly pestilence restrain.
O pow'r all-flourishing, abundant, bright,
Apollo's honour'd offspring, God of light;
Husband of blameless Health, the constant foe
Of dread disease, the minister of woe:
Come, blessed saviour, human health defend,[2]
And to the mortal life afford a prosp'rous end.

---

1 This deity, as I have before observed, subsists in Apollo. Proclus, in his very elegant hymn to the Sun, says that Esculapius springs into light from the bland dance of the Sun.

Σης δ' απο μειλιχοδωρος αλεξικακου θιασειης
Παιηων βλαστησεν, εην δ' επετασσεν υγειην,
Πλησας αρμονιης παναπημονος ευρεα κοσμον.

i.e. "From thy bland dance repelling deadly ill,
Salubrious Pæon blossoms into light,
Health far diffusing, and th'extended world
With streams of harmony innoxious fills."

2 In the hymn to Apollo, Orpheus, or, as he wrote these hymns for the Mysteries, the initiating priest, *prays for the welfare of all mankind.* Hence, as Esculapius subsists in Apollo, the poet very properly invokes the *healing God* to defend *human* health, or the health of *all men.*

LXVIII

TO HEALTH

THE FUMIGATION FROM MANNA

O much desir'd, prolific, gen'ral queen.
Hear me, life-bearing Health, of beauteous mien,
Mother of all; by thee diseases dire,
Of bliss destructive, from our life retire;
And ev'ry house is flourishing and fair,
If with rejoicing aspect thou art there.
Each dædal art thy vig'rous force inspires,
And all the world thy helping hand desires.
Pluto, life's bane, alone resists thy will,
And ever hates thy all-preserving skill.
O fertile queen, from thee for ever flows
To mortal life from agony repose;
And men without thy all-sustaining ease
Find nothing useful, nothing form'd to please.
Without thy aid, not Pluto's self can thrive,
Nor man to much afflicted age arrive;
For thou alone, of countenance serene,
Dost govern all things, universal queen.
Assist thy mystics with propitious mind,
And far avert disease of ev'ry kind.

LXIX

TO THE FURIES[1]

THE FUMIGATION FROM AROMATICS

Vociferous Bacchanalian Furies hear!
Ye I invoke, dread pow'rs, whom all revere;
Nightly, profound, in secret who retire,
Tisiphone, Alecto, and Megara dire:
Deep in a cavern merg'd, involv'd in night,
Near where Styx flows impervious to the sight.
To mankind's impious counsels ever nigh,
Fateful, and fierce to punish these you fly.
Revenge and sorrows dire to you belong,
Hid in a savage vest, severe and strong.
Terrific virgins, who for ever dwell,
Endu'd with various forms, in deepest hell;
Aerial, and unseen by human kind,
And swiftly coursing, rapid as the mind.
In vain the sun with wing'd effulgence bright,[2]
In vain the moon far darting milder light,
Wisdom and virtue may attempt in vain,
And pleasing art, our transport to obtain;
Unless with these you readily conspire,
And far avert your all-destructive ire.
The boundless tribe of mortals you descry,
And justly rule with Right's impartial eye.
Come, snaky-hair'd, Fates many-form'd, divine,
Suppress your rage, and to our rites incline.

---

1 See the note on Hymn lix, to the Fates. The Chaldean Oracle observes, "that the Furies are the bonds of men,"

Αι ποιναι μεροπων αγκτειραι.

i.e. as Psellus explains it, the powers that punish guilty souls bind them to their material passions, and in these, as it were, suffocate them; such punishment being finally the means of purification. Nor do these powers only afflict the vicious, but even such as convert themselves to an immaterial essence: for these through their connection with matter require a purification of this kind. This illustrates what is said in the seventeenth and three following lines of this hymn.

2 Ruhnkenius thinks that this and the five following lines should be transferred from hence to the hymn to the Graces; and Hermann adopting this opinion has omitted them in the present hymn, and inserted them in hymn lx. to the Graces. To me, however, it appears that they properly belong to this hymn to the Furies; and therefore I have not transferred them.

LXX

TO THE FURIES

THE FUMIGATION FROM AROMATICS

Hear me, illustrious Furies, mighty nam'd,
Terrific pow'rs, for prudent counsel fam'd;
Holy and pure, from Jove terrestrial born,
And Proserpine, whom lovely locks adorn:
Whose piercing sight with vision unconfin'd
Surveys the deeds of all the impious kind.
On Fate attendant, punishing the race
(With wrath severe) of deeds unjust and base.
Dark-colour'd queens, whose glittering eyes are bright
With dreadful, radiant, life-destroying light:
Eternal rulers, terrible and strong,
To whom revenge and tortures dire belong;
Fateful, and *horrid to the human sight*,
With snaky tresses,[1] wand'ring in the night:
Hither approach, and in these rites rejoice,
For ye I call with holy suppliant voice.

---

1 "Eschylus (says Pausanias, in Attic. cap. 28) was the first that represented the Furies with snakes in their hair." On this passage I have observed in a note in my translation of Pausanias as follows: Those who are of opinion that the Orphic hymns are spurious compositions will doubtless imagine that their opinion is indisputably confirmed by the present passage: for the Furies, in the above hymn, are called οφιοπλοκαμοι, or *snaky-haired*; and consequently, it may be said, they must have been written posterior to the time of Eschylus, if what Pausanias asserts be true. It must, however, be remembered, that Eschylus was accused of inserting in his tragedies things belonging to the Mysteries; and we have shown, in the Introduction to these Hymns, that they were used in the Eleusinian Mysteries. If this be the case, either Pausanias is mistaken in what he asserts of Eschylus in this place; or, which appears to me to be more probable, being a man religiously fearful of disclosing any particulars belonging to the mysteries, he means that no one prior to Eschylus *openly* represented the Furies with snakes in their hair. There is also a passage in the Cataplus of Lucian which very much corroborates my opinion. The passage is as follows: ειπε μοι, ετελεσθης γαρ, ω Κυνισκε τα Ελευσινι, ουχ ομοια τοις εκει τα ενθαδε σοι δοκει; ΚΥΝ. ευ λεγεις· ιδου ουν προσερχεται τις δᾳδουχουσα, φοβερον τι, και

απειλητικον προσβλεπουσα· ἢ αρα που Ερινυς εστιν; *i.e.* Tell me, Cynic, for you are initiated in the *Eleusinian Mysteries*, do not the present particulars appear to you to be similar to those which take place in the Mysteries? Cyn. Very much so. See then, here comes a certain torch-bearer with *a dreadful and threatening countenance. Is it, therefore, one of the Furies?* It is evident from this passage, that the Furies in the Mysteries were of a terrible appearance, which Pausanias informs us was not the case with their statues; and it is from this circumstance of the statues of these divinities not being dreadful in their appearance, that he infers Eschylus was the first that represented them to be so. Hence, as the Mysteries were instituted long before Eschylus, it is evident that the terrible aspects of the Furies were not invented by him: and it is more than probable that this dreadful appearance was principally caused by the snakes in their hair. The present hymn too calls the Furies φοβερωπες, *i.e. terrific to the sight.*

But from what Natales Comes narrates from Menander, it is evident that the snaky tresses of the Furies were not the invention of Eschylus. For he informs us that Menander says, in one of his plays, "it is fabulously reported that Tisiphone became enamoured of a certain beautiful youth, whose name was Cytheron, and that her love for him being very ardent, she contrived the means of conversing with him. He, however, being terrified at her formidable aspect, did not deign to answer her; on which she took one of the *snakes* from her hair and threw it at him, which occasioned his death. But through the commiseration of the Gods, the mountain which was before called Asterius was from him denominated Cytheron." "Fabulati sunt antiqui neque has quidem severissimas Deas Cupidinis vim potuisse devitare, quando scriptum reliquit Mænander in rebus fabulosis, Tisiphonem in amorem cujusdam pueri formosi Cytheronis nomine incidisse, cujus desiderium cum ferre non posset, verba de congressu ad illum proferenda curavit. At is formidandum aspectum veritus, neque responso quidem dignam fecit, quo illa unum e suis draconibus e capillis convulsum in eum conjicit, quem serpens intra nodos constringens interemit, ubi Deorum misericordia mons ab illo dictus fuit, qui prius Asterius dicebatur." Natalis Comit. Mythol. lib. iii. p. 216. As none of the ancient tragedians, therefore, were the inventors of the fables which are the subjects of their dramas, but derived them from authors more ancient than themselves, it is not at all probable that this fable was invented by Eschylus, and taken by Menander from him.

LXXI

TO MELINOE

THE FUMIGATION FROM AROMATICS

I call, Melinoe, saffron-veil'd, terrene,
Who from dread Pluto's venerable queen,
Mixt with Saturnian Jupiter, arose,
Near where Cocytus' mournful river flows;
When, under Pluto's semblance, Jove divine
Deceiv'd with guileful arts dark Proserpine.
Hence, partly black thy limbs and partly white,
From Pluto dark, from Jove etherial bright.
Thy colour'd members, men by night inspire
When seen in spectred forms, with terrors dire;
Now darkly visible, involv'd in night,
Perspicuous now they meet the fearful sight.
Terrestrial queen, expel wherever found
The soul's mad fears to earth's remotest bound;
With holy aspect on our incense shine,
And bless thy mystics, and the rites divine.

LXXII

TO FORTUNE

THE FUMIGATION FROM FRANKINCENSE

Approach, queen Fortune, with propitious mind
And rich abundance, to my pray'r inclin'd:
Placid and gentle Trivia, mighty nam'd,
Imperial Dian,[1] born of Pluto fam'd,
Mankind's unconquer'd endless praise is thine,
Sepulch'ral, widely wand'ring pow'r divine!
In thee our various mortal life is found,
And some from thee in copious wealth abound;
While others mourn thy hand averse to bless,
In all the bitterness of deep distress.
Be present, Goddess, to thy vot'ries kind,
And give abundance with benignant mind.

1 Fortune, according to the Platonic, which is the same with the Orphic theology, is that divine power which disposes things differing from each other, and happening contrary to expectation, to beneficent purposes. Or it may be defined to be that divine distribution which causes every thing to fill up the lot assigned to it by the condition of its being. This divinity, too, congregates all sublunary causes, and enables them to confer on sublunary effects that particular good which their nature and merits eminently deserve. "But the power of Fortune (says Simplicius, in Aristot. Physic. [see *The Works of Aristotle I*, TTS vol. XIX, p. 281]) particularly disposes in an orderly manner the sublunary part of the universe, in which the nature of what is contingent is contained, and which being essentially disordered, Fortune, in conjunction with other primary causes, directs, places in order, and governs. Hence she is represented guiding a rudder, because she governs things sailing on the sea of generation [*i.e.* of the sublunary world]. Her rudder too is fixed on a globe, because she directs that which is unstable in generation. In her other hand she holds the horn of Amalthea, which is full of fruits, because she is the cause of obtaining all divine fruits. And on this account we venerate the fortunes of cities and houses, and of each individual; because being very remote from divine union, we are in danger of being deprived of its participation, and require, in order to obtain it, the assistance of the Goddess Fortune, and of those natures superior to the human, who possess the characteristics of this Divinity. *Indeed, every fortune*

is good; for every attainment respects something good, nor does any thing evil subsist from divinity. But of things that are good, some are precedaneous, and others are of a punishing or revenging characteristic, which we are accustomed to call evils. Hence we speak of two Fortunes, one of which we denominate GOOD, *and which is the cause of our obtaining precedaneous good; but the other* EVIL, *which prepares us to receive punishment or revenge."*

From this beautiful passage, it is easy to see why *Fortune*, in this hymn, is called *Diana*; for each of these divinities governs the sublunary world. See the original of the above admirable extract from Simplicius in the notes to my Pausanias.

LXXIII

TO THE DÆMON[1]

THE FUMIGATION FROM FRANKINCENSE

Thee, mighty ruling Dæmon dread, I call,
Mild Jove, life-giving, and the source of all:
Great Jove, much wand'ring, terrible and strong,
To whom revenge and tortures dire belong.
Mankind from thee in plenteous wealth abound,
When in their dwellings joyful thou art found;
Or pass thro' life afflicted and distress'd,
The needful means of bliss by thee suppress'd.
'Tis thine alone, endu'd with boundless might,
To keep the keys of sorrow and delight.
O holy *blessed* father, hear my pray'r,
Disperse the seeds of life-consuming care,
With fav'ring mind the sacred rites attend,
And grant to life a glorious blessed end.

---

1 According to the Egyptians, as we are informed by Macrobius (in Saturnal, lib. i. cap 19), "the Gods that preside over man at the time of his birth are these four, the *Dæmon, Fortune, Love,* and *Necessity.*" He adds "that by the two former they signified the Sun and Moon; because the Sun, who is the source of spirit, heat, and light, is the generator and guardian of human life; and on this account he is believed to be the dæmon, that is, God of him who is born. But by Fortune they indicated the Moon, because she presides over bodies which are tossed about through the variety of fortuitous events." Conformably to this, Proclus, in his very elegant hymn to the Sun, invokes that divinity as *a blessed dæmon,*

Αλλα θεων αριστε, πυριστεφες, ολβιε δαιμων.

LXXIV

TO LEUCOTHEA

THE FUMIGATION FROM AROMATICS

I call, Leucothea, of great Cadmus born,
And Bacchus' nurse, whom ivy leaves adorn.
Hear, powerful Goddess, in the mighty deep
Vast-bosom'd, destin'd thy domain to keep:
In waves rejoicing, guardian of mankind;
For ships from thee alone deliv'rance find,
Amidst the fury of th'unstable main,
When art no more avails, and strength is vain.
When rushing billows with tempestuous ire
O'erwhelm the mariner in ruin dire,
Thou hear'st with pity touch'd his suppliant pray'r,
Resolv'd his life to succour and to spare.
Be ever present, Goddess! in distress,
Waft ships along with prosp'rous success:
Thy mystics thro' the stormy sea defend,
And safe conduct them to their destin'd end.

LXXV

TO PALÆMON

THE FUMIGATION FROM MANNA

O Nurs'd with Dionysius, doom'd to keep
Thy dwelling in the widely spreading deep;
With joyful aspect to my pray'r incline,
Propitious come, and bless the rites divine;
Thy mystics thro' the earth and sea attend,
And from old Ocean's stormy waves defend:
For ships their safety ever owe to thee,
Who wand'rest with them thro' the raging sea.
Come, guardian pow'r, whom mortal tribes desire,
And far avert the deep's destructive ire.

LXXVI

TO THE MUSES[1]

THE FUMIGATION FROM FRANKINCENSE

Daughters of Jove, loud-sounding, and divine,
Renown'd, Pierian, sweetly speaking Nine;
To those whose breasts your sacred furies fire,
Much form'd, the objects of supreme desire.
Sources of blameless virtue to mankind,
Who form to excellence the youthful mind:
Who nurse the soul, and give her to descry
The paths of right with reason's steady eye.
Commanding queens, who lead to sacred light
The intellect refin'd from error's night;
And to mankind each holy rite disclose,
For mystic knowledge from your nature flows.
Clio, and Erato who charms the sight,
With thee, Euterpe, minist'ring delight:
Thalia flourishing, Polymnia fam'd,
Melpomene from skill in music nam'd:
Terpsichore, Urania heav'nly bright,
With thee who gav'st me to behold the light.[†]
Come, venerable, various pow'rs divine,
With fav'ring aspect on your mystics shine;
Bring glorious, ardent, lovely, fam'd desire,
And warm my bosom with your sacred fire.

---

1 "The Muses (says Proclus, in Hesiod Op. p. 6) derive their appellation from *investigation*: for they are the sources of erudition." He adds "that Jupiter is said to be the father, and Mnemosyne the mother of the Muses, because the learner ought to possess both intelligence and memory, the latter of which Mnemosyne imparts, and the former Jupiter." See more concerning the Muses in the additional notes.

[†] In the original text the Muse Kalliope is named here. PT.

LXXVII

TO MNEMOSYNE
or the
GODDESS OF MEMORY

THE FUMIGATION FROM FRANKINCENSE

The consort I invoke of Jove divine,
Source of the holy, sweetly speaking Nine;
Free from th'oblivion of the fallen mind,
By whom the soul with intellect is join'd.[1]
Reason's increase and thought to thee belong,
All-powerful, pleasant, vigilant, and strong.
'Tis thine to waken from lethargic rest
All thoughts deposited within the breast;
And nought neglecting, vig'rous to excite
The mental eye from dark oblivion's night.
*Come, blessed pow'r, thy mystics' mem'ry wake
To holy rites, and Lethe's fetters break.*

---

1 "Memory (says Plotinus [En. IV, iii, 28, TTS vol. III]) leads to the object of memory." (αγει γαρ η μνημη προς το μνημονευτον.) But the object of memory to the soul is intellect, and the forms or ideas it contains, to which the soul tends through reminiscence; so that the Goddess of Memory is very properly said by Orpheus to conjoin the soul with intellect.

LXXVIII

TO AURORA

THE FUMIGATION FROM MANNA

Hear me, O Goddess, whose emerging ray
Leads on the broad refulgence of the day;
Blushing Aurora, whose celestial light
Beams on the world with redd'ning splendours bright.
Angel of Titan, whom with constant round
Thy orient beams recall from night profound:
Labour of ev'ry kind to lead is thine,
Of mortal life the minister divine.
Mankind in thee eternally delight,
And none presumes to shun thy beauteous sight.
Soon as thy splendours break the bands of rest,
And eyes unclose, with pleasing sleep oppress'd;
Men, reptiles, birds, and beasts, with gen'ral voice,
And all the nations of the deep rejoice;
For all the culture of our life is thine.
Come, blessed pow'r, and to these rites incline:
Thy holy light increase, and unconfin'd
Diffuse its radiance on thy mystics' mind.

LXXIX

TO THEMIS

THE FUMIGATION FROM FRANKINCENSE

Illustrious Themis, of celestial birth,
Thee I invoke, young blossom of the earth.[1]
All-beauteous virgin; first from thee alone
Prophetic oracles to men were known,
Giv'n from the deep recesses of the fane
In sacred Pytho, where renown'd you reign.
From thee Apollo's oracles arose,
And from thy pow'r his inspiration flows.
Honour'd by all, of form divinely bright,
Majestic virgin, wand'ring in the night.
Mankind from thee first learnt perfective rites,
And Bacchus' nightly choirs thy soul delights;
For the God's honours to disclose is thine,
And holy mysteries and rites divine.
Be present, Goddess, to my pray'r inclin'd,
And bless thy Teletæ with fav'ring mind.

---

1 Themis is one of the progeny of the intellectual Earth resident in Phanes. See the note on Hymn XII, to Hercules.

LXXX

TO BOREAS[1]

THE FUMIGATION FROM FRANKINCENSE

Boreas, whose wintry blasts, terrific, tear
The bosom of the deep surrounding air;
Cold icy pow'r, approach, and fav'ring blow,
And Thrace awhile desert, expos'd to snow:
The air's all-misty dark'ning state dissolve,
With pregnant clouds whose frames in show'rs resolve.
Serenely temper all within the sky,
And wipe from moisture Ether's splendid eye.

---

1 "Orpheus (says Simplicius, in Aristot. de Anima, lib. i.) appears to have called the aptitude of bodies, with respect to life, *respiration; but the total and universal causes winds,* without which *partial* causes cannot make bodies properly adapted animated."

LXXXI

TO ZEPHYRUS

THE FUMIGATION FROM FRANKINCENSE

Sea-born, aerial, blowing from the west,
Sweet gales, who give to weary'd labour rest.
Vernal and grassy, and of murm'ring sound,
To ships delightful through the sea profound;
For these, impell'd by you with gentle force,
Pursue with prosp'rous fate their destin'd course.
With blameless gales regard my suppliant pray'r,
Zephyrs unseen, light-wing'd, and form'd from air.

LXXXII

TO THE SOUTH WIND

THE FUMIGATION FROM FRANKINCENSE

Wide-coursing gales, whose lightly leaping feet
With rapid wings the air's wet bosom beat,
Approach, benevolent, swift-whirling pow'rs,
With humid clouds the principles of show'rs;
For show'ry clouds are portion'd to your care,
To send on earth from all-surrounding air.
Hear, blessed pow'r, these holy rites attend,
And fruitful rains on earth all-parent send.

151

LXXXIII

TO OCEAN[1]

THE FUMIGATION FROM AROMATICS

Ocean I call, whose nature ever flows,
From whom at first both Gods and men arose;
Sire incorruptible, whose waves surround,
And earth's all-terminating circle bound:
Hence every river, hence the spreading sea,
And earth's pure bubbling fountains spring from thee.
Hear, mighty sire, for boundless bliss is thine,
Greatest cathartic of the pow'rs divine:
Earth's friendly limit, fountain of the pole,
Whose waves wide spreading and circumfluent roll.
Approach benevolent, with placid mind,
And be for ever to thy mystics kind.

1 Ocean, as I have before observed in the note on the hymn to Hercules, according to its first subsistence, is one of the offspring of the first intellectual Earth. "And of the divine Titannic hebdomads (says Proclus, in Tim. 292F ff. TTS vol. XVI p. 889) Ocean both abides and proceeds, uniting himself to his father [Heaven] and not departing from his kingdom. But all the rest of the Titans, rejoicing in progression, are said to have given completion to the will of Earth, but to have assaulted their father, dividing themselves from his kingdom, and proceeding into another order. Or rather, of all the celestial genera, some alone abide in their principles, as the two first triads." "For (says Orpheus) as soon as Heaven understood that they had an implacable heart and a lawless nature, he hurled them into Tartarus, the profundity of the earth." He concealed them, therefore, in the unapparent, through transcendency of power. But others both abide in and proceed from their principles, as Ocean and Tethys. For when the other Titans proceeded to assault their father Heaven, Ocean prohibited them from obeying the mandates of their mother, being dubious of their rectitude.

"But Ocean (says Orpheus) remained within his place of abode, considering to what he should direct his attention, and whether he should deprive his father of strength, and unjustly mutilate him in conjunction with Saturn, and the other brethren, who were obedient to their dear mother; or leaving these, stay quietly at home. After much fluctuation of thought, however, he remained peaceably at home, being angry with his mother, but still more so with his brethren." He therefore abides, and at the same time proceeds together with Tethys; for she is conjoined with him according to the first progeny. But the other Titans are induced to separation and progression. And the leader of these is the mighty Saturn, as the theologist says; though he evinces that Saturn is superior to Ocean, by saying that Saturn himself received the celestial Olympus, and that there being throned, he reigns over the Titans; but that Ocean obtained all the middle allotment. For he says, "that Ocean dwells in the divine streams which are posterior to Olympus, and that he environs the Heaven which is there, and not the highest Heaven, but as the fable says, that which fell from Olympus, and was there arranged."

As the latter part of what is here said from Proclus, is a very remarkable Orphic fragment, and is not to be found in the Collection of the Orphic remains by either Gesner or Hermann, I shall give the original for the sake of the learned reader. Και τοι γε οτι ο Κρονος υπερτερος εστι του Ωκεανου, δεδηλωκεν ο θεολογος παλιν λεγων· τον μεν Κρονον ουτον καταλαμβανειν τον ουρανιον Ολυμπον, κᾳκει θρονισθεντα, βασιλευειν των Τιτανων· τον δε Ωκεανον την ληξιν απασαν την μεσην· ναιειν γαρ αυτον εν τοις θεσπεσιοις ρειθροις τοις μετα τον Ολυμπον, και τον εκει περιεπειν Ουρανον, αλλ' ου τον ακροτατον, ως δε φησιν ο μυθος, τον εμπεσοντα του Ουλυμπου, και εκει τεταγμενον.

Proclus also, in Tim. [298A], speaking of the nine deities mentioned by Plato in the *Timæus*, according to their *sublunary* allotment; for they originally proceed from the intellectual order, says: "Heaven terminates, Earth corroborates, and *Ocean* moves all generation. But Tethys establishes every thing in its proper motion; intellectual essences in intellectual, middle essences in psychical [or such as pertain to soul], and such as are corporeal in physical motion; *Ocean* at the same time collectively moving all things. Saturn alone divides intellectually; Rhea vivifies; Phorcys distributes spermatic productive principles; Jupiter perfects things apparent from such as are unapparent; and Juno evolves according to the all-various mutations of visible natures."

LXXXIV

TO VESTA[1]

THE FUMIGATION FROM AROMATICS

Daughter of Saturn, venerable dame,
Who dwell'st amidst great fire's eternal flame;
In sacred rites these ministers are thine,
Mystics much blessed, holy, and divine.
In thee the Gods have fix'd their dwelling place,
Strong, stable basis of the mortal race.
Eternal, much form'd, ever florid queen,
Laughing[2] and blessed, and of lovely mien;
Accept these rites, accord each just desire,
And gentle health and needful good inspire.

---

1 Saturn (says Proclus, in Cratyl, [139, *The Works of Plato V*, TTS vol. XIII, p. 590]) in conjunction with Rhea, produced Vesta and Juno, who are coordinate with the demiurgic causes. For Vesta imparts from herself to the Gods an uninclining permanency and seat in themselves, and an indissoluble essence. But Juno imparts progression, and a multiplication into things secondary. She is also the vivifying fountain of wholes, and the mother of prolific powers; and on this account she is said to have proceeded together with Jupiter the Demiurgus; and through this communion she generates maternally such things as Jupiter generates paternally. But Vesta abides in herself, possessing an undefiled virginity, and being the cause of sameness to all things. Each of these divinities, however, together with her own proper perfection, possesses according to participation the power of the other. Hence some say that Vesta is denominated from *essence*, (απο της εσσιας,[†] lege ουσιας) looking to her proper hyparxis. But others, surveying her vivific and motive power, which she derives from Juno, say that she is thus denominated as *being the cause of impulsion.* (ως ωσεως ουσαν αιτιαν.) For all divine natures are in all, and particularly such as are co-ordinate with each other, participate of, and subsist in each other. Each, therefore, of the demiurgic and vivific orders participates

---

[†] My manuscript has εστιας· but the edition of this work, by the very learned Professor Boissonade, Leipsic, 1820, has εσσιας. The true reading however is doubtless ουσιας.

the form by which it is characterized from Vesta. The orbs of the planets, likewise, possess the sameness of their revolutions from her; and the poles and centres are always allotted from her their permanent rest. Vesta, however, does not manifest essence, but the abiding and firm establishment of essence in itself; and hence this Goddess proceeds into light after the mighty Saturn. For the Divinities prior to Saturn have not a subsistence in themselves and in another, but this originates from Saturn. And a subsistence in *self* is the peculiarity of Vesta, but in *another* of Juno." What is here said by Proclus about a subsistence in *self* and in *another*, the reader will find explained in the notes on my translation of the *Parmenides* of Plato.

In addition to the above admirable development of the nature of Vesta by Proclus, it is necessary to add, that this Goddess, according to her mundane allotment, is the Divinity of the Earth; and as such she is celebrated in the present hymn. Hence Philolaus, in a fragment preserved by Stobæus (Eclog. Phys. p. 51), says, "that there is a fire in the middle at the centre, which is the Vesta of the universe, the house of Jupiter, the mother of the Gods, and the basis, coherence, and measure of nature." Hence it appears that they are greatly mistaken who suppose the Pythagoreans meant the Sun by the fire at the centre; and this is still more evident from what Simplicius says in his Commentary on Arist. de Cœlo, lib. ii. for he there observes, "that the Pythagoreans supposing the decad to be a perfect number, were willing to collect the bodies that are moved in a circle into the decadic number. Hence they say, that the inerratic sphere, the seven planets, this our earth, and the antichthon complete the decad; and in this manner Aristotle understands the assertions of the Pythagoreans." He then adds: Οι δε γνησιεστερον αυτων μετασχοντες, το μεν πυρ εν τω μεσω φασι την δημιουργικην δυναμιν, εκ του μεσου οληv την γην τρεφουσαν, και το ψυχομενον αυτης ανεγειρουσαν· δι ο, οι μεν Ζηνος πυργον αυτο καλουσιν, ωσ αυτος εν τοις Πυθαγορειοις διηγσατο· οι δε Διος φυλακην, ως εν τουτοις· οι δε Διος θρονον· ως αλλοι φασιν· αντρον δε την γην ελεγον, ως οργανον και αυτην του χρονου· ημερων γαρ εστιν αυτη, και νυκτων, αιτια. *i.e.* "But those who more genuinely participate of the Pythagorean doctrines say that the fire in the middle is a demiurgic power, nourishing the whole earth from the middle, and exciting whatever it contains of a frigid nature. Hence some call it the tower of Jupiter, as he (*i.e.* Aristotle) narrates in his *Pythagorics*. But others denominate it the guardian of Jupiter, as Aristotle relates in the present treatise. And according to others it is the throne of Jupiter. They called, however, the earth a cavern, as being itself an instrument of time: for it is the cause of day and night." In that part of this remarkable passage, in which it is said that the Pythagoreans called the earth *a cavern*, it is necessary for ,αντρον to read αστρον, *a star*. For a little before both Aristotle and Simplicius inform us, that the Pythagoreans asserted that *the earth exists as one of the stars*. And this is confirmed by their calling the earth one of the *instruments of time*: for the stars are thus denominated by Plato in the *Timæus*. Meursius, in his Denarius Pythagoricus, p. 19, thinks we should read κεντρον for αντρον; but he was evidently mistaken.

From this account, given by Simplicius, it appears that the above-mentioned decad of the Pythagoreans consists of the inerratic sphere, the seven planets, the earth, and the fire in the centre of the earth.

2 "The *laughter* of the Gods (says Proclus, in Plat. Polit. p. 384) must be defined to be their exuberant energy in the universe, and the cause of the gladness of all mundane natures. But as such a providence is incomprehensible, and the communication of all good from the Gods is never failing, Homer very properly calls their laughter unextinguished." He adds, "fables, however, do not assert that the Gods always weep, but that they laugh without ceasing. For tears are symbols of their providence in mortal and frail concerns, and which now rise into existence, and then perish; but laughter is a sign of their energy in wholes, and those perfect natures in the universe which are perpetually moved with undeviating sameness. On which account, I think, when we divide demiurgic productions into Gods and men, we attribute laughter to the generation of the Gods, but tears to the formation of men and animals; whence a certain poet, in his hymn to the Sun, says

> Mankind's laborious race thy tears excite,
> But the Gods, *laughing*, blossom'd into light.

But when we make a division into things celestial and sublunary, again, after the same manner, we must assign *laughter* to the former and tears to the latter. And when we reason concerning the generations and corruptions of sublunary natures themselves, we must refer the former to the *laughter*, and the latter to the *tears* of the Gods. Hence in the mysteries also, those who preside over sacred institutions order both these to be celebrated at stated times."

LXXXV

TO SLEEP

THE FUMIGATION FROM A POPPY

Sleep, king of Gods, and men of mortal birth,
Sov'reign of all, sustain'd by mother Earth;
For thy dominion is supreme alone,
O'er all extended, and by all things known.
'Tis thine all bodies with benignant mind
In other bands than those of brass to bind.
Tamer of cares, to weary toil repose,
And from whom sacred solace in affliction flows.
Thy pleasing gentle chains preserve the soul,
And e'en the dreadful cares of death control;
For Death, and Lethe with oblivious stream,
Mankind thy genuine brothers justly deem.
With fav'ring aspect to my pray'r incline,
And save thy mystics in their works divine.

LXXXVI

TO THE DIVINITY OF DREAMS

THE FUMIGATION FROM AROMATICS

Thee I invoke, blest pow'r of dreams divine,
Angel of future fates, swift wings are thine.
Great source of oracles to human kind,
When stealing soft, and whisp'ring to the mind,
Thro' sleep's sweet silence, and the gloom of night,
Thy pow'r awakes th'intellectual sight;
To silent souls the will of heaven relates,
And silently reveals their future fates.
Forever friendly to the upright mind,
Sacred and pure, to holy rites inclin'd;
For these with pleasing hope thy dreams inspire:
Bliss to anticipate, which all desire.
Thy visions manifest of fate disclose,
What methods best may mitigate our woes;
Reveal what rites the Gods immortal please,
And what the means their anger to appease;
For ever tranquil is the good man's end,
Whose life thy dreams admonish and defend.
But from the wicked turn'd averse to bless,
Thy form unseen, the angel of distress;
No means to check approaching ill they find,
Pensive with fears, and to the future blind.
Come, blessed pow'r, the signatures reveal
Which heav'n's decrees mysteriously conceal,
Signs only present to the worthy mind,
Nor omens ill disclose of monstrous kind.

LXXXVII

TO DEATH[1]

THE FUMIGATION FROM MANNA

Hear me, O Death, whose empire unconfin'd
Extends to mortal tribes of ev'ry kind.
On thee the portion of our time depends,
Whose absence lengthens life, whose presence ends.
Thy sleep perpetual bursts the vivid folds
By which the soul attracting body holds:[2]
Common to all, of ev'ry sex and age,
For nought escapes thy all-destructive rage.
Not youth itself thy clemency can gain,
Vig'rous and strong, by thee untimely slain.
In thee the end of nature's works is known,
In thee all judgment is absolv'd alone.
No suppliant arts thy dreadful rage control,
No vows revoke the purpose of thy soul.
O blessed pow'r, regard my ardent pray'r,
And human life to age abundant spare.

---

1 Hermann's edition of these Orphic *Teletai* ends with a hymn to Mars, which is found among the hymns ascribed to Homer; both he and Ruhnkenius being of opinion that it is more Orphic than Homeric. I, however, should say, that it was written by any one rather than by Orpheus. For can it for a moment be supposed that Orpheus would pray that he might be able

> Θυμου τ' αυ μενος οξυ κατισχεμεν, ος μ' ερεθησι
> Φυλοπιδος κρυεπης επιβαινεμεν. -

"To restrain the impetuous force of anger, which excites him to engage in horrid war!"

2 What is said in this and the preceding line is well explained by Porphyry in his excellent treatise entitled Αφορμαι προς τα νοητα, or *Auxiliaries to the Perception of Intelligibles*,† viz. "That which nature binds, nature also dissolves: and that which the soul binds, the soul likewise dissolves. Nature, indeed,

---

† Section I, 6. See *Select Works of Porphyry*, TTS volume II, p. 169.

bound the body to the soul; but the soul binds herself to the body. Nature, therefore, liberates the body from the soul; but the soul liberates herself from the body." And again, in the next sentence, "Hence there is a twofold death; the one, indeed, universally known, in which the body is liberated from the soul; but the other peculiar to philosophers, in which the soul is liberated from the body. Nor does the one entirely follow the other." The meaning of this twofold death is as follows: Though the body, by the death which is universally known, may be loosened from the soul, yet while material passions and affections reside in the soul, the soul will continually verge to another body, and as long as this inclination continues, remain connected with body. But when, from the predominance of an intellectual nature, the soul is separated from material affections, it is truly liberated from the body; though the body at the same time verges and clings to the soul, as to the immediate cause of its support.

Additional Notes

The following Additional Notes are given for the purpose of elucidating the Orphic theology, with which the preceding hymns are replete. They form the greater part of the Scholia of Proclus on the *Cratylus* of Plato,[†] a work inestimably valuable to the student of the Grecian theology, and which has been recently published with very valuable critical notes by the most learned Professor Boissonade. The following translation, however, was made by me many years ago from a manuscript of this work, which is a copy of an original in the possession of Mr. Heber, and which is so very rare that it is not to be found either in the Bodleian Library or the British Museum, nor, I believe, in any of the public libraries of Great Britain. I have given the translation of these Scholia in the order in which they occur in the original, as I could not have done otherwise without omitting some part of them, which, on account of their great importance, I was unwilling to do.

Jupiter is not *said to be*, but *is*, the father of those who genuinely preserve the proper form of life, such as Hercules and the Dioscuri; but of those who are never at any time able to convert themselves to a divine nature, he never *is* nor is *said to be* the father. Such therefore, as having been partakers of a certain energy above human nature, have again fallen into *the sea of dissimilitude*,[‡] and for honour among men have embraced error towards the Gods, - of these Jupiter is *said to be* the father.

The paternal cause originates supernally from the intelligible and occult Gods; for there the first fathers of wholes subsist; but it proceeds through all the intellectual Gods into the demiurgic order. For *Timæus* celebrates this order as at the same time *fabricative* and *paternal*; since he calls Jupiter the *demiurgus* and *father*. The fathers, however, who are superior to the one fabrication are called Gods of Gods, but the demiurgus is the father of Gods and men. Farther still, Jupiter is said to be *peculiarly* the father of some, as of Hercules, who immutably preserve a Jovian and ruling life during their converse with the realms of

---

[†] See *The Works of Plato V*, TTS vol. XIII, for a fuller translation of the Scholia; this also carries the Tuebner text line numbering.

[‡] Plato, in the *Politicus*, thus calls the realm of generation, *i.e.* the whole of a visible nature.

generation. Jupiter, therefore, is triply father, of gods, partial souls, and of souls that embrace an intellectual and Jovian life. The intellectual order of the gods, therefore, is supernally bounded by the king[†] of the total divine genera, and who has a paternal transcendency with respect to all the intellectual Gods. This king, according to Orpheus, is called by the blessed immortals that dwell on lofty Olympus, Phanes Protogonus. But this order proceeds through the three Nights, and the celestial orders, into the Titanic or Saturnian series, where it first separates itself from the fathers, and changes the kingdom of the *Synoches*[‡] for a distributive government of wholes, and unfolds every demiurgic genus of the Gods from all the above-mentioned ruling and royal causes, but proximately from Saturn, the leader of the Titanic orders. Prior, however, to other fabricators (δημιουργοι) it unfolds Jupiter, who is allotted the unical strength of the whole demiurgic series, and who produces and gives subsistence to all unapparent and apparent natures. And he is indeed intellectual, according to the order in which he ranks, but he produces the species and the genera of beings into the order of sensibles. He is likewise filled with the Gods above himself, but imparts from himself a progression into being to all mundane natures. Hence Orpheus[§] represents him fabricating every celestial race, making the sun and moon and the other starry Gods, together with the sublunary elements, and diversifying the latter with forms which before had a disordered subsistence. He likewise represents him presiding over the Gods who are distributed about the whole world, and who are suspended from him; and in the character of a legislator assigning distributions of providence in the universe according to desert to all the mundane Gods. Homer too, following Orpheus, celebrates him as the common father of Gods and men, as leader and king, and as the supreme of rulers. He also says that all the multitude of mundane Gods is collected about him, abides in and is perfected by him. For all the mundane Gods are converted to Jupiter through Themis,

---

[†] That is, intelligible intellect, the extremity of the intelligible order.

[‡] That is, the divinities who compose the middle of that order of Gods which is denominated intelligible and at the same time intellectual.

[§] As what is here said from Orpheus concerning Jupiter is very remarkable, and is no where else to be found, I give the original for the sake of the learned reader. διο και Ορφευς δημιουργουντα μεν αυτον την ουρανιαν πασαν γενεαν παραδιδωσι, και ηλιον ποιουντα και σεληνην, και τους αλλους αστρῳους θεους· δημιουργουντα δε τα υποσεληνην στοιχεια, και διακρινοντα τοις ειδεσιν ατακτως εχοντα προτερον· σειρας δ' εφισταντα θεων περι ολον τον κοσμον εις αυτον ανηρτημενας, και διαθεσμοθετουντα πασι τοις εγκοσμιοις θεοις κατ' αξιαν διανομας της εν τῳ παντι προνοιας.

ζευς δε θεμιστα κελευσε θεους, αγορην δε καλεσσαι.
. . . . ηδ, αρα παντη
φοιτησασα κελευσε Διος προς δωμα νεεσθαι.
Iliad, xx, 4.

i.e. "But Jupiter orders Themis to call the Gods to council; and she directing her course every where commands them to go to the house of Jupiter," All of them therefore are excited according to the one of will Jupiter, and become διος ενδον,[†] *within Jupiter*, as the poet says. Jupiter too again separates them within himself, according to two coordinations, and excites them to providential energies about secondary natures; he at the same time, as Timæus says,[‡] abiding after his accustomed manner;

ως εφατο κρονιδης πολεμον δ' αλιαστον εγειρεν.
Iliad, xx, 32.

i.e. "Thus spoke Saturnian Jupiter, and excited inevitable war." Jupiter however is separate and exempt from all mundane natures; whence also the most total and leading of the other Gods, though they appear to have in a certain respect equal authority with Jupiter, through a progression from the same causes, yet call him father. For both Neptune and Juno celebrate him by this appellation. And though Juno speaks to him as one who is of the same order,

και γαρ εγο θεος ειμι· γενος δε μοι ενθεν οθενσοι,
και με πρεσβυτατην τεκετο κρονος αγκυλομητις.
Iliad, iv, 58.

i.e. "For I also am a divinity, and Saturn, of inflected council, endowed me with the greatest dignity, when he begot me."
And though Neptune says,

τρεις· γαρ τ' εκ κρονου ειμεν αδελφεοι, ους τεκε Ρειη,
Ζευς και εγω, τριτατος δ' Αϊδης ενεροισιν ανασσων.
Iliad, xv, 187.

i.e. "For we are three brothers from Saturn, whom Rhea bore, Jupiter and I, and the third is Pluto, who governs the infernal realms:"
Yet Jupiter is called father by both these divinities; and this because he comprehends in himself the one and impartible cause of all fabrication;

[†] See the 14th line.

[‡] *Timæus* 42e.

is prior to the Saturnian triad;[†] connectedly contains the three fathers; and comprehends on all sides the vivification of Juno. Hence, at the same time that this goddess gives animation to the universe, he also, together with other Gods, gives subsistence to souls. Very properly therefore do we say that the demiurgus in the *Timæus*[‡] is the mighty Jupiter. For he it is who produces mundane intellects and souls, who adorns all bodies with figures and numbers, and inserts in them one union, and an indissoluble friendship and bond. For Night also, in Orpheus, advises Jupiter to employ things of this kind in the fabrication of the universe.

αυταρ επην δεσμον κρατερον περι πασι ταννασης.

i.e. But when your power around the whole has spread
A strong coercive bond.-

(Frag. 22)

The proximate bond indeed of mundane natures is that which subsists through analogy; but the more perfect bond is derived from intellect and soul. Hence Timæus calls the communion of the elements through analogy, and the indissoluble union from life, a bond [*Timæus.* 31c]. For he says, animals were generated bound with animated bonds [38e]. But a more venerable bond than these subsists from the demiurgic will. "For my will (says Jupiter in the *Timæus,* [41b]) is a greater and more principal bond, &c."

Firmly adhering therefore to this conception respecting the mighty Jupiter, *viz.* that he is the demiurgus and father of the universe, that he is an all-perfect imparticipable[§] intellect, and that he fills all things both with other goods, and with life, let us survey how from names Socrates unfolds the mystic truth concerning this divinity. Timæus then says [28c] that it is difficult to know the essence of the demiurgus, and Socrates now says that it is not easy to understand his name, which manifests his power and energy [*Crat.* 396a].

[†] For the Saturnian triad belongs to that order of Gods which is called supermundane, and which immediately subsists after the intellectual order; so that the Jupiter who ranks at the summit of this triad is different from and inferior to the demiurgus.

[‡] *Timæus* 32c.

[§] That is, he is not an intellect consubsistent with soul.

Again, our soul knows partibly the impartible nature of the energy of the Gods, and that which is characterized by unity in this energy, in a multiplied manner: and this especially takes place about the demiurgus who expands intellectual forms, and calls forth intelligible causes, and evolves them to the fabrication of the universe. For Parmenides[†] characterizes him by sameness and difference. According to Homer [*Iliad* xxiv, 527], two tubs are placed near him; and the most mystic tradition and the oracles of the Gods say that the duad is seated with him. For thus they speak: "He possesses both; containing intelligibles in intellect, but introducing sense to the worlds." These oracles likewise call him *twice beyond*, and *twice there* (δις επεκεινα και δις εκει). And, in short, they celebrate him through the duad. For the demiurgus comprehends in himself unitedly every thing *prolific*,[‡] and which gives subsistence to mundane natures. Very properly therefore is his name twofold, of which δια manifests *the cause through which*, and this is paternal goodness; but ζηνα signifies *vivification*, the first causes of which in the universe the demiurgus unically comprehends. The former too is a symbol of the Saturnian and paternal series; but the latter of the vivific and maternal Rhea. So far likewise as Jupiter receives the whole of Saturn, he gives subsistence to a triple essence, the impartible, the partible, and that which subsists between these; but according to the Rhea which he contains in himself, he scatters as from a fountain, intellectual, psychical, and corporeal life. But by his demiurgic powers and energies, he gives a formal subsistence to these, and separates them from forms of a prior order, and from each other. He is also the ruler and king of all things: and is exempt from the three demiurgi. For they, as Socrates says in the *Gorgias* [523a], divide the kingdom of their father; but Jupiter the demiurgus at once, without division, reigns over the three, and unically governs them.

He is therefore the cause of the paternal triad, and of all fabrication; but he connectedly contains the three demiurgi. And he is a *king* indeed, as being coordinated with the fathers; but a *ruler*, as being proximately established above the demiurgic triad, and comprehending the uniform cause of it. Plato therefore, by considering his name in two ways, evinces that images receive partibly the unical causes of paradigms, and that this is adapted to him who establishes the intellectual duad in himself. For he gives subsistence to twofold orders, the celestial and the

---

[†] *Parmenides* 146a.

[‡] And the duad, considered as a divine form or idea, is the source of fecundity.

super-celestial; whence also the theologist Orpheus says, that his sceptre consists of four and twenty measures, as ruling over a twofold twelve.†

Farther still, the soul of the world gives life to alter-motive natures; for to these it becomes the fountain and principle of motion, as Plato says in the *Phædrus* [245e] and *Laws* [892a]. But the demiurgus simply imparts to all things life divine, intellectual, psychical, and that which is divisible about bodies. No one however should think that the Gods in their generations of secondary natures are diminished; or that they sustain a division of their proper essence in giving subsistence to things subordinate; or that they expose their progeny to the view, externally to themselves, in the same manner as the causes of mortal offspring. Nor in short, must we suppose that they generate with motion or mutation, but that abiding in themselves, they produce by their very essence posterior natures, comprehend on all sides their progeny, and supernally perfect the productions and energies of their offspring. Nor again, when it is said that Gods are the sons of more total Gods, must it be supposed that they are disjoined from more ancient causes, and are cut off from a union with them: or that they receive the peculiarity of their hyparxis through motion, and an indefiniteness converting itself to bound. For there is nothing irrational and without measure in the natures superior to us. But we must conceive that their progressions are effected through similitude; and that there is one communion of essence, and an indivisible continuity of powers and energies, between the sons of Gods and their fathers; all those Gods that rank in the second order being established in such as are more ancient; and the more ancient imparting much of perfection, vigour, and efficacious production to the subordinate. And after this manner we must understand that Jupiter is said to be the son of Saturn.‡ For Jupiter, being the demiurgic intellect, proceeds from another intellect, superior and more uniform, which increases indeed its proper intellections, but converts the multitude of them to union; and multiplies its intellectual powers, but elevates their all-various evolutions to impartible sameness. Jupiter therefore proximately establishing a communion with this divinity, and being filled from him with total intellectual good, is very properly said to be

---

† *i.e.* The twelve Gods who first subsist in the *liberated* or super-celestial order, and who are divided into four triads, and the twelve mundane Gods, Jupiter, Neptune, Vulcan; Vesta, Minerva, Mars; Ceres, Juno, Diana; and Mercury, Venus, Apollo. The first of these triads is *fabricative*; the second *defensive*; the third *vivific*; and the fourth *anagogic* or *elevating*, as is shown by Proclus in the sixth book of his Theology.

‡ *Crat.* 396b.

the son of Saturn, both in hymns and in invocations, as unfolding into light that which is occult, expanding that which is contracted, and dividing that which is impartible in the Saturnian monad; and as emitting a second more partial kingdom, instead of that which is more total, a demiurgic instead of a paternal dominion, and an empire which proceeds every where instead of that which stably abides in itself.

Why does Socrates apprehend the name of king Saturn to be υβριστικον, *insolent*, and looking to what does he assert this? We reply, that according to the poets *satiety* (κορος) is the cause of *insolence*; for they thus denominate immoderation and repletion; and they say that *Satiety* brought forth *Insolence* (υβριν φασιν τικτει κορος). He therefore who looks without attention to the name of Saturn will consider it as signifying *insolence*. For to him who suddenly hears it, it manifests satiety and repletion. Why therefore, since a name of this kind is expressive of insolence, do we not pass it over in silence, as not being auspicious and adapted to the Gods? May we not say that the royal series[†] of the Gods, beginning with Phanes and ending in Bacchus, and producing the same sceptre supernally as far as to the last kingdom,

---

[†] This royal series consists of Phanes, Night, Heaven, Saturn, Jupiter, Bacchus. "Ancient theologists (says Syrianus, in his Commentary on the fourteenth book of Aristotle's *Metaphysics* [*The Works of Aristotle V*, TTS vol. XXV, p. 462]) assert that Night and Heaven reigned, and prior to these the mighty father of Night and Heaven, who distributed the world to Gods and mortals, and who first possessed royal authority, the illustrious Ericapæus.

τοιον ελων διενειμε θεοις, θνητοισι δε κοσμον
ου πρωτος βασιλευε περικλυτος ηρικεπαιος.

Night succeeded Ericapæus, in the hands of whom she has a sceptre:

σκεπτρον εχουσ' εν χερσιν ηρικεπαιου.

To Night Heaven succeeded, who first reigned over the Gods after mother Night.

ος πρωτος βασιλευε θεων μετα μητερα νυκτα.

Chaos transcends the habitude of sovereign dominion: and, with respect to Jupiter, the oracles given to him by Night manifestly call him not the first, but the fifth immortal king of the Gods.

αθανατον βασιλεα θεων πεμπτον γενεσθαι.

"According to these theologists therefore, that principle which is most eminently the first, is *The One* or *The Good*, after which, according to Pythagoras, are those two principles Æther and Chaos, which are superior to the possession of sovereign dominion. In the next place succeed the first and occult genera of the Gods, in which first shines forth the father and king of all wholes, and whom on this account they call *Phanes*."

Saturn being allotted the fourth royal order, appears according to the fabulous pretext, differently from the other kings, to have received the sceptre insolently from Heaven, and to have given it to Jupiter? For Night receives the sceptre from Phanes; Heaven derives from Night the dominion over wholes; and Bacchus, who is the last king of the Gods, receives the kingdom from Jupiter. For the father (Jupiter) establishes him in the royal throne, puts into his hand the sceptre, and makes him the king of all the mundane Gods. "Hear me, ye Gods, I place over you a king."

κλυτε θεοι τον δ'υμμιν βασιλεα τιθημι,
Orph. fr. 190

says Jupiter to the junior Gods. But Saturn alone perfectly deprives Heaven of the kingdom, and concedes dominion to Jupiter, cutting and being cut off, as the fable says [Orph. fr. 114]. Plato therefore seeing this succession, which in Saturn is called by theologists *insolent* (υβριστικη), thought it worth while to mention the appearance of insolence in the name; that from this he might evince the name is adapted to the God, and that it bears an image of the insolence which is ascribed to him in fables. At the same time he teaches us to refer mythical devices to the truth concerning the Gods, and the apparent absurdity which they contain to scientific conceptions.

The great, when ascribed to the Gods, must not be considered as belonging to interval, but as subsisting intellectually, and according to the power of cause, but not according to partible transcendency. But why does Plato now call Saturn διανοια, the dianoetic part of the soul? May we not say, that it is because he looks to the multitude of intellectual conceptions in him, the orders of intelligibles, and the evolution of forms which he contains; since also in the *Timæus*, he represents the demiurgic intellect as reasoning, and making the world, dianoetically energizing: and this in consequence of looking to his partible and divided intellections, according to which he fabricates not only wholes, but parts. When Saturn, however, is called intellect, Jupiter has the order of the dianoetic part: and when again, Saturn is called the dianoetic part, we must say that he is so called according to analogy with reference to a certain other intellect of a higher order. Whether therefore you are willing to speak of intelligible and occult intellect, or of that which unfolds into light (εκφαντορικος νους), or of that which connectedly contains (συνεκτικος νους), or of that which imparts perfection† (τελεσιουργος νους), Saturn will be as the dianoetic part to all these. For he produces united intellection into multitude, and fills himself wholly with excited intelligibles. Whence also he is said to be the leader of the Titanic race, and the source of all-various separation and diversifying power. And perhaps Plato here primarily delivers twofold interpretations of the name of the Titans, which Iamblicus and Amelius afterwards adopted. For the one interprets this name from the Titans extending their powers to all things; but the other from *something insectile* (παρα το τι ατομον), because the division and separation of wholes into parts receives its beginning from the Titans. Socrates therefore now indicates both these interpretations, by asserting of the king of the Titans that he is a *certain great dianoetic power*. For the term *great* is a symbol of power pervading to all things; but the term *a certain*, of power proceeding to the most partial natures.

The name Saturn is now triply analyzed; of which the first asserting this God to be the plenitude of intellectual good, and to be the satiety of a divine intellect, from its conveying an image of the satiety and repletion which are reprobated by the many, is rejected as insolent. The second also, which exhibits the imperfect and the puerile, is in like manner rejected. But the third, which celebrates this God as full of purity, and as the leader of undefiled intelligence, and an undeviating life, is approved. For king Saturn is intellect, and the supplier of all intellectual life; but he is an intelligible exempt from coordination with sensibles, immaterial and separate, and converted to himself. He likewise converts his progeny, and after producing them into light again embosoms and firmly establishes them in himself. For the demiurgus of the universe, though he is a divine intellect, yet he orderly arranges sensibles, and provides for subordinate natures. But the mighty Saturn is essentialized in separate intellections, and which transcend wholes. "For the fire which is beyond the first (says the Chaldean Oracle [TT. fr. 113]) does not incline its power downwards." But the demiurgus is suspended and proceeds from Saturn, being himself an intellect subsisting about an immaterial intellect, energising about it as the intelligible, and producing that which is occult in it, into the apparent. For the maker of the world is an intellect of intellect. And it appears to me, that as Saturn is the summit of those Gods that are properly called intellectual,

---

† Of these intellects the first is Phanes, the second Heaven, the third Earth, and the fourth the Subcelestial Arch, which is celebrated in the *Phædrus*, viz. νους νοητος ο φανης, εκφαντορικος νους ο Ουρανος, συνεκτικος νους η γη, τελεσιουργος δε νους η υπ' ουρανιος αψις.

he is intellect, as with reference to the intelligible genus of Gods. For all the intellectual adhere to the intelligible genus of Gods, and are conjoined with them through intellections. "Ye who understand the supermundane paternal profundity," says the hymn to them. But Saturn is intelligible, with reference to all the intellectual Gods. *Purity*, therefore, indicates this impartible and imparticipable transcendency of Saturn. For the not coming into contact with matter, the impartible, and an exemption from habitude, are signified by purity. Such, indeed, is the transcendency of this God with respect to all coordination with things subordinate, and such his undefiled union with the intelligible, that he does not require a Curetic guard, like Rhea, Jupiter, and Proserpine. For all these, through their progressions into secondary natures, require the immutable defence of the Curetes. But Saturn being firmly established in himself, and hastily withdrawing himself from all subordinate natures, is established above the guardianship of the Curetes. He contains, however, the cause of these uniformly in himself. For this purity, and the undefiled which he possesses, give subsistence to all the progressions of the Curetes. Hence, in the Oracles, he is said to comprehend the first fountain of the Amilicti, and to ride on all the others. "The intellect of the father riding on attenuated rulers, they become refulgent with the furrows of inflexible and implacable fire."

Νους πατρος αραιοις εποχουμενος ιθυντηρσιν
Ακναμπτου αστραπτουσιν αμειλικτου πυρος ολκοις.
TT Chaldæan Fr. 99

He is therefore *pure intellect*, as giving subsistence to the undefiled order, and as being the leader of the whole intellectual series.

Αυτου γαρ εκθρωσκουσιν αμειλικτοι τε κεραυνοι,
Και πρηστηροδοχοι κολποι παμφεγγεος αλκης·
Πατρογενους Εκατης, και υπεζωκος πυρος ανθος,
Ηδε κραταιον πνευμα πολων πυριων επεκεινα.
TT Chaldæan Fr. 89

i.e. "From him leap forth the implacable thunders, and the prester-capacious bosoms of the all-splendid strength of the father-begotten Hecate, together with the environed flower of fire, and the strong spirit which is beyond the fiery poles."

For he convolves all the hebdomad of the fountains,† and gives subsistence to it, from his unical and intelligible summit. For he is, as the Oracles say, αμιστυλλευτος, uncut into fragments, uniform, and undistributed, and connectedly contains all the fountains, converting and uniting all of them to himself, and being separate from all things with immaculate purity. Hence he is κορονους, as an immaterial and pure intellect, and as establishing himself in the paternal silence. He is also celebrated as the father of fathers. Saturn, therefore, is a father, and intelligible, as with reference to the intellectual Gods.

Again, every intellect either abides, and is then intelligible, as being better than motion; or it is moved, and is then intellectual; or it is both, and is then intelligible, and at the same time intellectual. The first of these is Phanes; the second, which is alone moved, is Saturn; and the third, which is both moved and permanent, is Heaven.

Saturn, from his impartible, unical, paternal, and beneficent subsistence in the intellectual orders, has been considered by some as the same with the one cause of all things. He is, however, only analogous to this cause, just as Orpheus [fr. 50] calls the first cause *Time* (χρονος) nearly homonymously with Saturn (κρονος). But the Oracles of the Gods characterize this deity by the epithet of *the once* (τῳ απαξ); calling him *once beyond* (απαξ επεκεινα). For *the once* is allied to *The One*.

Heaven, the father of Saturn, is an intellect understanding himself indeed, but united to the first intelligibles; in which he is also firmly established; and connectedly contains all the intellectual orders, by abiding in intelligible union. This God too is *connective*, just as Saturn is of a *separating* peculiarity; and on this account he is *father*. For connecting precede separating causes; and the intelligible and at the same time intellectual such as are intellectual only. Whence also *Heaven* being the *Synocheys* (συνοχευς) of wholes, according to one union gives subsistence to the Titanic series, and prior to this, to other orders of the Gods; some of which abide only in him, which he retains in himself; but others both abide and proceed, which he is said to have concealed after they were unfolded into light. And after all these, he gives subsistence to those divine orders which proceed into the universe, and are separated from their father. For he produces twofold monads, and triads, and hebdomads equal in number to the monads. These things, however, will be investigated more fully elsewhere. But this deity is denominated according to the similitude of the apparent Heaven. For each of them

---

† That is of the whole intellectual order, which consists of Saturn, Rhea, Jupiter, the three Curetes, and the separating monad Ocean.

compresses and connects all the multitude which it contains, and causes the sympathy and connection of the whole world to be one. For connection is second to unifying power, and proceeds from it. In the *Phædrus*, therefore, Plato delivers to us the production of all secondary natures by Heaven, and shows us how this divinity leads upwards and convolves all things to the intelligible. He likewise teaches us what its summit is, what the profundity of its whole order, and what the boundary of the whole of its progression. Here, therefore, investigating the truth of things from names, he declares its energy with respect to things more elevated and simple, and which are arranged nearer to *The One*. He also clearly appears here to consider the order of Heaven as intelligible and at the same time intellectual. For if it sees things on high, it energizes intellectually, and there is prior to it the intelligible genus of Gods, to which looking it is intellectual; just as it is intelligible to the natures which proceed from it. What then are the things on high which it beholds? Is it not evident that they are the supercelestial place, an essence without colour, without figure, and without the touch, and all the intelligible extent? An extent comprehending, as Plato would say, intelligible animals,[†] the one cause of all eternal natures, and the occult principles of these; but, as the followers of Orpheus would say, bounded by æther upwards, and by Phanes downwards. For all between these two gives completion to the intelligible order. But Plato[‡] now calls this both singularly and plurally; since all things are there united, and at the same time each is separated peculiarly; and this according to the highest union and separation.

With respect to the term μετεωρολογοι, *i.e. those who discourse on sublime affairs*, we must now consider it in a manner adapted to those who choose an anagogic life, who live intellectually, and who do not gravitate to earth, but sublimely tend to a theoretic life. For that which is called Earth there maternally gives subsistence to such things as Heaven, which is coordinate to that Earth, produces paternally. And he who energizes there, may be properly called μετεωρολογος, or *one who discourses about things on high*. Heaven, therefore, being of a *connective* nature, is expanded above the Saturnian orders, and all the intellectual series; and produces from himself all the Titanic race; and prior to this, the perfective and defensive orders: and, in short, is the leader of every good to the intellectual Gods. Plato, therefore, having celebrated Saturn

---

[†] *Timæus* 31a.

[‡] *Cratylus* 397b.

for his intelligence, which is without habitude to mundane natures; and for his life, which is converted to his own exalted place of survey, now celebrates Heaven for another more perfect energy. For to be conjoined to more elevated natures is a greater good than to be converted to oneself. Let no one however think, that on this account the abovementioned energies are distributed in the Gods; as, for instance, that there is providence alone in Jupiter, a conversion alone to himself in Saturn, and an elevation alone to the intelligible in Heaven. For Jupiter no otherwise provides for mundane natures than by looking to the intelligible; since, as Plato says in the *Timæus* [39e], intellect understanding ideas in animal itself, thought it requisite that as many and such as it there perceived should be contained in the universe; but as Orpheus[†] says with a divinely inspired mouth, "Jupiter swallows his progenitor Phanes, embosoms all his powers, and becomes all things intellectually which Phanes is intelligibly." Saturn also imparts to Jupiter the principles of fabrication and of providential attention to sensibles, and understanding himself, he becomes united to first intelligibles, and is filled with the goods which are thence derived. Hence also the theologist (Orpheus) says "that he was nursed by Night."[‡] If, therefore, the intelligible is nutriment, Saturn is replete not only with the intelligibles coordinated with him, but also with the highest and occult intellections. Heaven himself also fills all secondary natures with his proper goods, but guards all things by his own most vigorous powers; and the father supernally committed to him the connecting and guarding the causes of eternal animal. But he intellectually perceives himself, and is converted to the intelligibles which he contains; and this his intelligence, Plato in the *Phædrus* [247c] calls circulation. For as that which is moved in a circle is moved about its own centre, so Heaven energizes about its own intelligible, according to intellectual circulation. But all the Gods subsisting in all, and each possessing all energies, one transcends more in this, and another in a different energy, and each is particularly characterized according to that in which it transcends. Thus Jupiter is characterized by providence, and hence his name is now thus analyzed; but Saturn by a conversion to himself, whence also he is *inflected counsel*, αγκυλομητις; and Heaven by habitude to things more excellent; from which also he receives his

---

[†] ως δ' Ορφευς ενθεῳ στοματι λεγει, και καταπινει τον προγονον αυτου τον φανητα, και εγκολπιζεται πασας αυτου τας δυναμεις ο ζευς, και γινεται παντα νοερως, οσαπερ ην εκεινος νοητως. Orph. fr. 123.

[‡] διο και τρεφεσθαι φησιν αυτον ο θεολογος υπο της νυκτος. "εκ παντων δε κρονον νυξ ετρεφεν ηδ ατιταλλεν." Orph. fr. 98.

appellation. For his giving subsistence to a pure and the Saturnian intellect represents his energy on the other part. But as there are many powers in Heaven, such as the connective, guardian, and convertive, you will find that this name is appropriately adapted to all these. For the connective is signified through bounding the intellectual Gods; since the connective bounds the multitude which he contains. The power which guards wholes subsists through the termination and security of an intellectual essence. And the convertive power subsists through converting, seeing, and intellectually energizing natures, to things on high. But all these are adapted to Heaven. For there is no fear that the Gods will be dissipated, and that on this account they require connective causes; or that they will sustain mutation, and that on this account they stand in need of the saving aid of guardian causes; but now Socrates at once manifests all the powers of Heaven, through convertive energy. For this is to behold things on high, to be converted to them, and through this to be connected and defended. And it appears to me that Heaven possesses this peculiarity according to analogy to the intelligible eternity and the intelligible wholeness. For Timæus[†] particularly characterizes eternity by this, *viz.* by abiding in the one prior to it, and by being established in the summit of intelligibles; and Socrates says that Heaven surveys things on high, *viz.* the supercelestial place, and such things as are comprehended in the god-nourished silence of the fathers. (και οσα τη θεοθρεμμονι σιγη περιειληπται των πατερων).[‡] As, therefore, Parmenides[§] signifies each of these orders through *wholeness*, the one through intelligible, and the other through intellectual wholeness; in like manner both Timæus and Socrates characterize them by a conversion to more excellent natures. But the conversion as well as the wholeness is different. For that of eternity is intelligible, on which account Timæus does not say that it looks to its intelligible, but only that it stably abides. But the conversion of Heaven is intellectual, and on this account Socrates says, that it sees things on high, and through this converts, guards, and connects all things posterior to itself. Whence also in the *Phædrus* [247c], it is said by the circulation of itself, to lead all things to the supercelestial place, and the summit of the first intelligibles.

[†] *Timæus* 37d.

[‡] Chaldæan Oracle TT fr. 58 - TTS vol. VII.

[§] *Parmenides* 142d.

As there are three fathers and kings, of which Socrates here makes mention, Saturn alone appears to have received the government from his father, and to have transmitted it to Jupiter, by violence. Mythologists therefore celebrate the sections of Heaven and Saturn. But the cause of this is, that Heaven is of the connective, Saturn of the Titanic, and Jupiter of the demiurgic order. Again, the Titanic genus rejoices in separations and differences, progressions and multiplications of powers. Saturn, therefore, as a dividing God, separates his kingdom from that of Heaven; but as a pure intellect he is exempt from a fabricative energy proceeding into matter. Hence also the demiurgic genus is again separated from him. Section therefore is on both sides of him. For so far as he is a Titan, he is cut off from the connective causes, but so far as he does not give himself to material fabrication, he is cut off from the demiurgus Jupiter.

With respect, however, to the supercelestial place to which Heaven extends his intellectual life, some characterize it by ineffable symbols; but others, after giving it a name, celebrate it as unknown, neither being able to speak of its form or figure. And proceeding somewhat higher than this, they have been able to manifest the boundary[†] of the intelligible Gods by name alone. But the natures which are beyond this, they signify through analogy alone, these natures being ineffable and incomprehensible. Since that God who closes the paternal order is said by the wise to be the only deity among the intelligible Gods, that is denominated: and theurgy ascends as far as to this order. Since, therefore, the natures prior to Heaven are allotted such a transcendency of uniform subsistence that some of them are said to be effable, and at the same time ineffable, known, and at the same time unknown, through their alliance to *The One*, Socrates very properly restrains the discourse about them, in consequence of names not being able to represent their hyparxis; and, in short, because it requires a certain wonderful employment to separate the effable and ineffable, of their hyparxis or power. He accuses, therefore, his memory, not as disbelieving in the fables, which assert that there are certain more ancient causes beyond Heaven, nor as not thinking it worth while to mention them. For in the *Phædrus* [247c] he himself celebrates the supercelestial place. But he says this, because the first of beings cannot become known by the exercise of memory and through phantasy, or opinion, or the dianoetic part. For we are alone naturally adapted to be conjoined to them, with

---

† That is Phanes, intelligible intellect, or in the language of Plato αυτοζωον, *animal itself*.

the flower of intellect and the hyparxis of our essence; and through these we receive the sensation of their unknown nature. Socrates therefore says, that what in them is exempt, both from our gnostic and recollective life, is the cause of our inability to give them a name; for they are not naturally adapted to be known through names. Theologists, likewise, would not remotely signify them, and through the analogy of things apparent to them, if they could be named, and apprehended by knowledge.

Homer[†] does not ascend beyond the Saturnian order, but evincing that Saturn is the proximate cause of the demiurgus, he calls Jupiter, who is the demiurgus, the son of Saturn. He also calls the divinities coordinate with him Juno, Neptune, and Mars; and he denominates Jupiter the father of men and Gods. But he does not introduce Saturn as either energizing or saying anything but as truly $\alpha\gamma\kappa\upsilon\lambda o\mu\eta\tau\iota\varsigma$, in consequence of being converted to himself.

Orpheus greatly availed himself of the license of fables, and manifests every thing prior to Heaven by names, as far as to the first cause. He also denominates the ineffable, who transcends the intelligible unities, *Time*; whether because *Time* presubsists as the cause of all generation, or because, as delivering the generation of true beings, he thus denominates the ineffable, that he may indicate the order of true beings, and the transcendency of the more total to the more partial; that a subsistence according to Time may be the same with a subsistence according to cause; in the same manner as generation with an arranged progression. But Hesiod venerates many of the divine natures in silence, and does not in short name the first. For that what is posterior to the first proceeds from something else, is evident from the verse,

"Chaos of all things was the first produced."

Theog. 116

For it is perfectly impossible that it could be produced without a cause; but he does not say what that is which gave subsistence to Chaos. He is silent indeed with respect to both the fathers[‡] of intelligibles, the exempt, and the coordinate; for they are perfectly ineffable. And with respect to the two coordinations, the natures which are coordinate with the one, he passes by in silence, but those alone which are coordinate

---

[†] Homer, however, appears to have ascended as far as to the Goddess Night, or the summit of the intelligible and at the same time intellectual order.

[‡] That is to say, *the first cause, and bound* which is called by Orpheus *æther*.

with the indefinite duad, he unfolds through genealogy. And on this account Plato now thinks Hesiod deserves to be mentioned, for passing by the natures prior to Heaven, as being ineffable. For this also is indicated concerning them by the Oracles, which likewise add, "they possess mystic silence." And Socrates himself, in the *Phædrus* [250c], calls the intellectual perception of them μνησις and εποπτεια, *in which nearly the whole business is ineffable and unknown.*

The theology of Hesiod from the monad Rhea produces, according to things which are more excellent in the coordination, Vesta; but according to those which are subordinate, Juno; and according to those which subsist between, Ceres. But according to Orpheus, Ceres is in a certain respect the same with the whole of vivification, and in a certain respect is not the same. For on high she is Rhea, but below, in conjunction with Jupiter, she is Ceres: for here the things begotten are similar to the begetters, and are nearly the same.

Again, we ought to receive with caution what is now said concerning effluxions and motions. For Socrates does not descend to the material flowing of Heraclitus; for this is false,[†] and unworthy the dianoetic conceptions of Plato. But since it is lawful to interpret things divine analogously, through appropriate images, Socrates very properly assimilates fontal and Saturnian deities to streams; in so doing jesting and at the same time acting seriously, because good is always derived as it were in streams from on high, to things below. Hence, according to the image of rivers, after the fontal deities, who eternally devolve streams of good, the deities who subsist as principles are celebrated. For after the *fountain* of a river the place where it *begins* to flow is surveyed.

But those divinities who are peculiarly denominated total intellectual Gods, of whom the great Saturn is the father, are properly called fontal. For "from him leap forth the implacable thunders," says the Oracle concerning Saturn. But concerning the vivific fountain Rhea, from which all life, divine, intellectual, psychical, and mundane is generated, the Chaldean Oracles thus speak,

Ρειη τοι νοερων μακαρων πηγη τε ροη τε.
Παντων γαρ πρωτη δυναμεις κολποισιν αφραστοις
Δεξαμενη, γενεην επι παν προχεει τροχαουσαν.

[†] That is to say, it is false to assert of intellectual and divine natures they are in a perpetual flux; for they are eternally stable themselves, and are the sources of stability to other things.

i.e. "Rhea[†] is the fountain and river of the blessed intellectual Gods. For first receiving the powers of all things in her ineffable bosoms, she pours running generation into every thing."

For this divinity gives subsistence to the infinite diffusion of all life, and to all never failing powers. She likewise moves all things according to the measures of divine motions, and converts them to herself; establishing all things in herself, as being coordinate to Saturn. Rhea, therefore, is so called from causing a perpetual influx of good, and through being the cause of divine *facility*, since the life of the gods is attended with *ease* (θεοι ρεια ζωντες).

Ocean is the cause to all the Gods of acute and vigorous energy, and bounds the separations of the first, middle, and last orders; converting himself to himself, and to his proper principles, through swiftness of intellect, but moving all things from himself, to energies accommodated to their natures; perfecting their powers, and causing them to have a never failing subsistence. But Tethys imparts permanency to the natures which are moved by Ocean, and stability to the beings which are excited by him to the generation of secondary natures. She is also the source of purity of essence to those beings who perpetually desire to produce all things; as sustaining every thing in the divine essences which, as it were, *leaps forth and percolates*. For each of first causes, though it imparts to secondary natures a participation of good, yet at the same time retains with itself that which is undefiled, unmingled, and pure from participation. Thus, for instance, intellect is filled with life, being, and intelligence, with which also it fills soul; but establishing in itself that which in each of these is genuine and exempt, it also illuminates from itself to beings of a subordinate rank, inferior measures of these goods. And vigour of energy, indeed, is present with more ancient natures, through Ocean; but the leaping forth and percolating through Tethys. For every thing which is imparted from superior to subordinate natures, whether it be essence, life, or intelligence, is *percolated*. And such of these as are primary are established in themselves; but such as are more imperfect are transferred to things of a subject order. Just as with respect to streams of water, such of them as are nearer their source are purer, but the more remote are more turbid. Both Ocean and Tethys, therefore, are fontal Gods, according to their first subsistence. Hence Socrates now calls them the fathers of streams. But they also proceed into other orders of Gods, exhibiting the same powers among the Gods

---

[†] Gesner, misled by Patricius, has inserted these lines among the Orphic fragments, in his edition of the works of Orpheus.

who rank as principles or rulers, among those of a liberated, and those of a celestial characteristic; and appropriately in each of these. Timæus, however, celebrates their sublunary orders, calling them fathers of Saturn and Rhea, but the progeny of Heaven and Earth. But their last processions are their divisible allotments about the earth; both those which are apparent on its surface, and those which under the earth separate the kingdom of Hades from the dominion of Neptune.

Saturn is conjoined both to Rhea and Jupiter, but to the former as father to prolific power, but to the latter as father to intelligible[†] intellect.

Ocean is said to have married Tethys, and Jupiter Juno, and the like, as establishing a communion with her, conformably to the generation of subordinate natures. For an according co-arrangement of the Gods, and a connascent cooperation in their productions, is called by theologians *marriage*.

Tethys is denominated from leaping forth and *straining* or *cleansing*, being as it were *Diatethys*, and by taking away the first two syllables *Tethys*.[‡]

Saturn is the monad of the Titanic order of the Gods, but Jupiter of the demiurgic. This last divinity, however, is twofold, the one exempt and coordinated with Saturn, being a fontal God, and, in short, ranking with the intellectual fathers, and convolving the extremity of them; but the other being connumerated with the sons of Saturn, and allotted a Saturnian summit and dominion in this triad; concerning which also the Homeric Neptune says,

τρεις γαρ τ' εκ Κρονου ειμεν αδελφεοι, ους τεκε Ρειη.

As brother Gods we three from Saturn came,
And Rhea bore us.

Iliad xv, 187.

And the first Jupiter indeed, as being the demiurgus of wholes, is the king of things first, middle, and last, concerning whom Socrates also had just said, that he is the ruler and king of all things; and life and salvation are imparted to all things through him.

[†] Proclus here means that there is the same analogy between Saturn, Rhea, and Jupiter, as in the intelligible triad, between father, power, and intellect.

[‡] Οτι ωνομασται η Τηθυς παρα το διαττομενον και ηθουμενον, οιον Διατηθυς, και αφαιρεσει των πρωτων δυσσυλλαβων Τηθυς.

But the ruling Jupiter, who ranks as a principle, and who is coordinate with the three sons of Saturn, governs the third part of the whole of things, according to that of Homer,

τριχθα δε παντα δεδασται . . . .

A triple distribution all things own.

Iliad xv, 189.

He is also the summit of the three, has the same name with the fontal Jupiter, is united to him, and is monadically called Jupiter. But the second is called dyadically, marine Jupiter, and Neptune. And the third is triadically denominated terrestrial Jupiter, Pluto, and Hades. The first of these also preserves, fabricates, and vivifies summits, but the second, things of a second rank, and the third those of a third order. Hence this last is said to have ravished Proserpine, that together with her he might animate the extremities of the universe.

The Titanic order dividing itself from the connecting order of Heaven, but having also something in itself abiding, and connascent with that order, Saturn is the leader of the separation, and on this account he both arms others against his father, and receives the scythe[†] from his mother, through which he divides his own kingdom from that of Heaven. But Ocean is coordinated with those that abide in the manners of the father, and guards the middle of the two orders; so far as a Titan being connumerated with the Gods that subsist with Saturn; but so far as rejoicing in a coordination with Heaven, conjoining himself with the Synoches. For it is fit that he who bounds the first and second orders should be arranged in the middle of the natures that are bounded. But every where this God is allotted a power of this kind, and separates the genera of the Gods, the Titanic from the connecting (των συνοχικων), and the vivific from the demiurgic. Whence also ancient rumour calls Ocean the God who separates the apparent part of Heaven from the unapparent; and on this account poets say, that the sun and the other stars rise from the ocean. What is now said therefore by Plato, comprehends all the Titanic order through these two conjunctions; this order abiding, and at the same time proceeding. And through the Saturnian order, indeed, it comprehends every thing separated from the fathers; but through that of Ocean, every thing conjoined with the connecting Gods. Or if you had rather so speak, through the Saturnian

---

[†] See the Theogony of Hesiod, v 176 ff.

order, he comprehends every maternal cause, but through the other, every thing subservient to the paternal cause. For the female is the cause of progression and separation, but the male of union and stable permanency.

Of the demiurgic triad[†] which divides the whole world, and distributes the indivisible, one, and whole fabrication of the first Jupiter, the summit, and which has the relation of father, is Jupiter, who, through union with the whole demiurgic intellect having the same appellation with it, is for this reason not mentioned here by Plato. But Neptune is allotted the middle, and that which binds together both the extremes; being filled indeed from the essence of Jupiter, but filling Pluto. For of the whole of this triad, Jupiter indeed is the father, but Neptune the power, and Pluto the intellect. And all, indeed, are in all; but each receives a different character of subsistence. Thus Jupiter subsists according to *being*; but Neptune according to *power*, and Pluto according to *intellect*. And though all these divinities are the causes of the life of all things, yet one is so *essentially*, another *vitally*, and another *intellectually*. Whence also the theologist Orpheus says, that the extremes fabricate in conjunction with Proserpine things first and last; the middle being co-arranged with generative cause from his own allotment, without Proserpine. Hence *violence* is said to have been offered to Proserpine by Jupiter; but she is said to have been *ravished* by Pluto (διο και φασι την κορην υπο μεν του διος βιαζεσθαι, υπο δε του πλουτωνος αρπαζεσθαι). But the middle is said to be the cause of motion to all things. Hence, also, he is called *earthshaker*, as being the origin of motion. And among those who are allotted the kingdom of Saturn, the middle allotment, and the agile sea (η ευκινητος θαλασσα) are assigned to him. According to every division, therefore, the summits are Jovian, the middles belong to Neptune, and the extremes to Pluto. And if you look to the centres, such as the east, that of mid-heaven, and the west; if also you divide the whole world, as for instance into the inerratic, planetary, and sublunary spheres; - or again, if you divide that which is generated into the fiery, terrestrial, and that which subsists between; or the earth into its summits, middle, and hollow, and subterranean parts, this triad every where distributes the first, middle, and last differences of things fabricated in demiurgic boundaries.

The name Neptune is now triply analyzed. For Neptune is the trident-bearer; and the Tritons and Amphitrite are the familiars of this

---

[†] That is, of the first triad of the supermundane, which subsists immediately after the intellectual order.

God. And the first analyzation of his name is from the allotment over which he presides, and from souls coming into generation, in whom the circle of sameness is fettered; since the sea is analogous to generation. But the second is from communion with the first.

αλλα ζευς προτερος γεγονει, και πλειονα ηδει.†

But Jove was born the first, and more he knows.

For a Jupiter of this kind is the proximate intelligible of Neptune. But the third analysis of his name is from his energy in externals. For he is motive of nature, and vivific of things last. He is also the guardian of the earth, and excites it to generations.

Neptune is an intellectual demiurgic God, who receives souls descending into generation; but Hades is an intellectual demiurgic God, who frees souls from generation. For as our whole period receives a triple division, into a life prior to generation, which is Jovian, into a life of generation, which is Neptunian, and into a life posterior to generation, which is Plutonian; Pluto, who is characterized by intellect, very properly converts ends to beginnings, effecting a circle without a beginning and without an end, not only in souls, but also in every fabrication of bodies, and in short, of all periods; - which circle also he perpetually convolves. Thus for instance, he converts the ends to the beginnings of the souls of the stars, and the convolutions of souls about generation, and the like. And hence Jupiter is the guardian of the life of souls prior to generation.

Some, however, badly analyze the name of Pluto into wealth from the earth, through fruits and metals; but Hades into the invisible, dark, and dreadful. These Socrates now reprobates, bringing the two names to the same signification; referring the name of Pluto, as intellect, to the wealth of prudence, but that of Hades to an intellect knowing all things. For this God is a sophist, who, purifying souls after death, frees them from generation. For Hades is not, as some improperly explain it, evil: for neither is death evil; though Hades to some appears to be attended with perturbations (εμπαθως); but it is invisible, and better than the apparent; such as is every thing intelligible. Intellect, therefore, in every triad of beings, convolves itself to being, and the paternal cause, imitating in its energy the circle.

Men who are lovers of body badly refer to themselves the passions of the animated nature, and on this account consider death to be dreadful,

---

† Homer's Iliad.

as being the cause of corruption. The truth, however, is, that it is much better for man to die, and live in Hades a life according to nature, since a life in conjunction with body is contrary to nature, and is an impediment to intellectual energy. Hence it is necessary to divest ourselves of the fleshly garments with which we are clothed, as Ulysses did of his ragged vestments, and no longer like a wretched mendicant, together with the indigence of body, put on our rags. For, as the Chaldean Oracle says, "Things divine cannot be obtained by those whose intellectual eye is directed to body; but those only can arrive at the possession of them who stript of their garments hasten to the summit."

Neptune, when compared with Jupiter, is said to know *many* things; but Hades, compared with souls to whom he imparts knowledge, is said to know *all* things; though Neptune is more total than Hades.

As it is necessary to analyze Pluto, not only into the obvious wealth from the earth, but also into the wealth of wisdom, so likewise Ceres must be analyzed not only into corporeal nutriment; but beginning from the Gods themselves it is requisite to conceive her to be the supplier of aliment, first to the Gods themselves, afterwards to the natures posterior to the Gods; and in the last place, that the series of this beneficent energy extends as far as to corporeal nutriment. For the characteristic of love shines forth first of all in the Gods; and this is the case with the medicinal and prophetic powers of Apollo, and with those of every other divinity. But nutriment, when considered with reference to the Gods, is the communication of intellectual plenitude from more exalted natures to those of an inferior rank. Gods, therefore, are nourished, when they view with the eye of intellect Gods prior to themselves; and when they are perfected and view intelligible beauties, such as justice itself, temperance itself, and the like, as it is said in the *Phædrus*.

From sportive conceptions about the Gods, it is possible for those to energize entheastically, or according to a divinely inspired energy, who apply themselves to things in a more intellectual manner. Thus, for instance, according to the material conceptions of the multitude, Venus derives her origin from foam; and foam corresponds to seed. Hence, according to them, the pleasure arising from this in coition is Venus. Who, however, is so stupid as not to survey primary and eternal natures, prior to such as are last and corruptible? I will therefore unfold the divine conception respecting Venus.

They say then that the first Venus was produced from twofold causes, the one as that *through which*,[†] co-operating with her progression, as calling forth the prolific power of the father, and imparting it to the intellectual orders; but Heaven as the maker and cause unfolding the goddess into light, from his own generative abundance. For whence could that which congregates different genera, according to one desire of beauty, receive its subsistence except from the *synochical* power of Heaven? From the foam, therefore, of his own prolific parts thrown into the sea, Heaven produced this Goddess, as Orpheus says. But the second Venus Jupiter produces from his own generative powers, in conjunction with Dione; and this goddess likewise proceeds from foam, after the same manner with the more ancient Venus, as Orpheus evinces. These goddesses therefore differ from each other, according to the causes of their production, their orders and their powers. For she that proceeds from the genitals of Heaven is supermundane, leads upwards to intelligible beauty, is the supplier of an unpolluted life, and separates from generation. But the Venus that proceeds from Dione governs all the coordinations in the celestial world and the earth, binds them to each other, and perfects their generative progressions, through a kindred conjunction. These divinities too are united with each other through a similitude of subsistence: for they both proceed from generative powers; one from that of the connectedly containing power of Heaven, and the other from Jupiter the demiurgus. But the sea signifies an expanded and circumscribed life; its profundity, the universally extended progression of such a life; and its foam, the greatest purity of nature, that which is full of prolific light and power, and that which swims upon all life, and is as it were its highest flower.

According to Orpheus, Ceres is the same with Rhea. For he says, that subsisting on high in unproceeding union with Saturn, she is *Rhea*, but that by emitting and generating Jupiter, she is *Ceres*. For thus he speaks,

$$\text{Ρειην το πριν εουσαν, επει διος επλετο μητηρ}$$
$$\text{Γεγονε δημητηρ.}^{‡}$$

i.e. The goddess who was *Rhea*, when she bore Jove became Ceres.

[†] This cause is Saturn, who according to the fable cut off the genital parts of Heaven. See the *Theogony* of Hesiod.

[‡] This Orphic fragment is not to be found in Gesner's or Hermann's collection of the Orphic remains.

But Hesiod says that Ceres is the daughter of Rhea. It is however evident that these theologists harmonize: for whether this goddess proceeds from union with Saturn to a secondary order, or whether she is the first progeny of Rhea, she is still the same. Ceres, therefore, thus subsisting, and receiving the most ancient and ruling order from the whole vivific Rhea (της ολης ζωογονου ρεας), and comprehending the middle centres of whole vivification (της ολης ζωογονιας), she fills all supermundane natures with the rivers of all-perfect life, pouring upon all things vitally, indivisibly, and uniformly.

Prior however to all this, she unfolds to us the demiurgic intellect (Jupiter), and imparts to him the power of vivifying wholes. For as Saturn supplies her from on high with the cause of being; so Ceres from on high, and from her own prolific bosoms, pours forth vivification to the demiurgus. But possessing herself the middle of all vivific deity, she governs the whole fountains which she contains, and comprehends the one bond of the first and last powers of life. She stably convolves too, and contains all secondary fountains. But she leads forth the uniform causes of prior natures to the generation of others. This goddess too comprehends *Vesta* and *Juno*: in her right hand parts Juno, who pours forth the whole order of souls; but in her left hand parts Vesta, who leads forth all the light of virtue. Hence Ceres is with great propriety called by Plato[†] *mother*, and at the same time the *supplier of aliment*. For, so far as she comprehends in herself the cause of Juno, she is a mother; but as containing Vesta in her essence, she is the supplier of aliment. But the paradigm of this goddess is *Night: for immortal Night is called the nurse of the Gods*. Night however is the cause of aliment intelligibly:[‡] for that which is intelligible is, according to the oracle,[§] the aliment of the intellectual orders of Gods. But Ceres first of all separates the two kinds of aliment in the Gods, as Orpheus says:

> Μησατο γαρ προπολους, και αμφιπολους, και οπαδους·
> Μησατο δ' αμβροσιην, και ερυθρου νεκταρος αρθρον·
> Μησατο δ' αγλαα εργα μελισσαων εριβομβων.[◊]

[†] Cratylus 404b, *The Works of Plato V*, TTS vol. XIII.

[‡] Because Night subsists at the summit of *the intelligible and at the same time intellectual* order, and is wholly absorbed in the intelligible.

[§] That is, according to one of the Chaldean Oracles [fr. 71 TTS vol. VII]

[◊] These verses likewise are not in Gesner's and Hermann's collection.

i.e. She cares for pow'rs ministrant, whether they
Or Gods *precede*, or *follow*, or *surround*:
Ambrosia, and *tenacious nectar red*
Are too the objects of her bounteous care.
Last to the bee her providence extends,
Who gathers honey with resounding hum.

Ceres, therefore, our sovereign mistress (δεσποινα) not only generates life, but that which gives perfection to life; and this from supernal natures to such as are last: *for virtue is the perfection of souls*. Hence mothers who are connected with the circulations of time, bring forth their offspring in imitation of this twofold and eternal generation of Ceres. For, at the same time that they send forth their young into the light, they extend to them milk naturally produced as their food.

Again, the conjunction of the demiurgic intellect with the vivific causes is triple: for it is conjoined with the fountains prior to itself: is present with its kindred coordinate natures; and coenergizes with the orders posterior to itself. For it is present with the mother prior to itself, *convertively* (επιστρεπτικως); with Proserpine posterior to itself, *providentially* (προνοητικως); and with Juno coordinate to itself with an *amatory energy* (ερασμιως). Hence Jupiter is said to be enamoured of Juno,

> ως σεο νυν εραμαι.
>
> As now I love thee, -
>
> *Iliad* xiv, 328.

And this love indeed is legal, but the other two appear to be illegal. This Goddess therefore produces from herself, in conjunction with the demiurgus and father, all the genera of souls, the supermundane and mundane, the celestial and sublunary, the divine, angelic, dæmoniacal, and partial. After a certain manner too, she is divided from the demiurgus, but in a certain respect she is united to him: for Jupiter is said, in the *Philebus*, to contain a royal intellect and a royal soul. For he contains uniformly the paternal and maternal cause of the world; and the fountain of souls is said to be in Jupiter; just as again the intelligence of Jupiter is said to be first participated by Juno. For no other divinity, says Jupiter in Homer, knows my mind prior to Juno. Through this ineffable union therefore of these divinities, the world participates of intellectual souls. They also give subsistence to intellects who are carried in souls, and who together with them give completion to the whole fabrication of things.

The series of our sovereign mistress Juno, beginning from on high, pervades to the last of things; and her allotment in the sublunary region is the air. For *air* is a symbol of *soul*, according to which also soul is called a *spirit* (πνευμα); just as *fire* is an image of *intellect*, but *water* of *nature*, by which the world is nourished (της κοσμοτροφου φυσεως), through which all nutriment and increase are produced. But *earth* is the image of *body*, through its gross and material nature. Hence Homer, obscurely signifying this, represents Juno suspended with two anvils under her feet: for the air is allotted two heavy elements beneath itself. For

ηλιον δ' ακαμαντα βοωπις ποτνια ηρη
πεμψεν επ' ωκεανοιο ροας.

i.e. "Fair-eyed venerable Juno sent the sun to the streams of the ocean," - is from the same conception.

For he calls the thick cloud produced by Juno the setting of the sun. The assertion likewise that the end of this name will be conjoined with the beginning, if any one frequently repeats the name of the Goddess, evinces the conversion of rational souls to her which proceed from her; and that voice is air that is struck. On this account also the voice of rational animals is especially dedicated to this Goddess, who made the horse of Achilles to become vocal. But Socrates now delivers these three vivific monads in a consequent order, *viz.* Ceres, Juno, Proserpine; calling the first the mother, the second the sister, and the third the daughter of the demiurgus. All of them however are partakers of the whole of fabrication; the first in an exempt manner and intellectually, the second in a fontal manner, and at the same time in a way adapted to a principle (αρχικως), and the third in a manner adapted to a principle and leader (αρχικως και ηγεμονοκως).

Of these Goddesses the last possesses triple powers, and impartibly and uniformly comprehends three monads of Gods. But she is called Core (κορη) through the purity of her essence, and her undefiled transcendency in her generations. She also possesses a first, middle, and last empire. And according to her summit, indeed, she is called Diana by Orpheus; but according to her middle Proserpine; and according to the extremity of the order Minerva. Likewise, according to an hyparxis transcending the other powers of this triple vivific order, the dominion of Hecate is established; but according to a middle power, and which is generative of wholes, that of Soul; and according to intellectual conversion that of Virtue.† Core therefore, subsisting on high, and among the supermundane Gods, uniformly extends this triple order of divinities; and together with Jupiter generates Bacchus, who impartibly presides over partible fabrication. But beneath, in conjunction with Pluto, she is particularly beheld according to the middle peculiarity; for it is this which proceeding every where imparts vivification to the last of things. Hence she is called Proserpine, because she especially associates with Pluto, and together with him orderly distributes the extremities of the universe. And according to her extremities indeed, she is said to be a virgin, and to remain undefiled: but according to her middle, to be conjoined with Hades, and to beget the Furies in the subterranean regions. She therefore is also called Core, but after another manner than the supermundane and ruling Core. For the one is the connective unity of the three vivific principles; but the other is the middle of them, in herself possessing the peculiarities of the extremes. Hence in the Proserpine conjoined with Pluto, you will find the peculiarities of Hecate and Minerva; but these extremes subsist in her occultly, while the peculiarity of the middle shines forth, and that which is characteristic of ruling soul, which in the supermundane Core was of a *ruling*‡ nature, but here subsists according to a mundane peculiarity.

Proserpine is denominated, either through judging of forms and separating them from each other, thus obscurely signifying the ablation of slaughter (δια το κρινειν τα ειδη και χωριζειν αλληλων, ως του φονου την αναιρεσιν αινιττομενον), or through separating souls perfectly from bodies, through a conversion to things on high, which is the most fortunate slaughter and death, to such as are worthy of it (η δια το χωριζειν τας ψυχας τελεως εκ των σωματων δια της προς τα ανω επιστροφης, οπερ εστιν ευτυχεστατος φονος και θανατος τοις αξιουμενοις τουτου). But the name φερεφαττα, *Pherephatta*, according to a contract with generation, is adapted to Proserpine; but according to wisdom and counsel to Minerva. At the same time, however, all the appellations by which she is distinguished are adapted to the perfection of soul. On this account also she is called Proserpine, and not by the names of the extremes; since that which was ravished by Pluto is the middle; the extremes at the same time being firmly established in themselves, according to which Core is said to remain a virgin.

---

† Proclus says this conformably to the theology of the Chaldeans. For according to that theology, the first monad of the vivific triad is *Hecate*, the second *Soul*, and the third *Virtue*.

‡ That is, of a supermundane nature: for the *ruling* are the *supermundane* Gods.

With respect to our sovereign mistress Diana, Plato delivers three peculiarities of her, the undefiled, the mundane, and the anagogic. And through the first of these indeed, the goddess is said to be a lover of virginity; but through the second, according to which she is perfective of works (τελεσιουργος) she is said to be the inspective guardian of virtue; and through the third she is said to hate the impulses arising from generation. Of these three, likewise, the first is especially adapted to the progression of the goddess, according to which she is allotted an hyparxis in the vivific triad of the supermundane Gods; whether we call this deity Hecatic, as Theurgists say, or Diana with Orpheus. For there being established, she is filled with undefiled powers from the Gods called *Amilicti*.[†] But she looks to the fountain of virtue, and embraces its virginity. For the virginity which is there does not proceed forth, as the Oracle says, but abiding gives subsistence to Diana, and to supermundane virtue, and is exempt from all communion, conjunction, and progression, according to generation. Hence Core also, according to the Diana and Minerva which she contains, is said to remain a virgin; but according to the prolific power of Proserpine, she is said to proceed forth, and to be conjoined with the third demiurgus, and to bring forth, as Orpheus says, "nine azure-eyed, flower-producing daughters;"

εννεα θυγατερας γλαυκωπιδας ανθεσιουργους·

since the Diana and the Minerva which she contains preserve their virginity always the same. For the former of these is characterized according to her stability, but the latter according to her convertive energy. But that which is generative is allotted in her a middle order. They say too, that she aspires after virginity, since the form of her is comprehended in the vivific fountain, and she understands fontal virtue, gives subsistence to supermundane and anagogic virtue, and despises all material sexual connexion, though she inspects the fruits arising from it.

She appears also to be averse to the generations and progressions of things, but to introduce perfections to them. And she gives perfection indeed to souls through a life according to virtue; but to mortal animals she imparts a restitution to form. But that there is a great union between Diana, the mundane Hecate, and Core, is evident to those that are in the least degree conversant with the writings of Orpheus; from which it appears that Latona is comprehended in Ceres, and together with Jupiter gives subsistence to Core, and the mundane Hecate. To

---

† That is, the Corybantes.

which we may also add, that Orpheus[†] calls Diana Hecate. So that it is nothing wonderful, if we should elsewhere call the Diana contained in Core Hecate.

The wise man venerates the last and mundane progressions of the Gods, though, as Plato says, they are sports through these Gods [*i.e.* Venus and Bacchus] being lovers of sport. For as he says of the terminations of the other Gods, that they are terrible, and that they avenge and punish, and thus give perfection to souls; as for instance, that Justice follows Jupiter, the avenger of the divine law, and that this divinity is benevolent to those whose manners are orderly, and who live according to intellect; but that she is baneful to those who mingle their life with insolence and ignorance, until she has entirely subverted them, their houses, and cities; - in like manner, he venerates the terminations of Bacchus and Venus, which produce γλυκυθυμια, *sweetness of sensation*; every where purifying our conceptions concerning the Gods, and preparing us to understand that all things look to the best end, whatever it may be. For because the terminations of these divinities strengthen the infirmity of the mortal nature, and recall corporeal molestation, on this account the Gods, the causes of these things, are φιλοπαιγμονες, *lovers of sport*. Hence of statues, they make some of them laughing and dancing, and exhibiting relaxation, but others austere, astonishing and terrible to the view, analogously to the mundane allotments of the Gods.

That theologists frequently call Bacchus *wine*, from the last of his gifts, as for instance Orpheus,

οινου παντα μελη κοσμω λαβε, και μοι ενεικε.

i.e. "Take all the members of wine (that are distributed) in the world and bring them to me."

But if the God is thus denominated, certainly his first and middle energies will be thus called, as well as his last; so that Socrates now looking to this, calls the God διδοινυσος, beginning from wine, which, as we have said, manifests all the powers of the God. Thus also in the *Phædrus*, Socrates calls love in common *great*, both that which is divine and that which is a lover of body. By this epithet *wine*, therefore, we must understand that the peculiarity of a partial intellect is in common presented to our view. For the word οιουν, *such as*, is nothing else than intellectual form separated from a total intellect, and in consequence of this becoming participated, *particular* and *alone*. For an all-perfect

---

[†] Η δ' αρα εκατη παιδος μελη αυθι λυωουσα
Αητους ευωλοκαμοιο κορη ωροσεβησατ' ολυμπον.

intellect is all things, and energizes according to all things with invariable sameness; but a partial and participated intellect is indeed all things, but this according to one form, such as a solar, lunar, or mercurial form. This therefore, the peculiarity of which is to be separated from the rest, wine indicates, signifying an intellect *such as* and *particular* (σημαινων τον οιον και τινα νουν). Since therefore every partial fabrication is suspended from the Dionysiacal monad, which distributes participated mundane intellects from total intellect [or the intellect which ranks as a whole], many souls from one soul, and all sensible forms from their proper totalities; on this account theologists call both this God and all his fabrications *wine*. For all these are the progeny of intellect; and some things participate of the partial distribution of intellect in a more distant, but others in a nearer degree. *Wine* therefore energizes in things analogously to its subsistence in them; in body, indeed, after the manner of an image, according to a false opinion and imagination; but in intellectual natures according to an intellectual energy and fabrication; since in the laceration of Bacchus by the Titans, the heart of the God [*i.e.* the indivisible essence of intellect] is said to have alone remained undistributed.

Again, theologists especially celebrate two powers of our sovereign mistress Minerva, the *defensive* and the *perfective*; the former preserving the order of wholes undefiled, and unvanquished by matter, and the latter filling all things with intellectual light, and converting them to their cause. And on this account, Plato also in the *Timæus*, analogously celebrates Minerva as *philopolemic* and *philosophic*. But three orders of this Goddess are delivered by theologists; the one fontal and intellectual, according to which she establishes herself in her father Jupiter, and subsists in unproceeding union with him; but the second ranks among the supermundane Gods, according to which she is present with Core, and bounds and converts all the progression of that Goddess to herself. And the third is *liberated*, according to which she perfects and guards the whole world, and circularly invests it with her powers, as with a veil; binding together all the mundane summits, and giving subsistence to all the allotments in the heavens, and to those which proceed into the sublunary region. Now therefore Socrates celebrates her *guardian* power, through the name of *Pallas*; but her *perfective* power through that of *Minerva*. She is the cause therefore of orderly and measured motion, which she first imparts to the Curetic order, and afterwards to the other Gods. For Minerva, according to this power, is the leader of the Curetes, as Orpheus says, whence also, as well as those divinities she is adorned with empyrean arms, through which she represses all disorder, preserves the demiurgic series immovable, and unfolds dancing through rhythmical motion. She also guards reason as it proceeds from intellect; through this power vanquishing matter. For the visible region, says Timæus, is mingled from intellect and necessity, the latter being obedient to the former, and all material causes being in subjection to the will of the father. It is this Goddess therefore who arranges necessity under the productions of intellect, raises the universe to the participation of Jupiter, excites and establishes it in the port of its father, and eternally guards and defends it. Hence, if the universe is said to be indissoluble, it is this goddess who supplies its permanency; and if it moves in measured motion, through the whole of time, according to one reason and order, she is the source of this supply. She watchfully surveys therefore all the fabrication of her father, and connects and converts it to him; and vanquishes all material indefiniteness. Hence she is called *Victory* and *Health*; the former because she causes intellect to rule over necessity, and form over matter; and the latter, because she preserves the world† perpetually whole, perfect, exempt from age, and free from disease. It is the property therefore of this Goddess to elevate and distribute, and through an intellectual dance as it were, to connect, establish, and defend inferior natures in such as are more divine.‡

---

† In the very learned Professor Boissonade's edition of this work, for τον κοσμον in this place, there is nothing more than το κον; and my manuscript has very erroneously το κακον. But the true reading is undoubtedly τον κοσμον. For Proclus, in what he here says, alludes to the following words of Plato in the *Timæus*, δια δε την αιτιαν και τον λογισμον τονδε, εν ολον εξ απαντων τελεον και αγηρων και ανοσον αυτον [*i.e.* τον κοσμον] εκτηνατο. In all the editions of Plato's works, however, there is a very erroneous omission in this passage. For from the text of Proclus, and also from what Plato previously says, instead of εν ολον εξ απαντων, it is necessary to read εν ολον εξ ολων απαντων. And then the passage will be in English, "Through this cause, and from this reasoning process he [*i.e.* the Demiurgus] fashioned the world one perfect whole, consisting of all wholes, exempt from age and free from disease."

‡ The whole of this sentence is in my manuscript as follows: Οικειον ουν της θεου ταυτης και το αναγειν και μεριζειν, και δια της νοερας χορειας συναπτειν τοις θειοτεροις, και ενιδρυειν και φρουρειν εν αυτοις. But after the word μεριζειν, it is necessary either to add or conceive to be implied τα δευτερα. The last word, αυτοις, is wanting in the Professor's edition.

HYMNS

of

THOMAS TAYLOR

To The Intelligible

To Being

To Life

To Intellect

To the order of Gods denominated *Intelligible* and at the same time *Intellectual*

To The Artificer of the Universe

To the Liberated order of Gods or that which exists between the Supermundane and Mundane Gods

To Apollo

To Apollo and the Sun

To the Rising Sun

To the Sun and his Attendants

To Jupiter

To Minerva (1)

To Minerva (2)

To Minerva (3)

To Vesta

To Mercury (1)

To Ceres

To Venus

To Love

To Neptune

To Mercury (2)

To Latona

To Osiris

To Isis

TO THE INTELLIGIBLE

or

*To the Whole of a pure intellectual essence,
considered as forming One Intelligible World.*

O Fairest Offspring of a fire unknown!
Splendour immense, all-comprehending god;
Thy blest intelligible world I'll sing
And celebrate the beauty it contains.
Witness, ye shining stars, that nightly roll
With ever-wakeful and rejoicing fires:
Witness, thou moon, whose ever-changing orb
Gives due perfection to material forms:
And thou, O sun! bright ruler of the stars,
And sacred arbiter of pious souls,
Witness the constant tribute of my praise;
Witness the mystic ardour of my soul,
To thee my wings, from Hyle's dire abode
I stretch, impatient of a speedy flight;
That rapid to thy palace I may rise,
And in *The Good's* bright vestibule exult.
For there the great intelligible gods,
Like dazzling lamps, in spheres of crystal shine;
Ineffably announcing by their light
Th'abode of deity's o'erflowing fount.
All-perfect father, may thy piercing eye
Shine on my soul with sacred hymns replete,
And rouse conceptions bright with mental fire!
Now from the barriers of the race divine,
Urged by the Muse's vivid fire, I start;
And rapid to the goal of sacred verse,
To gain the soul's Olympic honours, run.
A voice divine in intellect's retreats,
Now gently murmurs with inspiring sound.
O blessed father, deity sublime!
Propitious listen to my suppliant prayer,
And haste my union with thy beauteous world:

Thy world with every excellence endued,
And with ideas omniform replete.
There shines the sun with intellectual light,
And ev'ry star is there a mental sun.
Each contains all, yet separate and distinct
Particulars their proper character preserve.
There all is truly all, immensely great,
Motion is pure, *abiding* without change;
And every part exists a perfect whole.
O grant my soul the lynx's piercing eye,
That I may penetrate the depth divine
Thy blest intelligible world contains.
There each inhabitant, with boundless view,
Light within light perpetually perceives;
Nor finds in ought vacuity to check
Th'unweary'd energies of mental sight.
But all things there with power untamed subsist,
And each by seeing more abundant sees.
Now in my phantasy from sense refined,
A lucid image of a globe appears,
Throughout diaphanous; whose orb contains
The sun, and stars, and ev'ry mundane form,
And all things shine in each divinely fair.
And while this lucid spectacle remains,
My soul attempts to frame a brighter sphere:
Devoid of bulk, subsisting without place,
And from the images of matter free.
Come then, blest parent of that sphere divine,
Whose mental image anxious I explore;
Come with thy own intelligible world,
And all the gods its beauteous realms contain.
With all things come conspiring into one:
That thus with thee, in perfect union join'd,
My soul may recognize thy matchless fire;
May vig'rous rise to his occult retreats,
And fly alone to solitary Good.

TO BEING ITSELF

or

The First Monad of the Intelligible Triad

The highest order of the gods I sing,
First shining forth from Unity's retreats,
And with intelligible good replete.
Essence divine, all-comprehending God!
Whose nature, ever vigilant and fair,
The most united multitude contains:
And as *The Good's* bright vestibule displays
With dazzling grandeur undecaying light.
Thy matchless nature, O transcendent king,
From stable *bound* and *infinite* consists.
For after the subsistence of *The One*,
That solitary darkness thrice unknown
That God of gods, of unities the fount,
Than silence more ineffably occult,
Than deepest intellection more profound
With light immense the first of beings shines
And veils the uncaus'd glories of *The Good*.
O first begotten, of the first unknown!
Great *unity* partaking of *The One*,
And *duad* mixt of *infinite* and *bound*
Triadic god, with symmetry adorn'd.
Truth ever pure, and beauty's sacred light!
Hence, through the union symmetry affords,
Thy being shines an all-containing one;
And from the purity of perfect truth,
Thy nature is not only one, but true.
And last, through beauty's all-perfective power,
Thou reign'st the first intelligible god,
The *bound* thy essence secretly contains,
Proceeds from imparticipable Good,
And shines the first intelligible height.
Hence it both measures all things and defines;
And each paternal genus of the gods,

With energy ineffable sustains.
But *infinite* thy never-failing power,
And distributions generative shows;
Which from thy essence omniform proceed
To matter's utmost, dark, rebounding seat.
O mighty god, enable me to rise
With winged speed from this terrene abode,
And the dark mists disperse of matter's night,
That essence true, substantial, I may view,
And generation's phantom scenes despise.
O haste my union with thy secret world,
That by a flight ineffably divine,
My soul may leave all mental forms behind,
And lose herself in solitary Good.

TO LIFE

or

The Second Monad of the Intelligible Triad

A fertile god, intelligible life,
The second triad from *The One*, I sing;
Whose boundless essence is a vital all,
And through the first infinity, subsists.
Hence it contains through untam'd endless power,
The middle of intelligible gods;
And from a union more sublime is fill'd,
But fills all natures subject to its own
With ever vig'rous and prolific powers.
O first intelligence! in thee is fix'd
Th'intelligible centre full of life,
And truth from thee its purity derives.
Eternity in thee too first resides;
For this in never-failing total life,
And in unsluggish energy subsists.
From thy unwearied essence Rhea flows:
And all the central orders of the gods
In union beautiful from thee proceed.
Knowledge to thee its situation owes,
Between th'intelligible object plac'd,
And Intellect's divinely piercing eye.
Hence too, all life, howe'er sublime or low
Is nought but Intellection's active light!
O ever true, all-comprehending god!
Enable me to rise from Lethe's life
Phantastic, false, with death and darkness mix'd,
And vig'rous fly with winged speed to thee.
Give me to see, that while in body 'merg'd,
I but receive the punishment of guilt,
And die the life of unembodied souls.
O aid me to depart from Matter's seat,
Stormy, and dark, and whirling without end:
A boundless chaos, where delusion dire

And true nonentity maintain their sway.
Dispel the phantoms of corporeal night,
The flying mock'ries of fictitious life;
Which, as they glide before the mental eye,
Arrest its sight with fascinating arts,
And fix in lethargy its active power.
O haste my union with thy perfect life,
That by a flight transcendently divine,
My soul may leave all vital forms behind,
And lose herself in solitary Good.

TO INTELLECT

or

The Third Monad of the Intelligible Triad

The third bright offspring of the thrice-unknown
Intelligible animal I sing,
Fairest of all things: for in this alone
The beautiful itself for ever dwells.
Th'intelligible *tetrad* here resides,
Of all that lives the hypostatic cause;
And this exhibits to the mental eye
The first ideas in perfection bright.
Hence from contemplating these splendid forms,
The demiurgus constitutes the world,
And shines a great intelligible all.
Hail, perfect animal, bright form of forms,
Only-begotten, intellect supreme!
Whose essence omniform alone unfolds
The single nature of the unknown Good;
Before its power, with light unbounded shines,
And to thine own self-perfect splendour draws
The pure desire which there occultly dwells.
For all things, though in different modes, possess
A silent, unapparent wish for good;
But beauty with astonishment excites,
And vig'rous agitates with strong desire;
Its light acutely penetrates the soul,
And mental natures to itself converts,
And, as in rites most holy and divine,
Before the mystic spectacles appear'd,
A stupor fill'd th'initiated soul,
So, prior to the influence of the good,
Beauty's unbounded and forerunning light,
Astonishes th'intelligible gods;
And seated in the vestibule supreme,
The secret nature of *The One* declares.
This highest beauty from that place proceeds,

On which the eyes of all the gods are fix'd.
And to their genera from thence extends,
And with its all-attractive light illumes,
Their unities than essence more divine.
All beings too, which from the gods depend,
The sacred influence of its splendour own,
Ev'n to th'apparent vehicles which shine
Amid the heavens with undecaying light.
And as through uncaus'd, solitary good,
The gods their nature binoform derive,
And through intelligible wisdom share
A knowledge seated beyond mind itself;
So, through true beauty's summit, they acquire
A form transcendently divine and fair:
Hence they replenish with its copious streams
Inferior natures subject to their own,
And vig'rous raise them to its powerful love,
As if with vivid, god-like fury fir'd.
This is the constant source of joy divine,
Of friendship and communion without end:
For all the gods through this in union join,
And in eternal amity subsist.
This beauty, from its anagogic power,
Which strongly agitates, is *lovely* call'd,
For this the amatory series leads
Walks silent on its shining feet's extremes;
And to itself perpetually excites
Whatever is, through wonder and desire.
But from the plenitude and joy serene,
Which this on secondary forms confers
Alluring, raising all things by its light,
This highest beauty *delicate* is nam'd.
And last, because this perfect beauty bounds
The triad of intelligible gods,
Majestic swims above the light of forms,
And with intelligible splendour shines,
The unknown union of the gods conceals,
And silently enunciates secret good, -
Hence it is *splendid, clear*, and *lucid* call'd.
O fairest offspring of an uncaus'd sire!
Give me to see that all material forms

Are only shadows of substantial life,
True beauties mock'ries, without check or stay,
Innum'rous flowing into matter's seat,
Where true nonentity and darkness reign.
O may thy light, replete with mystic joy,
Beam on my soul with energy divine,
And to my ravish'd mental eye disclose
Thy bright abode amidst the highest forms.
Come with thy fair, all-comprehending world,
Come with the gods its secret realms contain,
That thus my soul with rapturous delight
Thy splendid vestibule may quickly gain,
May pass beyond thy lovely vital forms,
And seated on the first intelligible height,
May view alone with supermental gaze
The gods' o'erflowing, solitary Fount.

TO THE ORDER OF GODS DENOMINATED *INTELLIGIBLE* and at the same time *INTELLECTUAL*

> The middle triad of the Gods I sing,
> Between th' Intelligible order plac'd,
> And Mind[†] with perfect purity endu'd.
> Whose lucid nature constantly supplies
> Progression, motion, and all-various life:
> And from the unities divine receives
> Perpetual stores of super-mental light;
> But to the Gods by intellect defin'd
> All-powerful, perfect multitude imparts.
> Each triad of these middle Gods contains
> *Essence and life, and intellect* combin'd.
> But in the first, th' *intelligible* sways,
> And *intellect* throughout the third prevails,
> While mix't from these the second rank contains
> The common property of each extreme.
> And as the first intelligible three
> Are mix'd from *essence, infinite* and *bound;*
> So here the first *essentially* exists,
> Compos'd of *essence, intellect,* and *life.*
> And as the second triad there subsists
> From unity than *essence* more divine,
> From *power* prolific of all vital forms,
> Where *life intelligible and occult;-*
> So *here* the second *vitally* partakes
> Of *essence, intellect, and life* combin'd.
> And lastly, as the third is *there* compos'd
> Of union, power, and intellect supreme;
> So the third triad of this rank contains
> Three Gods exalted above being's self,
> Who bound the series with prolific light,
> And from life, essence, intellect, are mix'd,
> But this according to a *mental* mode;
> And who with never-failing power supply

[†] *i.e.* Saturn, or the first Deity of the intellectual triad.

A state of being perfectly divine.
In this all-splendid multitude of Gods
A place subsists with perfect joy replete,
Super-celestial; and a lucid Heav'n,
Intelligible in its ev'ry part;
The source of rapt'rous vision to the mind,
And power prolific to the mundane Gods.
But Jupiter endu'd with sov'reign might,
Intent the vision of this place to gain,
His winged chariot summoning in haste,
Begins th' arduous supermundane march,
Disposing all things in his swift ascent,
In order fit with providential care.
The *liberated* and the *mundane* Gods,
And godlike dæmons in eleven parts
Attend his lofty course with winged speed.
Vesta alone immoveable remains,
Fixt in the sacred dwellings of the Gods.
And ev'ry God belonging to the twelve,
Rules o'er the office to his charge assign'd.
Within the regions of this mental heav'n,
Objects replete with perfect bliss reside,
On which the eyes of all the Gods are fixt,
As each accomplishes his due employ.
But *will* and *power* perpetually attend
The blest immortals in their sacred course,
For baneful Envy from the choir of Gods
Divinely happy, is fore'er expell'd.
But when th' immortals to the banquet haste,
The banquet of intelligible food,
The *beautiful itself*, the *wise*, the *good*,
They march sublimely to the *mental* heav'n,
And at the *subcelestial arch* arrive,
Which largely scatters intellectual light,
The second genera of Gods contains;
And gives perfection to whate'er ascends
To Truth's intelligible, fertile plain.
Indeed, the lucid chariots of the Gods,
Are well adapted to the guiding reins,
And balanc'd equally proceed with ease.
But other natures anxious to obtain

The blessed vision of this mental Heav'n,
Direct their vehicles with mighty toil.
For in this arduous course the brutal horse
Oft gravitates, and restive in his course
Thro' want of proper discipline, inclines
And strongly draws the charioteer to earth.
But when th' immortal Gods the summit gain,
They march beyond this shining Heav'ns extreme,
On its intelligible back abide,
And thus unmov'd intelligence aquire.
But while establish'd in this high abode,
And carry'd by the bright circumference round,
Thro' which they rapid energy obtain,
And life divinely flourishing enjoy,
With vision beatific they survey
Th' unknown pulchritudes of mystic forms,
Which shine apparent in the lucid place,
Beyond this sacred intellectual Heav'n.
O fountains of intelligence, illume
My soul with true intelligible light,
That thus by you inspir'd my mystic song
May show the beauties of this secret place.
Devoid of *colour*, *figure*, and the *touch*,
As true substantial essence it subsists,
And intellect contemplative employs.
Hence thro' the dignity of cause this height
Excells th' immediately posterior Gods,
Who form the lucid intellectual Heav'n.
For *colour* the celestial order shows,
Containing in intelligible light,
The bright ideas of whate'er exists.
And hence the light proceeding from *The Good*,
Which in the inaccessible retreats
Of all the Gods is secret and unknown,
Here shines apparent with prolific rays.
But *figure* shows the subcelestial arch
Immensely bright thro' intellectual bound.
And *touch* occultly signifies the top
Of intellectual and paternal forms.
But as first being's progeny divine
This place is *true substantial essence* call'd.

And *intellect contemplative* employs,
Because amidst the intellectual Gods
Intelligible excellence it shares.
Here too revolving with the Heav'ns and Jove,
Each of these blessed uncorrupted souls,
Science, and temperance, and justice views,
Not such as in dark Lethe's realms reside;
For these are true, intelligible Gods.
And *science* is the perfect constant source
Of an intelligence unmov'd and pure.
But *temperance* to all the Gods supplies
A never-failing, self-convertive power.
And *justice* is the distributive fount
Of good according to desert and rank.
And hence thro' science ev'ry God percieves
Whate'er exists superior to himself,
And with intelligible unity is fill'd:
But to himself thro' *temperance* returns,
And secondary union hence enjoys.
And last thro' *justice* ev'ry God is rais'd,
And o'er posterior natures silent rules,
To each supplying distribution fit.
Add too, that when these uncorrupted souls
Have similarly other truths beheld,
And perfect nourishment from hence reciev'd,
Again they enter in this mental Heav'n,
And to their proper blissful home return.
But when return'd the winged charioteer[†]
His steady coursers at the manger stops,
And then supplies them with ambrosial food,
And copious draughts of nectar's streams divine.
But nectar here the power occultly shows
Indissoluble, liberal and pure,
Of providence pervading thro' *the all*;
While power in better natures stably plac'd,

[†] Johnson notes that the following lines followed here but were deleted before the continuation was written:

> With food ambrosial the repast of Gods
> Their hunger satiates; and with copious draughts
> Of nectar's streams divine

Is indicated by ambrosial food.
And last, *ambrosia* corresponds to bound,
Solid, and terminated by itself.
But *nectar* to infinity's alli'd,
Resembling moisture, and self-unconfin'd.
And hence *ambrosia* is perfection sure,
And to the Gods the never-failing source
Of an intelligence unmov'd and firm.
But *nectar* is prolific, and the cause
Of providential vigour to the whole.
Here too, th' extended lucid *plain of truth*,
And fertile *meadow* of the soul abides.
Thro' which her most exaltad power recieves
Convenient nutriment, and light divine.
Through which her wings are nourish'd and enlarg'd,
With vigour strength'ned, and with life inspir'd.
For *Truth's* expanded lofty *plain* implies
Th' unfolding of intelligible light;
And the prolific *meadow* is the sign
Of generative power, the constant source
Of various animals, and fertile forms.
And last, this lucid place beyond th' heav'ns
Is the first triad of the middle Gods,
Intelligibly, and by ways unknown
Possessing triple properties and power;
Thro' which these lucid deities *announce*,
Collect, and *guard* intelligible forms.
Hence from the triad of the highest Gods,
A plenitude of lucid forms they share;
And in their arcane essences receive
The whole of pure, intelligible light.
And while abiding in th' occult retreats
From whence th' intelligible triad shines,
Intelligibly they proceed from thence,
And thro' ineffable and secret powers,
Implanted by the images divine
Which in their mystic unities subsist,
Attract, and shine on all the *mental* Gods.
Hail glorious triad! from whose lucid plain
All life howe'er diversified proceeds;
And whence all sight corporeal or divine,

Largely participates of *light and life*.
For intellectual sight from life proceeds,
And all intelligence is full of light.
And hence, the clear resplendant solar rays,
Are said to be the swiftly penetrating sight
Pure and unbounded, of the mundane Gods.
Here too, *sufficiency, truth, wisdom* shine
With ever-vigilant, prolific rays;
The beauteous images of which are seen
Serenely seated in the beams of day.
O perfect Deities divinely bright,
Produc'd by the intelligible Gods,
Assist my flight from generation's life,
And body's cumbrous, all-surrounding shell.
The secret summit of my soul excite
To Truth's communion and supernal light,
And blest repletion with ambrosial food.
Here in phantastic images terrene
Of justice, temperance, and truth itself,
The soul percieves no beams of light divine;
But few thro' instruments obscure[†] can see
From flowing shadows, firm substantial forms.
But when united with th' immortal choir,
She happily surveys your blissful plain,
Together then with Deity she'll view
Beauty supremely splendid and divine.
Come blessed Deities possess my soul,
And all her powers with vivid light illume,
That join'd in mystic union with your world,
She thence may rise with vigour unconfin'd,
And in *The Good's* bright vestibule exult:
And last, relinquishing all mental forms
Th' o'er-flowing fountain of the Gods may view.

[†] *i.e.* through syllogisms.

To The

ARTIFICER OF THE UNIVERSE[1]

To thee great Demiurgus of the world,
With various intellectual sections bright,
My soul the tribute of her praise shall pay,
Unfeign'd and ardent, mystic and devout.
Thee shall she sing, when Morning's rosy beams
Lead on the broad effulgence of the day,
And when the hand of softly-treading Eve
Invests the world with solitary shade.
Artificer, and father of the whole!
With perfect good, and deity replete,
Through which the world perpetually receives
Exhaustless stores of intellectual good.
To thee belongs that all-sustaining power,
Which mind, and soul, and mundane life supports.
To thee, their fabrication bodies owe,
And things the due perfection of their kinds.
Through thee, each part of this amazing whole
Is link'd by sympathy's connecting hand,
And in the strongest, best proportions join'd;
And the world's various powers and pondrous weights
Are bound by thee in beautiful accord.
By thee, the world is formed a perfect whole,
From age exempt, unconscious of disease,
And with a shape adorn'd by far the first,
Most simple, most capacious, and the best.
By thee, this *all*, was self-sufficient fram'd,
And with a self-revolving power endu'd;
And motion intellectual owes to thee
Its never-ceasing energy, and life.
From thee, the soul derives her various frame,
Her distribution, and generic forms,
With all th'harmonic reasons she contains.
By thee she's stably seated in the world,
Like a self-motive, and immortal lyre,
The echo of whose life-inspiring sound

Is heard in Matter's dark, rebounding seat.
From thy own nature thou hast fashion'd time,
Whose fleeting essence, rolling without end,
Perpetually proceeds from life to life,
And imitates eternity's abiding state.
But far the most illustrious of the works
That glorious deity, the Sun, shines forth,
Whose sacred light from thy occult retreats
Was first enkindled; that its nature hence
Might shine exempt from all the mundane gods,
And reign the sov'reign of this lower world.
The stars, heav'n's joyful, ever-wakeful fires,
That roll incessant in harmonic dance,
Own thee, the parent of their splendid frames.
Exalted æther, blossom bright of fire,
From thee derives its eminent abode;
And constant covers, by thy dread command,
Dark Hyle's[2] fluctuating, boist'rous back,
And hides its unsubstantial naked shape,
Odious and horrid, from the sight of gods.
In intellectual hymns, the glorious choir
Of deathless angels celebrates thy name;
And while one part, with fixt attention views
Thy nature fill'd with intellectual forms,
And thence true beauty's principle collects,
A different part surveys the mundane spheres,
O'er the world's unknown altitude presides,
And e'en to matter's utmost realms extends
The fertile power of ornament divine.
To thee that intellect its being owes,
Which, falling into Lethe's dark abyss,
Is totally diffus'd through every part,
And, plac'd in various forms, preserves the whole;
But when degraded in a terrene form,
And from its parents and its kindred torn,
It then becomes a secondary god,
Is fill'd with dark oblivion of itself,
And eagerly regards the flowing shades
Of human scenes, ridiculous and vain.
Yet still indignant of their fallen state,
Some vivid rays of heav'nly light remain

In eyes with earth's obscurity suffus'd;
Some portion still of anagogic power
In miserable captive souls survives,
Through which, emerging from life's bitter waves,
These exiles to thy bosom may return,
From whence at first through mad desire they fell.
Blessed, thrice blessed! who with winged speed,
From Hyle's dread voracious barking flies,
And leaving earth's obscurity behind,
By a light leap directs his steps to thee.
Blessed! who after having well fulfill'd
The terms ordain'd by Destiny's decree;
Who, after mighty toils and anxious cares,
At length surveys in intellectual paths
A depth resplendent with a light divine.
Great is the labour for the captive soul
To soar on high with all her ruffled wings
Of anagogic, intellectual Loves.
But thou, O king, th'impulsive power confirm,
Which bears me up to intellect light,
And Truth's intelligible plain unfold,
Divinely lucid, and with bliss replete.
O! haste my flight from all material forms,
That I may drink of perfect beauty's streams,
And rise to mystic union with its fount;
For thus my nature shall be all divine,
And deity in deity exult.

1   According to the theology of Orpheus, Pythagoras, and Plato, the immediate artificer of the universe is not the ineffable principle of things: and this not from any defect, but, on the contrary, through transcendency of power. For as the essence of the first cause, if it be lawful so to speak, is full of deity, his immediate energy must be deific, and his first progeny must be gods; just as souls are the immediate progeny of one first soul, and natures of one first nature. As the immediate offspring, therefore, of the first cause, are wholly absorbed in deity, and are as it were stamped throughout with the characteristics of the ineffable, so as to be *secondarily* what the first god is *primarily*; and as the universe from its *corporeal* subsistence is not a thing of this kind, it is not the *immediate* progeny of the ineffable. Hence, as the world is replete with all various forms, its immediate artificer is a divine essence characterized by intellect; for intellect is the primary seat of forms. At the same time it must be observed, that among causes which produce from their very essence, whatever the inferior cause produces is also

produced by the superior, but the manner in which it proceeds from the superior transcends that in which it proceeds from the inferior. For processions are according to the characteristics of the natures from which they proceed. Hence, as the first principle of things is ineffable and super-essential, all things proceed from him ineffably and super-essentially, and other intermediate causes are necessary to the evolution of things into *distinct* subsistence. See this most interesting of all subjects copiously unfolded in the Introduction to my translation of Plato's works.

2 *i.e.* Matter

TO THE LIBERATED ORDER OF GODS

OR THAT WHICH EXISTS BETWEEN THE SUPERMUNDANE AND MUNDANE GODS

The mighty liberated Gods I call,
Between th' exalted supermundane powers,
And those of mundane character arrang'd.
Jove I invoke of demiurgic Gods
The first; from whom supernally proceed
Motion, and separate energy, and life.
Ruler of souls and bodies; and whose care
To all extended, with convertive power,
Leads secondary natures up to first.
Great Neptune! of the fabricative Gods
The centre; from whose all-prolific power
Soul's middle order, and the dreary realms
Of fluctuating Generation are evolv'd.
And Vulcan, from whose all-inspiring fount
The natures scatter'd about bodies flow,
And by whose plastic demiurgic skill
The seats of all the mundane Gods were fram'd.
I call th' immutable and guardian powers!
Who next succeed the fabricative Gods.
Firm Vesta, from whose all-preserving might
Being proceeds, and essence undefil'd.
Pallas who guards thro' intellectual light
All middle lives, and from th' incursions keeps
Of Hyle, thro' self-energizing life.
And Mars who body from on high illumes,
And natural forms, with all-victorious pow'r.
Next, the vivific triad I invoke,
Ceres, from whom all mundane life proceeds,
Whether or psychical, or mental nam'd,
Or in the dark, inexplicable turns
Of body's labyrinth inseparably fixt.
Great Juno the vivific central queen!
From whom the soul's progressions are evolv'd.
And then Diana! midwife of the world:
For with resuscitating force 'tis thine
Nature's spermatic dormant powers to wake

To energy, and to perfection bring
Matter's imperfect essence, formless, void.
The anagogic triad last I call:
Hermes, of blest philosophy the source,
The greatest of the gifts of Gods to men;
Thro' which he leads the apostate wand'ring soul,
Back to her fountain and her orb of light,
And raises by the dialectic powers,
Partial and total souls, to good itself.
Venus, the beauteous, and primordial cause
Of amatory influence, which pervades
With ceaseless vigour thro' this mighty whole;
And who familiarizes to the light
Of beauty, all the lives she upwards leads.
And bright Apollo who perfection gives
To all things thro' the power of harmony divine,
And all things draws to mental truth and light.
All-bounteous powers regard my fervent prayer;
May unimpeded energy be mine,
And from material knowledge wholly free.
Give me from souls ignoble to retire,
The impious vulgar of this barren age.
Keep me from servile, all-degrading cares,
That drag th' aspiring mind and chain to earth;
And when no more 'tis given me to unfold
Wisdom's deep mysteries, and truths divine,
Extend your hands, and with benignant aid,
My flight facilitate from Hyle's sea;
And raise my soul with num'rous ills opprest,
To your bright realms and Paradise of rest.

TO APOLLO

Thee, mighty ruler of the world, I sing!
Of life the splendour, and of light the king.
Sprung from a fire ineffably divine,
The world's bright eye, and leader of the Nine.
Whose unmixt rays prophetic truth inspire,
And leap exulting from an unknown fire:
Whose liberated power thro' matter's night
Widely pervades with purifying light:
Whose piercing darts malignant powers annoy,
And all immoderate lawless forms destroy;
And whose revolving motion is the sign
Of symphony collective and divine.
But not in matter's flowing realms alone
Thy matchless power and sacred light is known:
The supermundane realms confess thy might,
And intellectual gods from thee derive their light.
Thee, great Apollo, as their king they own,
And move in mental circles round thy throne.
Thee, too, each ruler of the world reveres,
Those shining eyes that deck th'æthereal spheres;
And as they roll with energy divine,
Declare that dignity supreme is thine,
Hence when thy beams, deep merg'd in mental night,
First shone thro' æther with unhop'd-for light,
The mundane gods, with Bacchic joy entranc'd,
Around thy orb in mystic measures danc'd;
And, lost in wonder, saw thy vivid ray
Strike darkness back, and give unbounded day.
Dæmons and heroes venerate thy nod,
Oh fairest image of the highest god!
With souls impassive, whom thy mental fire
Preserves from plunging into Hyle's mire,
Which at the bottom of life's stormy deep,
Polluted souls detain in deadly sleep.
Hail! sov'reign king, by mighty gods ador'd,
Parent of concord, universal lord.
Hear! and propitious to thy suppliant's prayer,

Disperse the seeds of life-consuming care;
Display the light of wisdom unconfin'd,
And pour its radiance on my dark'ned mind.
The stores of intellectual wealth be mine,
Peace ever tranquil, and a life divine:
And soon permit me, from the guileful ties
Of matter freed, from life's dark sea to rise,
And leave, expanding wide the wings of mind,
Its dreadful sounding billows far behind.
Here, from thy bosom torn, I sorrowing stay,
And meditate my flight from day to day;
Indignant in the realms of night I roam
And oft look up and gain a glimpse of home,
As some poor exile on a distant shore,
With mournful eye surveys the country o'er,
And oft looks back, and oft recalls to mind
The pleasing coast and friends he left behind,
Unwilling views the cheerful light of day,
And in ideal prospects pines away;
So grieves my soul while absent and distrest,
She roams an exile from her place of rest,
Oh! haste the period, when from body free,
This wretched captive shall return to thee;
Shall once more recognize her kindred soil,
And prove the blessing of her former toil;
Plac'd where no change impairs, no griefs corrode,
And shining 'midst th'immortal gods a god.

TO APOLLO and the SUN[1]

The Sun's resplendent deity I sing,
The beauteous offspring of almighty Jove,
Who, thro' the vivifying solar fount
Within his fabricative mind conceal'd,
A triad form'd of splendid solar gods;
From whence the world's all-various forms emerg'd
From mystic darkness into beauteous light,
Perfect, and full of intellectual goods.
Hail! Supermundane king of light divine,
And fairest image of the unknown good:
For, as the light proceeding from *The One*,
The god of gods, and beauty's matchless flower,
Intelligibles, with deific rays
Occult, illumes; so from Apollo's beams
Exulting glorious through harmonic power,
The mental world with elevating light
Is fill'd exub'rant: and th'apparent sun
Largely diffuses thro' the world of sense,
Light, all-prolific, beautiful, divine.
To thee, as bright Apollo, it belongs
All multitude in union to collect,
And many natures generate from one;
With vigour in thy essence to convolve
The diff'rent ranks of secondary forms;
And thro, one fair hyparxis[2] to combine
All-various essences and fertile powers.
'Tis thine, from multitude exempt, t'inspire
In forms subordinate, prophetic truth;
For *truth* and *pure simplicity* are one:
And of preserving unpolluted power,
Thy *liberated* essence is the source.
Fam'd mystic bards of old, in sacred song,
By thee inspir'd, as th'*arrow-darting* god,
Constant invok'd thee, with resistless sway,
Because thy vig'rous beams like arrows pierce,
And totally, whate'er of measure void the world
Inordinate or dark contains, destroy.

And last, thy revolution is the sign
Of motion, harmonizing into one
The various natures of this mighty whole.
Thy *first* bright *Monad*[3] hence, illustrious god,
Enunciates truth and intellectual light;
That light, which in the essence of the gods,
Subsists with rays uniting and unknown.
Thy *second*,[4] ev'ry thing confus'd destroys:
And from thy *third*,[5] the universe is bound
In beauteous symmetry and just consent,
Thro' splendid reasons and harmonic power.
Add, that thy essence, 'midst the mundane gods,
A super-mundane order is assign'd;
An unbegotten and supreme command
O'er all the ranks of generated forms;
And in the ever-flowing realms of sense,
An intellectual dignity of sway.
Progression two-fold, hence, to thee belongs, -
One in conjunction with the mundane gods,
The other supernat'ral and unknown:
For when the Demiurgus form'd the world,
He kindled in the solar sphere a light,
Unlike the splendour of the other orbs,
Drawn from his nature's most occult retreats,
A symbol fair of intellectual forms;
And openly announcing as it shines
To ev'ry part of this amazing whole,
The essence solitary and arcane
Of all the ruling, supermundane gods.
Hence too, when first thy beams the world adorn'd
The mundane gods were ravish'd at the sight;
And round thy orb, with emulative zeal
And symphony divine, desir'd to dance,
And draw abundant from thy fontal light.
'Tis thine by heat apparent to exalt
Corporeal natures from the sluggish earth,
Inspiring vivid, vegetative power;
And by a nature secretly divine,
And from the base alloy of matter free,
Inherent in thy all-productive rays,
Thou draw'st to union with thy wond'rous form,

Exalted souls, that in dark Hyle's realms
Indignant struggle for the courts of light:
All beauteous, *seven-rayed*, supermundane god!
Whose mystic essence secretly emits
The splendid fountains of celestial light.
For, midst the ruling, super-mundane gods
A solar world, and total light subsists;
A light, which as a fertile monad shines
Superior to the three corporeal worlds.
By sacred oracles of old, 'tis said,
Thy glorious orb beyond the starry sphere
And in the last etherial world revolves.
But in thy course, harmoniously divine,
Thy orb quadruply intersects these worlds;
And then twelve powers of radiant gods displays,
Thro' twelve divisions of the zone oblique.
And still abundant in productive might,
Each into three of diff'rent ranks divides.
Hence, from the fourfold elegance and grace
Of times and seasons, by thy course produc'd,
Mankind a triple benefit receive,
The circling Graces' never-failing gift.
All-bounteous god, by whom the soul is freed
From Generation's dark corporeal bands,
Assist THY OFFSPRING, borne on mental wings,
Beyond the reach of guileful Nature's hands
Swift to ascend, and gain thy beauteous world.
The subtle vestment of my soul refine,
Etherial, firm, and full of sacred light,
Her ancient vehicle by thee assign'd;
In which invelop'd, thro' the starry orbs,
Urg'd, by the impulse of insane desire,
She fail'd precipitate, till Lethe's shore,
Involv'd in night, unhappily she touch'd,
And lost all knowledge of her pristine state:
O best of gods, blest dæmon crown'd with fire,
My soul's sure refuge in the hour of woe,
My port paternal in the courts of light,
Hear, and from punishment my soul absolve,
The punishment incurr'd by pristine guilt,
Thro, Lethe's darkness and terrene desire:

And if for long-extended years I'm doom'd
In these drear realms Heav'n's exile to remain,
Oh! grant me soon the necessary means
To gain that good which solitude confers
On souls emerging from the bitter waves
Of fraudful Hyle's black, impetuous flood.
That thus retiring from the vulgar herd,
And *impious converse of the present age*,
My soul may triumph o'er her natal ills;
And oft with thee in blissful union join'd
Thro, energy ineffable, may soar
Beyond the highest super-mundane forms;
And in the vestibule supreme survey,
Emerging from th'intelligible deep,
Beauty's transcendent, solitary sun.

1 I have already observed in my account of Apollo and the Sun, in the first part of this Introduction, that though these divinities subsist in wonderful union with each other, yet they likewise inherit a proper distinction and diversity of nature.

2 *i.e* essence.   3 Mercury.   4 Venus.   5 Apollo

TO THE RISING SUN

See! how with thund'ring fiery feet,
Sol's ardent steeds the barriers beat,
   That bar their radiant way;
Yok'd by the circling hours they stand,
Impatient at the god's command,
   To bear the car of day.

See! led by morn, with dewy feet,
Apollo mounts his golden seat,
   Replete with seven-fold fire;
While dazzled by his conqu'ring light,
Heav'n's glittering host, and awful Night
   Submissively retire.

See! cloth'd with majesty and strength,
Through sacred Light's wide gates at length,
   The god exulting spring:
While lesser deities around,
And demon powers his praise resound,
   And hail their matchless king.

Through the dark portals of the deep,
The foaming steeds now furious leap,
   And thunder up the sky:
The god to strains now tunes his lyre,
Which Nature's harmony inspire,
   And ravish as they fly.

Ev'n dreadful Hyle's sea profound,
Feels the enchanting conqu'ring sound,
   And boils with rage no more;
The world's dark bound'ry Tart'rus hears,
The life inspiring strains reveres,
   And stills its wild uproar.

And while, through heav'n the god sublime,
Triumphant rides, see rev'rend Time
    Fast by his chariot run:
Observant of the fiery steeds,
Silent the hoary king proceeds,
    And hymns his parent sun.

See! as he comes, with gen'ral voice,
All Nature's living tribes rejoice,
    And own him as their king;
Ev'n rugged rocks their heads advance,
And forests on the mountains dance,
    And hills and valleys sing.

See! while his beauteous, glittering feet
In mystic measures aether beat,
    Enchanting to the sight;
Paeon, whose genial locks diffuse
Life-bearing health, ambrosial dews,
    Exulting springs to light.

Lo! as he comes, in heav'n's array,
And scattering wide the blaze of day
    Lifts high his scourge of fire,
Fierce demons, that in darkness dwell,
Foes of our race, and dogs of hell,
    Dread its avenging ire.

Hail, crown'd with light, creation's king!
Be mine the task thy praise to sing,
    And vindicate thy might;
Thy honours spread through barb'rous climes,
Ages unborn, and impious times,
    And realms involv'd in night.

---

1 That is, with his own proper fire, and the fire of the other planets.

TO THE SUN

*Considered as when rising,
attended by the Powers that preside over the planetary spheres,
and the four elements*

Tethys from hoary Ocean's deeps,
Now climbs Olympus' shining steeps,
    T'attend the god of day;
And frees the steeds that panting wait
Through sacred Light's refulgent gate
    To wing their spacious way.

Aurora, daughter of the Dawn,
Has sprinkled now the dewy lawn
    With rays of rosy light;
Apollo, crown'd with fire, is seen
Emerging now, with dazzling mien
    From Tartarus and Night.

Armies of gods and daemons round,
Now bursting from the dark profound,
    In solemn silence stand;
And from his lips, with mental speed,
Ere words of power immense proceed,
    Anticipate command.

The gods that roll the starry spheres,
And lead on hours, and days, and years,
    A shining synod form;
With those in fire and air who ride,
O'er winds and thunders who *preside*,
    Or rule the raging storm.

Before, behind, around the god,
Eager to mark his awful nod,
   And pleas'd his course t'attend,
With eyes undazzl'd by that light,
Whose beams o'erpower e'en angels' sight,
   See gods adoring bend.

Thron'd in a radiant amber car,
And scatt'ring milder light from far,
   See first great Dian comes;
And, hark! as deck'd with starry light,
Foremost proceeds the queen of night,
   Loud rattle Rhea's drums.

Gay Hermes next, fair Maia's son,
Glad round the king of light to run,
   And borne by fiery steeds -
The god who mounts the winged winds,
Fast to his feet his pinions binds,
   And gods ministrant leads.

The car of Venus, drawn by doves,
While close behind the Smiles and Loves,
   A blooming band are seen,
In order next attends the god,
Whose will is law, and fate his nod,
   And bears bright Beauty's queen.

See next advance terrific Mars,
Who joys in uproar, ruin, wars,
   With lance deep-bath'd in gore;
Fear, Fury, Flight, beside him stand,
Prompt to fulfil his dread command,
   His gold-rein'd steeds before.

But, lo! the mighty power[1] appears
Who guides the largest of the spheres,
   That round Apollo run -
See! how along sublimely roll'd
By brass-hoof'd steeds with manes of gold
   He hails the sov'reign Sun.

To close the band, Time's hoary sire,[2]
Who rides on guards of mental fire,[3]
   His winged chariot cites;
Slow through the shining tracts of Heav'n,
By dragons drawn, the god is driv'n
   From steep Olympian heights.

Each Dryad of the shady wood,
Each Sister of the silver flood,
   With these well-pleas'd advance;
Around creation's seven-ray'd king,
In strains that ravish Tart'rus sing,
   In mystic measures dance.

Glad earth perceives, and kindly pours
Unbidden herbs, spontaneous flow'rs,
   And forests tow'ring rise;
Old Ocean stills his raging deeps,
And Darkness flies, and Discord sleeps,
   And laugh th'exulting skies.

Let Nature's tribes, with gen'ral voice,
Unceasing in the god rejoice,
   Who pours the blaze of day;
Rocks, hills, and vales, one chorus raise,
Men, beasts, and birds, resound his praise,
   And bless his vivid ray.

1 Jupiter.   2 Saturn.

3 This is asserted of Saturn in the Chaldaic Theology. See my version of the *Chaldaic Oracles* [Fr. 90, TTS volume VII].

TO JUPITER

THE DEMIURGUS OF THE WORLD

Of the mundane gods the king,
Mighty Jupiter, I sing;
Whose unenvying, perfect will,
Can the world with order fill,
And throughout with life inspire,
And expel confusion dire.
Pregnant with paternal power,
Shining like a fiery flower,
Jove at first, thro' æther bright,
Gave the world unhop'd-for light.
Jove all-seeing, Bromius strong,
Various names to thee belong.
Secret, shining, holy god,
Nature trembles at thy nod.
Father of this mighty whole,
Number, harmony, and soul,
Thee, Minerva's sire, I sing,
Saturn's son, of gods the king:
Light and spirit, Jove, are thine,
Council, intellect divine.
Mighty parent, may thine eye,
Which can every thought descry,
Piercing, swift, divinely bright,
Round me scatter mental light.
Oh regard my fervent prayer!
Free me from degrading care;
From the toil which want requires,
From the flames of base desires.
Dæmons from my life expel,
That in matter's darkness dwell;
Noxious to the human race,
Dogs of hell, terrific, base.
Fraudful Hyle here prepares
Me to plunge thro' magic snares,
Deep in black Barbaric mire,

Torn from thee, my lawful sire.
From dark uproar where she dwells,
Now she raises by her spells,
Tempests potent to control,
And in horror wrap the soul.
Place me in celestial light,
Far beyond this horrid night;
Far beyond her dire domain,
And oblivion's drowsy plain.
While, involv'd in earthly folds,
Me indignant Hyle holds,
While I struggle to be free,
Burst my bonds and fly to thee,
Strengthen me with mental might,
Wide my pinions stretch for flight,
That my soul may rapid rise,
And regain her native skies.
Now my fallen state I mourn,
Bodies scenes phantastic scorn,
Which the soul in evil hour
Subject to earth's sluggish power,
Till thro' thee her bonds she breaks,
And herself to life betakes.
With the luscious drink ensnar'd,
By Oblivion's hands prepar'd,
Staggering and oppress'd with sleep,
Thro' dark Hyle's stormy deep,
Headlong borne with forceful sway,
And, unconscious of the way,
Far I fell, midst dire uproar,
Till I touch'd this gloomy shore.
But my soul, now rous'd by thee.
And enabled truth to see,
Scorns her fetters, and aspires,
Borne on wings of pure desires,
To thy meadows full of light;
Fill'd with fountains of delight.
Arbiter of mental life.
Thro' these realms of endless strife,
Thro' earth's dark Tartarian tomb,
May thy light my steps illume;

And disclose the arduous way
To the coasts of mental day.
Cut the reins, and loose the bands,
Wove by guileful Nature's hands,
Which, forgetful of her birth,
Keep the soul a slave to earth.
From the fount contain'd in thee,
Source of life's prolific sea,
Here a shining drop I fell,
Destin'd here at times to dwell.
Oh restore me back again
From dark Hyle's stormy main,
From these realms of ceaseless strife,
To thy lucid fount of life;
To thy fount divinely pure,
Ever tranquil and secure.
Gracious bid my sorrows end,
And my exil'd soul defend;
Exil'd from her place of rest,
Wand'ring, weary, and opprest.
To thy bosom haste my flight,
Where e'en gods to dwell delight;
Where the soul from anxious toil
Rests, as in her native soil;
Finds the period of her woes,
Joy unmixt with sorrow knows;
And to be divinely free,
Loses all herself in thee.

TO MINERVA

Great progeny of Jove, divinely bright,
Only-begotten source of mental light,
Whose beams the wise with vivid force inspire,
And leap resounding from a fount of fire,
Thee I invoke with supplicating voice,
Adore thy power, and in thy aid rejoyce:
To thee my wings from Hyle's stormy night
I stretch, impatient of a speedy flight;
For thee my soul far more than life desires,
And to thy light incessantly aspires.
By Vulcan's art thou fiercely sprung, 'tis said,
In splendid armour from thy father's head,
Shouting vehement, while with dire affright
Stood earth and heav'n astonished at the sight.
But this in symbols, obvious to the wise,
Thy amply-spreading government implies,
Which from the world's artificer extends,
And last in matter's lowest region ends;
While by the horror which thy wond'rous birth
Produc'd at first in heav'n and mother earth,
Thy power exempt from mundane forms we learn,
And its occult prerogative discern.
Thy shouts too shew, that energy divine,
With efficacious vigour fraught, is thine.
Thy dreadful shield, in mystic fables fam'd,
Occultly signifies the power untam'd
Which in thy essence first appears, and thence
Becomes the gods' invincible defence;
Thro' which from passion they remain secure,
And reign triumphant and divinely pure.
Thy spear, of all-pervading power's the sign,
(For nought can e'er thy matchless might confine)
Thro' which the gods, unconscious of control,
Pass without contact, thro' this mighty whole
Forms sublunary aid, and in their course
Base matter amputate with vig'rous force.
Hail, blue-ey'd maid, of countenance serene!

Who reign'st in heav'n apparent and unseen,
And thence, through Hyle's realms, involv'd in storms,
Pourst in abundant streams resplendent forms,
To thee triumphant, and of bounteous mind,
The ram celestial is by lot assign'd,
And equinoctial circle, where resides
A motive power that o'er the world presides.
Victorious virgin, may thy vivid light
Disperse the mists produc'd by Lethe's night,
My soul from earth's impurities refine,
And all her pow'rs expand through rites divine;
That wing'd and ardent with celestial fire,
She soon may gain the palace of her sire,
And there once more may rest from anxious toil,
Fix'd in her long-deserted native soil,

TO MINERVA

Great zoogonic monad, thee I sing!
Bright third procession from that lucid fount
Whose copious streams, all secondary ranks
Of generated forms, adorn and fill
With life's prolific, ever-flowing fire.
Hail triple virgin! by the wise of old
The philosophic Goddess justly call'd;
Because thy vital nature is replete,
With mental knowledge, and true wisdom's light.
Thee too they celebrate in sacred hymns
As pleas'd with war's loud-sounding horrid roar;
Because thy essence is the constant source
Of unpolluted, never-failing power,
And reigns o'er fortitude with boundless sway.
The wise invoke thee as a virgin fair;
Because thy nature is divinely pure
From all conversion to external forms:
And the world's various parts are bound by thee
In just consent, thro' all-containing power.
From thy full fount of intellectual life,
Thou pourst abundant streams of beauteous light,
Which flowing wide illume this mighty whole.
And by unific powers, with guardian care,
Thou rul'st th' opposing natures of the world.
Thee too, as radiant *Phosphor* they adore,
Because thy nature everywhere extends
The vivid beams of intellectual light.
And as thro' thee all partial minds subsist
Establish'd in Jove's universal mind;
Hence they invoke thee as *the saving* power.
But from thy rule o'er demiurgic works,
The fabricator thou art justly call'd.
And as the mighty father's works are bound
In mental beauty thro' thy arts divine,
In sacred hymns they call thee *artist fair*:
But *aegis-bearing*, as thro' power immense
Fate's all-connecting chain is moved by thee,
From whom its plastic energies proceed.

Thy *wond'rous veil with matchless art adorn'd*
In which the Giants' dreadful battle shines.
Thy mental wisdom secretly implies,
Widely diffus'd o'er Nature's varying realms.
And last, *the warlike dress of mighty Jove*
With which thy limbs are deck'd for horrid fight,
Shows thou at all times art prepar'd to rule
O'er ev'ry thing of natures more divine
Which in its ample orb the world contains.
Victorious virgin! may thy piercing eye,
Which guards, illumes, and vivifies the world,
Protect my life from danger and distress,
And shine upon me with propitious light.
My soul's etherial vehicle refine
From generation's deep, corrupting stains;
That ready-wing'd for flight, she soon may pass
Beyond dark Hyle's dire-resounding sea,
And gain her long-lost paradise of rest.

TO MINERVA

The untam'd deity sublimely pure
Of the first mental unities divine,
In demiurgic Jove contain'd I sing.
Thro' which the father of the world abides
In one immutable and equal state;
And whence his various progeny partake
Of power inflexible, and splendid truth:
Thro' which with intellection unconfin'd,
He sees collectively whate'er exists;
And rais'd sublime above the mighty *all*,
In solitary unity subsists.
Hail pure Minerva! from the awful head
Of sovereign Jupiter at first produc'd,
With armour shining like a brazen flower:
And who abiding in his essence fixt,
A separate intelligence dost shine,
Both demiurgic, and from matter free.
'Tis thine paternal wisdom to connect
In bonds unific, and divinely bright;
And hence in sacred and mysterious hymns
The philosophic Goddess thou art call'd.
Thee too the greatly wise of old invok'd,
As pleas'd with battle and contention dire;
Because th' opposing natures of the world,
Are ever uniformly rul'd by thee.
Thy essence in the Coric rank appears
The heptad lucid, and divinely pure;
And midst the Liberated Gods is seen,
With intellectual demiurgic light:
Thro' which the lunar deities derive
A nature perfectly unmixt and pure
From generation's ever-flowing forms.
Wherein among the ranks of partial souls
Resemblance to thy guardian essence shines,
Thy pure Minerval providence extends
Wisdom replete with intellectual light,
And strength superior to the power of Fate.
The guardian, mundane, Liberated Gods,

The dæmoniacal and ruling powers,
Largely thy twofold properties receive
As from an endless, ever-flowing fount.
Triumphant Goddess! may thy piercing eye,
Which guards, illumes, and vivifies the world,
Beam on my captive, yet aspiring soul
With anagogic and Olympian good:
And banish thence the dire gigantic forms
Phantastic, and the source of Lethe's life,
Which oft Imagination's realms invade,
And proudly strive the seats of *mind* to gain,
And hurl imperial Reason from her throne.
O beauteous virgin! may thy power excite
Far in the deep recesses of my soul
Conception of the Gods divinely pure,
And full of Truth's serenely splendid light.
That thus her vehicle from sense refin'd
And fraught with vivid intellectual fire,
May aid her to ascend with winged speed
Beyond the reach of guileful Lethe's hands,
And gain[†] her native, long-deserted home.

[†] In the original article *again* is wrongly printed for *gain*.

TO VESTA

Saturn's daughter, ancient dame,
Seat of fire's unweary'd frame,
Source of virtue's perfect light,
Juno's equal, Vesta bright,
Stable goddess, essence fair,
Gracious listen to my prayer;
And while ardent thee I sing,
Borne on pure devotion's wing,
With thy unpolluted fire
All my mental powers inspire.
From the gods by men divine
Liberated called, 'tis thine
Essence to illumine pure,
Uniform, unchang'd, and sure.
Hence the mundane gods we see,
Through thy stable deity,
Firmly in themselves abide,
And immutably preside
O'er the fluctuating forms,
O'er the dire resounding storms,
Of dark Hyle's rolling main,
Barren, impotent, and vain.
Thy abiding splendours hence
Firm stability dispense,
To the axis and the poles,
Round which heav'n incessant rolls;
And to earth's all-flow'ry frame,
Earth, prolific, central dame!
Blessed goddess, may thy light,
Beaming far thro' Lethe's night,
Widely scatt'ring virtue's fires,
Fill my soul with pure desires;
And disclose the arduous way
To the courts of mental day.
To thy stable, shining seat,
Wisdom's undisturb'd retreat,
Harbour of deific rest

To the wand'ring and opprest.
While on Hyle's stormy sea,
Wide I roam in search of thee,
Graciously thine arm extend,
And my soul from ill defend:
Gracious bid my sorrows cease;
Crown my future days with peace,
With the splendid gifts of health,
With the bliss of needful wealth;
And soon cut the fatal folds,
Through which guileful nature holds
Me indignant from thy sight,
Exil'd in the realms of night,
From my father's bosom torn,
Wand'ring, weary and forlorn,
That my soul with rapid wing,
From Oblivion's coast may spring,
May once more triumphant gain
Truth's immortal, shining plain,
And in her conceal'd abodes
Ravish'd view the god of gods.

TO MERCURY

Hermes I sing, a god supremely bright,
Who first emerging from Jove's fount of light,
Upborne on beauteous wings, from thence descends,
Till last his lucid course in Hades ends.
Angel of Jove, unfolding truth divine,
Propitious to thy vot'ry's prayer incline,
And while to thee my supplicant voice I raise,
Accept, well pleas'd, this tribute of my praise.
By ancient bards, in mystic verse, 'tis sung,
That thou, great god, from prudent Maia sprung:
But this in symbols, obvious to the wise,
Thy nature with invention fraught implies;
Since *search*, which into light *invention* leads,
First from fair Maia secretly proceeds,
And as unfolding mighty Jove's decree,
Mathesis owes its origin to thee;
Hence fallen souls, to deep research inclin'd,
By thee inspir'd, eternal truth may find;
When rous'd by discipline from Lethe's night,
They raise their eyes to intellectual light.
To thee unnumber'd benefits we owe;
From thee gymnastic, music, reasoning flow.
Hence thro' the first with vigour we inspire
In youth, the languid nature of desire;
And anger, merg'd in matter's gloomy deep,
Wake into energy from death-like sleep;
While thro' the power of melody divine
We force e'en rage its fury to resign,
And last, the seeds of truth in dormant state,
The vivid wings of reas'ning suscitate:
Hence, as of harmony the mighty sire,
The wise ador'd thee as the starry lyre,
Whose strains wide-spreading thro' the azure round,
The gods transport with deifying sound,
And even in the dark Tartarian gulf rebound.
And as 'tis thine o'er learning to preside,
The wise invok'd thee, as of souls the guide,

Who leadst them upwards to the splendid plain
Of sacred truth, from Hyle's dire domain,
Oblivion's sleep expelling from their sight,
And wide-expanding recollection's light.
All bounteous Hermes, hear my fervent prayer,
And make my future life thy constant care,
Teach me what rites th'offended gods may please,
And what the means their anger to appease:
For long thro' marine and material foes,
My soul has suffer'd complicated woes;
And all her efforts have as yet been vain
T'escape the fury of the avenging main.
Come, gracious god, thy saving arm extend,
And from her natal ills my soul defend;
Urge all her powers by baneful night oppress'd
To rise victorious to the goal of rest;
The splendid goal of loud-resounding fire,
And all-attractive centre of desire;
That wing'd and ardent, and from guilt refin'd,
She thus the end of all her woes may find.

TO CERES[1]

Bounteous Ceres, thee I sing,
Source of Jove the mighty king.
Goddess hail! of beauteous mien,
Splendid Rhea, Saturn's queen,
Gen'ral mother, nurse divine,
Nutriment to give is thine;
Food which first to gods extends,
And in sluggish body ends.
But the pure, immortal food,
Which supplies the gods with good,
From the beatific sight;
Springs of beauty's perfect light;
Springs, when gods themselves desire,
And th'inferior view the higher.
Ancient goddess, Saturn's wife,
Middle centre of all life,
Which for ever streams from thee,
All-prolific deity.
Juno, Vesta, ruling queen,
In thy vital fount are seen.
Juno, from whose fertile frame
Soul's self-motive, nature, came,
Whence its whole procession flows,
From thy right hand parts arose;
From thy left hand, Vesta bright,
Who wide scatters virtue's light.
Life not only, hence we see,
Springs, all-parent queen, from thee,
But life's bliss, fair virtue, streams
From thy fertile, mental beams:
And hence females offspring bear,
And from milky fountains rear.
Gracious goddess! may thy light
Beaming thro' oblivion's night,
Fill my soul with food divine,
Which to give alone is thine;
Fill my soul with mental fire,
Perfect virtue, wing'd desire;

> And from Hyle's stormy main,
> To her father back again,
> To her true immortal goal
> Lead my wand'ring, weary soul,
> Ardent panting to be blest,
> In her native place of rest.

1 According to Orpheus, as we are informed by Proclus on the *Cratylus*, this goddess, considered as united to Saturn, is called Rhea, and as producing Jupiter, Ceres: nor does this disagree with what Hesiod asserts in his *Theogony*, that Ceres is the daughter of Saturn; for considered as proceeding from her union with Saturn, to the production of Jupiter, she may be said to be the offspring of Saturn.

TO VENUS

A lucid, royal, foam-begotten fount,
The second monad of the solar gods,
By sov'reign Jupiter produc'd, I sing.
Hail parent goddess! secret, fav'ring Queen,
Whose all-prolific deity first shines
Harmonic 'midst the *supermundane* gods;
And thence according streams of beauteous light,
The source of union to material forms,
Diffuses wide thro' Nature's flowing realms.
The amatory impulse which pervades,
Allures, and raises all things by its power,
From thee, as from its fontal cause, proceeds:
And thy unbounded mental splendour draws
To beauty's self, its progeny divine.
Mother of Loves! a wing'd immortal tribe,
Whose triple order, with resistless sway,
The ever-changing race of mortals rules.
The greatly-wise of old, in sacred hymns,
Divinely mystic, thee as Night invok'd,
Because th'exemplar of thy splendid form
Subsists in union awfully occult,
Amid the great intelligible gods.
Thee too, as Lysian Bacchus, they ador'd,
Because thou pour'st, as from an endless fount,
Th'intoxicating streams of beauty's light,
Which vig'rous agitate th'enraptur'd soul,
And aid her to dissolve her natal bonds:
To fly indignant from the realms of night,
And gain th'eternal palace of her sire.
Once in truth's splendid and immortal plain,
With thee in blest deific union join'd,
Th'unknown pulchritudes of mystic forms,
Which shine apparent in a lucid place,
Beyond the sacred mental Heav'n, I saw.
But when the latent seeds of mad desire,
With gradual evolution silent spread,
And rous'd the baneful tendency to change;
My wretched soul her mental eye withdrew

From perfect beauty's progeny divine,
And all the splendid forms contain'd in thee,
And headless gaz'd on matter's fraudful face.
Then earthly images with guile replete,
Like thee appearing to my clouded fight,
The figur'd eye of phantasy assail'd,
And caus'd oblivion of supernal goods.
Unhappily from thee, I then retir'd,
And downward verg'd, as earthly love increas'd,
Till with insanity my soul was fill'd,
And into Hyle's stormy darkness hurl'd.
For then her former dignity impair'd,
My soul unable longer to extend
Intelligibly with the mighty world,
Her essence with all-various powers replete,
Through dark oblivion of thy beauteous form,
And wonder rais'd by Nature's guileful arts,
Lethargic tended towards solid forms,
Full of impetuous matter's base alloy.
Hence in her passage thro' th'ethereal orbs,
Whate'er replete with light and warmth she found,
And well-adapted body to connect,
This with avidity she madly seiz'd;
Herself involving in coercive bonds,
Form'd from these circles, and their moving lines,
And spreading round her like a filmy net.
But when thro' places near the moon she pass'd,
Which nat'rally a subtle air possess,
Mix'd with a spirit heavy and obscure;
Here, as she mov'd, by Nature's force impell'd,
A noise vehement in her course she rais'd,
And a moist spirit in herself receiv'd.
Then wide extending, as she gradual fell,
Each orb's entangling surfaces and lines,
And partly downwards thro' her spirit drawn,
And partly struggling for supernal forms,
Her spheric figure lost in lengthening rays,
She sunk, transmuted to a human shape.
In baneful hour thus fall'n and obscur'd,
And in dark Hyle's loud-resounding sea
Deep merg'd her vestment of etherial mould,

For one membraneous and terrene she chang'd.
The lines too, which before with fiery light,
And colour'd with a fiery redness shone,
She chang'd into the grosser form of nerves.
And last, from these inferior realms assum'd
A spirit pond'rous, humid, and obscure.
Thus with a nat'ral body cover'd o'er,
From certain surfaces membraneous form'd,
With spirit, nerves, and filmy lines combin'd,
Th'external body's harmony and root,
Thro' which its parts are nourish'd and sustain'd,
My clouded and lethargic soul at length
Thy perfect beauty and alluring light
Forgot, the source of energy divine.
All-bounteous Goddess, may thy splendid eye,
Whose beauteous rays the universe connect
With anagogic and harmonic bonds,
Beam on my soul with elevating power,
And freedom rouse unconscious of restraint.
Disperse these earthly unsubstantial forms,
Which oft attempt to fascinate my soul,
And fix in lethargy her active powers.
For magic Hyle, by her guileful arts,
With shadowy beauty charms the eye of sense,
And darkly imitates thy splendid form.
O gracious aid me by *theurgic* arts,
T'appease great Neptune's overwhelming ire;
And raise me by the power of mystic song,
Thy splendid palace in the plain of truth,
And anagogic centre to regain.
But grant my life, if long I'm doom'd to stray
A mourning captive from thy fair domain,
May peaceful glide, in solitude conceal'd,
And wrapt in blissful intellectual rest.
That thus with thee, in secret union join'd,
Ev'n while invested with this cumbrous shell,
My soul *first being's* vestibule may gain,
Borne on the flaming wings of holy love,
And seated there with solitary gaze,
The o'erflowing fountain of the Gods may view.

TO LOVE

Thee, mighty Daemon, anagogic Love,
First beauty's splendid progeny, I sing:
Whose mystic fire, descending from on high,
Diffuses wide intelligible light,
The source of union to material forms:
And seated in the vestibule sublime,
The secret entrance to the highest god,
All secondary natures upwards calls
With energetic and alluring voice.
Hail, beauteous son of aether, tender god!
All-spreading, dark-ey'd splendour, flaming flower.
Four circling eyes[1] adorn thy four-fold face,
And cause thy *perfect*, and unbounded sight:
Two golden wings emitting mental fire,
Impel thee rapid, thro' the mighty world:
And last, four different heads thy form compleat,
With aweful majesty, and grace combin'd.
For first the visage of a beauteous ram,
And then a bull's bedect with radiant horns:
A dragon's next, with ever-watchful eyes,
And tawny lion's front thy shape adorn.
And hence thy wond'rous nature is replete
With zoogonic, and defensive power.
Thy splendid essence in itself contains
The bright exemplar of all Daemon forms:
And hence thy summit 'midst the gods supreme,
United to the highest beauty shines.
But in the ranks of supermundane gods,
Thy middle process mentally appears;
And thro' the mighty world with fertile power,
And multifarious energies replete,
Thy third progression every where pervades.
But after thy uniting highest form,
And triple essence perfected from thence;
A various multitude of loves shines forth,
By thee adorn'd with intellectual light:
From whence th'angelic choirs are largely fill'd
With flaming zeal, and over-flowing love;

And all the middle ranks, of Daemon forms
Full of thy ardent deity attend
The gods to perfect beauty's self recall'd.
Hence too, the heroes anagogic band,
About first beauty rapidly revolves,
With boy divine, and bacchanalian rage.
But godlike human souls allied to thee,
And touch'd with thy transporting mental fire,
In dance harmonic, round true beauty move;
And into Hyle's stormy regions fall,
To benefit more dull lethargic souls;
Who lull'd to rest on Lethe's flow'ry brink,
Have lost all knowledge of their pristine state,
Merg'd in gross vapour, and in night profound.
Thy wond'rous middle nature first appear'd,
When beauteous Venus from the silver'd foam,
The sounding sea's bright blossom rose to light.
But this, in symbols obvious to the wise,
Shows thy production from that fertile power,
Who first shines forth as demiurgic life,
Amid the ruling supermundane gods.
'Tis said, thy all-connecting nature sprung
From wretched penury, with plenty join'd:
For mind consider'd as the seat of forms,
Resembles want, self-unconfin'd, and void;
But as its own intelligible good,
Is perfect plentitude, divinely fair.
Hence as intelligence thy nature shines,
For ever pregnant with some new desire:
Now from thy father's rich abundance full,
Now thro' thy mother, poverty extreme;
Blest Lysian god! regard my suppliant pray'r,
And free my captive, but indignant soul,
From guileful Lethe's fascinating realms.
Disperse the noxious race of earthly loves,
That eagerly with wanton flames contend
To rouse desires phantastic and impure.
My soul illume with beams of holy fire,
And all her vivid mental powers expand;
That thus her lucid car, from sense refin'd,
May rapid rise, on flaming pinions borne,

And joyful gain her anagogic goal.
Oh haste my flight to those paternal rays
From which my soul with mind invested came,
And in her passage pluck'd Empyrean flowers.
For this, O give my soul's immortal depth
O'er sense and phantasy to reign supreme,
And all her amatory eyes extend
To truth's wide-spreading and prolific plain;
From whence intelligible light evolv'd,
Proceeds redundant thro' the mighty world,
And vig'rous agitates material forms.
For now reluctant in the realms of night,
Of folly weary, and with labours sad,
And hourly panting to depart, I roam.
Haste then, blest power, and burst the magic bonds
Which first thro' earthly love my soul enchain'd;
Nor longer thus afflicted and forlorn,
Prolong this death-like, unsubstantial life,
For ever rolling with impetuous speed,
Like some dark river, into matter's sea.
Or if still longer I am doom'd to roam,
A wretched exile, from thy fair domain;
Oh grant me soon the necessary means
(That ardent object of my soul's desire)
To fly indignant from the vulgar throng,
And lead in solitude a life divine.

---

1 For Love, in the Orphic theology, is in a certain respect the same as Phanes; and the following verse, preserved by Hermias, in his MS Commentary on the Phaedrus, shows that he is adorned with four eyes.

$$\text{Τετρασιν οφθαλμοισιν ορωμενος ενθα και ενθα.}$$

ie "possessing through four eyes an unbounded vision."

And that Phanes has four heads is well known: from which it appears that each head possesses but one eye; for if this is denied, some one of the heads must be destitute of sight. Hence, since Love is the exemplar of all daemon forms, we may perhaps collect the reason why the Homeric Polyphemus is one-eyed, or a Cyclops.

TO NEPTUNE

The second monad of the *ruling* kings,
A vital, super-mundane god, I sing:
Whose power, all life and origin unfolds,
And into beautiful progression calls.
Hail, fertile Neptune! whose extended might,
O'er all the planetary system reigns;
And gives perfection to its rolling orbs,
With motions vig'rous, various, and divine.
Whate'er the middle elements contain,
With moisture's fluctuating form replete,
'Tis thine with ever-watchful eye to guard;
And thro' the whole of generation's realms,
Earthquakes, and hollows, and irriguous caves,
Sacred to Naiads, to thy sway belong:
Whence souls in matter's flow'ring regions toss'd,
Are under thy dominion said to live.
The middle centre of the mighty world
With fertile life replete to thee belongs;
And ev'ry middle station thro' the whole
Is rul'd by thee, from whom its nature flows.
And as from Jove, paternal monad! springs
The three *commanding demiurgic* gods;
So from thy essence centre of the three,
The vital order, full of fertile power
And unpolluted energy, proceeds.
Hence *Proserpine* for ever flows from thee,
As super-mundane's life's exhaustless fount.
The wise of old invok'd thee as the same
With sacred *Justice*; whose all-piercing eye,
With vision unconfin'd and pure, perceives
The life and conduct of the human race.
For *Justice* only has the power to join
From *truth*'s equality opposing forms:
And *life* connects in union and consent
The different species of this mighty whole.
Hence from the Sun's bright middle throne 'tis thine,
Diffus'd thro' all things, over all to rule.

Hence, too, 'tis said, the *ever-fertile* muse,
The fair *Thalia*, is conjoin'd with thee;
Because thou pour'st, as from an endless fount,
The vig'rous streams of all-producing life:
And, 'midst the liberated gods, 'tis thine
The ever-circling ranks of souls to rule.
Earth-shaking, dark-hair'd god, regard my prayer,
And aid my captive, but indignant, soul
From Hyle's dread voracious rage to fly,
And gain her native, long-deserted home,
And blissful union with thy splendid form.
For once in truth's wide-spreading fertile plain,
Merg'd in thy central deity, I saw
The unknown unities of all the gods
Enshrin'd in perfect beauty's boundless light.
But when the madd'ning impulse of desire,
Produc'd by Hyle's fluctuating life,
With silent evolution guileful spread,
And caus'd oblivion of supernal goods;
In evil hour, unconscious of my change,
And fraught with seeds of bitter woe, to earth
I rush'd impetuous; but in falling pass'd
Thro' various-colour'd widely-wand'ring streams,
With guilt and ruin partners of my flight.
First in a whirlpool, livid and obscure,
Widely-diffus'd, voluminous and cold,
And sluggish in its course, my soul was plung'd.
Then thro' a gentle milk-white stream she fell,
Whose silv'ry waves with silent motion glide;
And pass'd from hence to one of ruddy fire,
Whose rapid waters roll with headlong rage
In glittering currents and sulphureous whirls.
Then thro' a river, beautiful and wide,
Whose golden streams are bright with glitt'ring flames,
I sunk, enamoured of phantastic forms,
Pregnant with death, and eager to be lost.
But farther still descending in my flight,
Next thro' a stream divinely fair I fell,
A stream nectareous, more than amber pure:
And then thro' one in rapid whirlpools toss'd,
With various colours bright, I thoughtless plung'd.

Last, thro' a current,[1] whose meand'ring streams
Produce all waters, foaming as they flow,
With ev'ry river's humid seeds replete,
I fell; by love of outward form ensnar'd,
And guileful nature's fascinating charms:
Till plung'd in infancy and night profound,
And in this earthly cumbrous shell inclos'd,
The soul's dark prison and Tartarian tomb,
I lost all knowledge of my former state,
And ancient union with thy central fount.
Fertile, triadic, all-producing god!
Regard the fervent tribute of my praise,
And haste my passage to my native home.
Oh burst the bands of generation's life,
Dark and delusive, impotent and vain;
Like the black ocean, rolling without rest,
And wildly toss'd, with loud-resounding storms.
Or if still longer I am doom'd to stay
A mourning exile from the courts of light,
O gracious free me from the baneful rage
Of all my marine and material foes;
Nor suffer me, abandon'd, to sustain
Th'o'erwhelming billows of dark matter's flood;
Where flying mockeries of perfect life,
In swift succession rise and disappear;
And to the eye of cogitation seem
Like shadows on a sea of shadow toss'd,
Which rise and vanish with delusive play,
And vainly imitate substantial forms.
Give mental peace and necessary health,
From vulgar cares, and cruel labours rest,
And wealth sufficient for a life divine:
That thus my days, in solitude conceal'd,
May shine auspicious, and with transport glide;
Spent in pursuit of intellectual good,
Deific visions of the highest forms,
And central union with the *god of gods*.

---

1 These seven streams signify the seven planetary spheres. See Martianus Capella.

TO MERCURY

Hear, blessed Hermes, Maia's beauteous son,
And first bright monad of the solar gods,
Whose splendid power enunciates and unfolds
To secondary natures mental light,
All beings fills with universal truth,
And by harmonic, anagogic arts
Unites them with *the intellects divine*;
Jove's lucid angel, ruler of mankind,
Whose hand the rod of blameless peace contains;
Great life-supporter, prophet of discourse,
And in necessities to mortals kind;
Rejoicing power, by all the gods rever'd;
Holy, august, *the source of lawful rites*,
And the soul's leader to a blessed life.
When lost in error on the dreary coast
Of Circe's[1] magic realms I roam'd forlorn,
Thy friendly aid enabled me to brave
The dire effects of her transforming power;
The sov'reign plant thy bounteous hand bestow'd,
Repell'd the mischief of her venom'd cup,
And gave my reason to preserve her sway
O'er sensual appetite's debasing arts.
But, when departing from th'enchanted bower,
Replete with Fraud, Calypso in her cave
Irriguous, lucid, with detaining charms
My soul beguil'd, and with phantastic bliss
In vain attempted to secure my stay,
Inspir'd by thee, I then reluctant lay
Absorb'd in thought, in her desiring arms,
And inly pining for my native home,
Consum'd in wretched solitude my days.
O'er generation's loud-resounding sea,
Huge, horrid, dark, I roll'd my streaming eyes
Indignant, and to view the pleasing coast
From whence, *self-banished*, wretchedly I roam'd,
Attempted often, but th'attempt was vain.
At length th'ensnaring goddess, urg'd by thee,

Reluctant yielded to the will of Jove,
And sorrowing sent me from her shadowy isle.
Then on the dreadful-sounding sea I sail'd
Of wand'ring generation, in thy light
Rejoicing, which with guiding radiance shone
On the dark deep, and gave me to discern
The blissful coast, where, splendid as the day,
Thy palace charms the wand'ring trav'ller's eye.
There intellectual banquets fill the soul
With true, substantial, undecaying food,
And joy unmixt with sensual revels reigns;
While thoughts refin'd to recollection's lyre
To rapture strung, the dance responsive form.
Serenely seated in this lucid dome,
Inspir'd by thee with salutary grief,
I mourn'd the follies of my pristine state,
And with redoubled ardour sigh'd for home.
For then at length, the soul-awakening chords
Of recollection's lyre I touch'd, which long
Had lain forgotten, and in darkness hid
On flow'ry Lethe's sleep-inspiring brink:
Till thy sagacious eye, and powerful arts
Pierc'd and dispell'd the wide-encircling gloom,
And to my ravish'd view the heav'nly gift restor'd,
And last, in wond'rous vessels fram'd by thee,
Light as a bird, with intellect replete,
I flew transported o'er the *swelling* waves
Of scientific Reas'ning's mighty sea,
Dissolv'd in pleasing intellectual rest,
Till from the deep recesses of my soul
I banish'd, by Minerva's friendly aid,
Insidious appetite's destructive rout,
And the lost empire of my mind regain'd.
All-bounteous power, by whom the soul is rais'd
From sleep profound to energy divine;
And whose convertive purifying arts,
Her bright ethereal vehicle restore
To *truth*'s all-splendid and immortal plain:
O! place me far above dread Hyle's sea,
Profoundly-whirling, horrible and vast,
Where flying mockeries of perfect life

In swift succession rise and disappear;
And to the eye of cogitation seem
Like shadows on a sea of shadow toss'd,
Which rise and vanish with delusive play,
And vainly imitate substantial forms.
For now my soul abhors the realms of night,
And pants impatient for the shining coast
And lawful kindred which she left behind,
When ensnar'd through love of outward form
And mad desire of change, on earth she fell.
But if still longer I am doom'd to roam
A mourning exile from the courts of light,
O gracious free me from the hostile rage
Of all my marine and material foes,
That thus the seeds of life-consuming care,
Dispers'd by thine all-liberating power,
My weary soul may find desir'd repose,
And lead in solitude a life divine.

1 See my explanation of the fable of Ulysses, in my *On the Allegory of the Wandering of Ulysses* [in *Select Works of Porphyry*, TTS vol. II].

TO LATONA

O thou who are the mother of all vivific light, which preserves all things by heat, and who art thyself a vivific fountain comprehended in Ceres the fountain of all life. O thou who dost illuminate the intellectual essences of the Gods, the orders of souls, and the whole sensible heaven, generating mundane light and establishing the cause of this light in thy all-splendid offspring Apollo and Diana. O thou who dost cause all things to glitter with intellectual and vivific light, and dost impart to souls the consummation of virtue, and an illumination which leads them back to the intellectual port of their father, hastily withdrawing them from the winding paths of matter, the entanglements of vice, and the roughness of the passage over the sea of generation. Graciously be pleased to impart to me an ineffable energy, a voluntary and blameless life, gentleness of manners, sanctity, and intellectual tranquillity. Be pleased also O most benevolent Goddess, to produce in my soul an oblivion of those evils which I have experienced in this terrestrial abode, in order that I may be able to rise with unimpeded energy from a sensible to an intelligible essence, and that entirely forgetting the roughness and storms of the sea of generation, I may at length be perfectly established in the exuberantly vivific fountain of thy all-splendid divinity.

TO OSIRIS

O all-bountiful, all-powerful, and all-merciful Osiris, who art the chief of the great Gods, the highest of the greater, the greatest of the highest, and the ruler of the greatest Gods. Thro' thy benificent power remaining pure, and unmingled with contrary perturbation and error, the parts of the universe continue in their proper order. Graciously be pleased shortly to enable me to triumph over my natal ills, and grant me a constant supply of accessory wealth, that thus I may have more enlarged opportunities of disseminating divine wisdom to the latest posterity.

TO ISIS

O all-bountiful, all-powerful, and all-merciful Isis, who art Queen of all the elements, the primordial progeny of the ages, the sovereign of the spirits of the dead, the first of the celestials, and the uniform resemblance of Gods and Goddesses; and whose legislative decrees can never be rescinded. Thou art the wife and sister of Osiris, and the mother of king Orus, and among the constellations thou risest refulgent in the dog-star. Thou are all that was, is, and will be, and no mortal has ever withdrawn the veil by which thou art concealed. The fruit likewise which thou hast brought forth, is that mighty Divinity the Sun. The life too of all things remains pure and incorruptible, because the occult vivific beauties of the productive principles contained in thee do not decend into flowing body which is the object of sight. Thou rulest by thy nod the luminous summits of the heavens, the salubrious breezes of the sea, and the deplorable silences of the realms beneath; and thy one Divinity which comprehends in itself the peculiarities of many other Divinities, the whole orb of the earth anciently venerated under a manifold form, by different rites, and a variety of appellations. Hence the primogenial Phrygians called thee Pessinuntica the Mother of the Gods; the Attic Aborigines, Cecropian Minerva; the floating Cyprians, Paphian Venus; the arrow-bearing Cretans, Diana Dyctynna; the three-tongued Sicilians, Stygian Proserpine; and the Eleusinians, the ancient Goddess Ceres. Some also called thee Juno, others Bellona, others Hecate, and others Rhamnusia. And those who were illuminated by the incipient rays of that all-splendid Divinity the Sun when he rises, *viz.* the Ethiopians, the Arii, and the Egyptians skilled in ancient learning, worshipping thee by ceremonies perfectly appropriate, called thee by thy true name Queen Isis. Graciously be pleased O Goddess to look upon me with an eye of divine mercy; bring my sorrows to a speedy termination; check the avenging anger of my material foes; enable me shortly to triumph over my natal ills; and grant me a constant supply of accessory wealth, that thus I may be enabled to make a greater proficiency in divine wisdom, and may have more enlarged opportunities of disseminating it to the latest posterity.

HYMNS

of

ANCIENT AUTHORS

Proclus

To the Sun

To the Muses

To Venus (1)

To Venus (2)

To Minerva

A Common Hymn

Boethius

To Jove

The Emperor Julian

To the Mother of Gods

TO THE SUN

Hear golden Titan! king of mental fire,
Ruler of light; to thee supreme belongs
The splendid key of life's prolific fount;
And from on high thou pour'st harmonic streams
In rich abundance into matter's worlds.[1]
Hear! for high rais'd above th'ætherial plains,
And in the world's bright middle orb[2] thou reign'st,
Whilst all things by thy sov'reign power are fill'd
With mind-exciting, providential care.
The starry fires surround thy vig'rous fire,
And ever in unweary'd, ceaseless dance,
O'er earth wide-bosom'd, vivid dew diffuse.
By thy perpetual and repeated course
The hours and seasons in succession rise;
And hostile elements their conflicts cease,
Soon as they view thy awful beams, great king,
From deity ineffable and secret born.[3]
The steady Parcæ, at thy high command,
The fatal thread of mortal life roll back;
For wide-extended, sov'reign sway is thine.
From thy fair series of attractive song,
Divinely charming, Phœbus into light
Leaps forth exulting; and with god-like harp,
To rapture strung, the raging uproar lulls
Of dire-resounding Hyle's[4] mighty flood.
From thy bland dance, repelling deadly ill,
Salubrious Pæan blossoms into light,
Health far diffusing, and th'extended world
With streams of harmony innoxious fills.
Thee too they celebrate in sacred hymns
Th'illustrious source whence mighty Bacchus came;
And thee in matter's utmost stormy depths
Euion[5] Ate they for ever sing.
But others sound thy praise in tuneful verse,
As fam'd Adonis, delicate and fair.
Ferocious dæmons,[6] noxious to mankind,
Dread the dire anger of thy rapid scourge;

Dæmons, who machinate a thousand ills,
Pregnant with ruin to our wretched souls,
That merg'd beneath life's dreadful-sounding sea,
In body's chains severely they may toil,
Nor e'er remember in the dark abyss
The splendid palace of their sire sublime.
O best of gods, blest dæmon crown'd with fire,
Image of nature's all-producing god,[7]
And the soul's leader to the realms of light -
Hear! and refine me from the stains of guilt;
The supplication of my tears receive,
And heal my wounds defil'd with noxious gore;
The punishments incurr'd by sin remit,
And mitigate the swift, sagacious eye
Of sacred justice, boundless in its view.
By thy pure law, dread evil's constant foe,
Direct my steps, and pour thy sacred light
In rich abundance on my clouded soul:
Dispel the dismal and malignant shades
Of darkness, pregnant with invenom'd ills,
And to my body proper strength afford,
With health, whose presence splendid gifts imparts.
Give lasting fame; and may the sacred care
With which the fair-hair'd muses gifts, of old
My pious ancestors preserv'd, be mine.
Add, if it please thee, all-bestowing god,
Enduring riches, piety's reward;
For power omnipotent invests thy throne,
With strength immense and universal rule.
And if the whirling spindle of the fates
Threats from the starry webs pernicion dire,
Thy sounding shafts with force resistless send,
And vanquish ere it fall th'impending ill.

---

1 *Matter's worlds.* According to the Chaldaic theology, there are seven corporeal worlds, *viz.* one empyrean, three ætherial, and three material, which last three consist of the inerratic sphere, the seven planetary spheres, and the sublunary region. But the empyrean and etherial worlds, when compared with the three last, are said to be immaterial, not that they are void of matter, but because the matter from which they are composed bears the relation of an immaterial essence to that of the other worlds, from the

extreme purity and vitality of its nature. I only add, that according to the same theology, the sun moves beyond the inerratic sphere in the last of the etherial worlds. See more concerning this in my notes to the *Cratylus*.

2   That is, in the last ætherial world, which is of course the middle of the seven worlds.

3   That is, from the first cause, or *The Good*. But the Sun is said, by way of eminence, to be the progeny of this highest god, on account of the analogy which he bears to him in his illuminations. For as *The Good* is the source of the light of the intelligible world, so Apollo gives light to the supermundane, and the sun to the sensible, worlds.

4   I have used the word *Hyle*, or *matter*, instead of *generation*, γενεθλη, which is employed by Proclus, because it is better adapted to the measure of the verses; but the meaning of each word is nearly the same, for the regions of matter are the regions of generation.

5   An epithet of Bacchus.

6   According to the most accurate division of the Demoniacal order, there are six species of dæmons, as we learn from the excellent Olympiodorus, in his Commentary on the *Phædo* of Plato. The first of these species is called *divine*, from subsisting according to *The One*, or that which is super-essential in the mundane gods; the second is denominated *intellectual*, from subsisting according to the intellect of these gods; the third is *rational*, from subsisting according to the soul with which the mundane gods are connected; the fourth is *natural*, being characterised from the nature which depends on these gods; the fifth is *corporeal*, subsisting according to their bodies; and the sixth is *material*, subsisting according to the matter which depends on these divinities. Or we may say, that some of these dæmons are *celestial*, others *etherial*, and others *aerial*; that some are *aquatic*, others *terrestrial*, and others *subterranean*. Olympiodorus adds, that irrational dæmons commence from the aerial species; in proof of which he cites the following verse from some oracles, (most probably from the Zoroastrian oracles):

Ηεριων ελατηρα κυνων κθονιων τε και υγρων.

That is, "Being the charioteer of the *aërial*, terrestrial, and aquatic dogs." For evil dæmons, as I have shewn in my *Dissertation on the Mysteries*, appear in the shape of dogs. And perhaps in this verse the sun is the charioteer alluded to, as it wonderfully agrees with what Proclus says of that deity in the verses before us. I only add, that when irrational dæmons are said to be evil, this must not be understood as if they were essentially evil, but that they are noxious only from their employment; that is, from their either calling forth the vices of depraved souls that they may be punished and cured, or from their inflicting punishment alone: for, indeed, there is not any thing essentially evil in the universe; for as the cause of all is goodness itself, every thing subsisting from thence must be endued with the form of good; since it is not the property of fire to refrigerate, nor of light to give obscurity, nor of goodness to produce from itself any thing evil.

7 That is, image of the first cause.

TO THE MUSES[1]

A sacred light I sing, which leads on high
Jove's nine fam'd daughters, ruler of the sky,
Whose splendours beaming o'er this sea of life,
On souls hard struggling with its storms of strife,
Through mystic rites perfective and refin'd,
(From books which stimulate the sluggish mind)
From earth's dire evils leads them to that shore,
Where grief and labour can infest no more;
And well instructs them how, with ardent wing,
From Lethe's deep, wide-spreading flood to spring,
And how once more their kindred stars to gain,
And ancient seats in truth's immortal plain,
From whence they wand'ring fell, thro' mad desire
Of matter's regions and allotments dire.
In me this rage repress, illustrious Nine
And fill my mental eye with light divine.
Oh may the doctrines of the wise inspire
My soul with sacred Bacchanalian fire,
Lest men, with filthy piety[2] replete,
From paths of beauteous light divert my feet.
Conduct my erring soul to sacred light,
From wand'ring generation's stormy night:
Wise thro' your volumes hence, the task be mine,
To sing in praise of eloquence divine,
Whose soothing power can charm the troubled soul,
And throbbing anguish and despair controul.
Hear, splendid goddesses, of bounteous mind,
To whom the helm of wisdom is assign'd,
And who the soul with all-attractive flame
Lead to the blest immortals whence she came,
From night profound enabling her to rise,
Forsake dull earth, and gain her native skies,
And with unclouded splendour fill the mind,
By rites ineffable of hymns refin'd.
Hear, mighty saviours! and with holy light,
While reading works divine illume my sight,
And dissipate these mists, that I may learn

Immortal gods from mortals to discern;
Lest, plung'd in drowsy Lethe's black abyss,
Some baneful dæmon keep my soul from bliss;
And lest deep merg'd in Hyle's stormy mire,
Her powers reluctant suffer tortures dire,
And some chill Fury with her freezing chain,
In ling'ring lethargy my life detain.
All-radiant governours of wisdom's light,
To me now hast'ning from the realms of night,
And ardent panting for the coasts of day,
Thro' sacred rites benignant point the way,
And mystic knowledge to my view disclose,
Since this for ever from your nature flows.

1 Proclus, in his Scholia on the *Cratylus*, beautifully observes as follows, concerning the Muses: "The whole world is bound in indissoluble bonds from Apollo and the Muses, and is both one and all-perfect, through the communications of these divinities; possessing the former through the Apolloniacal monad,[†] but its all-perfect subsistence through the number of the Muses. For the number nine, which is generated from the first perfect number, (that is, three) is, through similitude and sameness, accommodated to the multiform causes of the mundane order and harmony; all of them at the same time being collected into one summit for the purpose of producing one consummate perfection; for the Muses generate the variety of reasons with which the world is replete; but Apollo comprehends in union all the multitude of these. And the Muses give subsistence to the harmony of soul; but Apollo is the leader of intellectual and indivisible harmony. The Muses distribute the phænomena according to harmonical reasons; but Apollo comprehends unapparent and separate harmony. And though both give subsistence to the same things, yet the Muses effect this according to number, but Apollo according to union. And the Muses indeed distribute the unity of Apollo; but Apollo unites and contain, harmonic multitude: for the multitude of the Muses proceeds from the essence of *Musagetes*, which is both separate and subsists according to the nature of *The One*."

2 Proclus here, I have no doubt, alludes to the Christians, and particularly to the Catholics, who were not in his days (the fifth century) a sect as they now are. But the reason why he calls them men full of *filthy piety* is, we

---

† Apollo is the monad of the Muses, *i.e.* is the proximately exempt producing cause of their multitude, and in which their summits are fixed like the roots of trees in the earth.

may presume, in the first place, because they worshipped a *mere man* as the first cause, which is certainly not only a *filthy*, but a *horrid* species of impiety; and in the next place, because they prayed to the departed souls of men who, when living, professed this *filthy piety*, which was still rendering their impiety more odious and impure.

TO VENUS[1]

A celebrated royal fount I sing,
From foam begotten, and of Loves the spring,
Those winged, deathless powers, whose gen'ral sway
In diff'rent modes all mortal tribes obey.
With mental darts some pierce the god-like soul,
And freedom rouse unconscious of controul;
That anxious hence the centre to explore
Which lead on high from matter's stormy shore,
The ardent soul may meditate her flight,
And view their mother's palaces of light.
But others, watchful of their father's will,
Attend his councils and his laws fulfil,
His bounteous providence o'er all extend,
And strengthen generation without end.
And others last, the most inferior kind,
Preside o'er marriage, and its contracts bind,
Intent a race immortal to supply
From man calamitous and doom'd to die.
While all Cythera's high commands obey,
And bland attention to her labours pay.
O venerable goddess ! hear my prayer,
For nought escapes thine universal ear:
Whether t'embrace the mighty heav'n is thine,
And send the world from thence a soul divine;
Or whether, seated in th'ætherial plain,
Above these seven-fold starry orbs you reign,
Imparting to our ties, with bounteous mind,
A power untam'd, a vigour unconfin'd; -
Hear me, O goddess, and my life defend,
With labours sad, and anxious for their end;
Transfix my soul with darts of holy fire,
And far avert the flames of base desire.

---

1 For an account of this divinity, consult my notes on the *Cratylus*.

TO VENUS

Thee, Venus, royal Lycian queen, I sing,
To whom of old by deity inspir'd,
In grateful signal of thy fav'ring aid,
Our country's guides, a sacred temple rais'd
In Lycia; of the intellectual rites
Symbolical, which link'd in Hymen's bands
Celestial Venus and the god of fire.
Olympian hence they called thee, by whose power
They oft avoided death's destructive ire,
To virtue looking; and from fertile beds
Through thee, an offspring provident and strong
Rose into light; while all their days were crown'd
With gentle peace, the source of tranquil bliss.
Illustrious queen! benignantly accept
The grateful tribute of this sacred hymn,
For we from Lycian blood derive our birth.
Expel base passions from my wand'ring soul,
And once more raise her to true beauty's light;
Averting far the irritation dire,
And rage insane, of earth-begotten love.

TO MINERVA

Daughter of ægis-bearing Jove, divine,
Propitious to thy vot'ries prayer incline;
From thy great father's fount supremely bright,
Like fire resounding, leaping into light.
Shield-bearing goddess, hear, to whom belong
A manly mind, and power to tame the strong!
Oh, sprung from matchless might, with joyful mind
Accept this hymn; benevolent and kind!
The holy gates of wisdom by thy hand
Are wide unfolded; and the daring band
Of earth-born giants, that in impious fight
Strove with thy sire, were vanquish'd by thy might.
Once by thy care, as sacred poets sing,
The heart of Bacchus, swiftly-slaughter'd king,
Was sav'd in æther, when, with fury fir'd,
The Titans fell against his life conspir'd;
And with relentless rage and thirst for gore,
Their hands his members into fragments tore:
But ever watchful of thy father's will,
Thy pow'r preserv'd him from succeeding ill,
Till from the secret counsels of his sire,
And born from Semele through heav'nly fire,
Great Dionysius to the world at length
Again appear'd with renovated strength.
Once, too, thy warlike axe, with matchless sway,
Lopp'd from their savage necks the heads away
Of furious beasts, and thus the pests destroy'd
Which long all-seeing Hecate annoy'd.
By thee benevolent great Juno's might
Was rous'd, to furnish mortals with delight:
And through life's wide and various range 'tis thine
Each part to beautify with arts divine:
Invigorated hence by thee, we find
A demiurgic impulse in the mind.
Towers proudly rais'd, and for protection strong,
To thee, dread guardian, deity belong,
As proper symbols of th'exalted height

Thy series claims amidst the courts of light.
Lands are belov'd by thee to learning prone,
And Athens, O Athena, is thy own!
Great goddess, hear! and on my dark'ned mind
Pour thy pure light in measure unconfin'd; -
That sacred light, O all-protecting queen,
Which beams eternal from thy face serene:
My soul, while wand'ring on the earth, inspire
With thy own blessed and impulsive fire;
And from thy fables, mystic and divine,
Give all her powers with holy light to shine.
Give love, give wisdom, and a power to love,
Incessant tending to the realms above;
Such as, unconscious of base earth's control,
Gently attracts the vice-subduing soul;
From night's dark region aids her to retire,
And once more gain the palace of her sire:
And if on me some just misfortune press,
Remove th'affliction, and thy suppliant bless.
All-Saving goddess, to my prayer incline![1]
Nor let those horrid punishments be mine[1]
Which guilty souls in Tartarus confine,[1]
With fetters fast'ned to its brazen floors,
And lock'd by hell's tremendous iron doors.
Hear me, and save (for power is all thy own)
A soul desirous to be thine alone.

---

1 These lines are wanting in the first edition of this hymn in my *Dissertation on the Mysteries*; and this because the verse to which they correspond in the Greek was not then properly corrected.

A COMMON HYMN

Hail, mother goddess! beauteous offspring fam'd:
Hail, strenuous Hecate! Prothyraea nam'd:
Grandfather Janus, undecaying Jove,
With Jove supreme, enthron'd all height above,
Hail! may the blissful road of life be mine,
With ev'ry good replete of light divine:
And from my members dire disease expel,
That splendid-gifted health with me may dwell.
My soul insanely wand'ring on the earth,
Though intellectual regions gave her birth,
Attract to heav'n with vigour unconfin'd,
Through mysteries which rouse the dormant mind.
Your helping hands, all-bounteous powers, extend,
And paths divine unfold as I ascend.
Give me to see those beams of glorious light,
Which aid the soul from Generation's night,
Dark, dreary, dire, indignantly to fly,
And rapidly regain her native sky.
Extend your hands, and with your fav'ring gales,
While bound for home I raise th'impatient sails,
Impel my vessel o'er life's stormy main,
Till the fair port of Piety I gain;
For there my soul, with mighty toils oppress'd,
Shall find her long-lost Paradise of rest.

A HYMN TO JOVE[1]

From Boethius' *Consolation of Philosophy*

Parent of nature, venerable mind,
Of pow'r immense, of wisdom unconfin'd;
Whose stable nature free from fate's control,
By endless reasons rules this mighty whole.
Supremely fair, yet not earth's beauteous plains,
But that from which the earth its beauty gains.
The river's beauty when with gentle course
It glides along, or rolls with rapid force;
The beauty of the heav'ns, with all the train
Of stars that glitter on the ethereal plain;
To thee, great source, their sev'ral beauties owe,
And from thy matchless charms their graces flow.
By thy command through endless ages past,
Time has endur'd, and shall for ever last;
Whose flowing nature without check or stay,
Like some swift stream glides rapidly away:
Unlike thy being, O supremely great,
Which, ever perfect, knows no change of state.
Thee no external causes could induce,
From matter's womb all nature to produce;
Inherent goodness destitute of spleen,
The plan devis'd, and rais'd the bounteous scene.
Hence by a just analogy we find,
A world more perfect in thy sov'reign mind;
Another sun, whose rays divinely bright,
Give to our source of day its vig'rous light;
Another moon, whose fertile beams supply
With mental light an intellectual sky:
For as the substance forms its following shade
So from the world divine this universe was made.
Through such a pattern, great beyond compare,
The perfect world has wholes[2] complete and fair.
Hence hostile elements no longer fight,
But bound in measure peaceably unite;
The cold and hot in perfect friendship join,

And moist and dry in firm embrace combine.
Imprison'd thus, the subtle force of heat
In vain aspires to gain its native seat;
And heavy parts of earth in vain may try,
To break the league, and in the centre lie.
From thee the soul derives her triple frame,
Form'd from two natures, *different* and *same*.
Hence, through apt limbs diffus'd, one general soul
Pervades and animates this mighty whole.
While in two orbs its vivid force divides,
And with unerring skill o'er all presides;
The circle,[3] one of intellectual life,
And one[4] the boundary of death and strife;
Where mutability maintains her sway,
And life immortal rises from decay.
But soon the scatter'd powers together meet,
And in their ancient source again retreat;
The mundane soul in one eternal round,
Encircling in her course the mind profound,
Derives of sov'reign good a large supply,
And in its beauteous image rolls the sky.
From thee proceeds the wide extended train
Of mundane gods o'er Truth's immortal plain;
With ardent love thy glories they survey,
And bask for ever in the dazzling ray.
In order next the daemon forms appear,
And heroes close the long majestic rear.
By thee fit bodies are to each applied,
And each, with star-like vehicles supplied;
While ev'ry rank a different charge assign'd,
In heaven presides, or is to earth confin'd.
And as from thee proceeds their life divine,
To thee alone their glorious forms incline;
In endless circles round thy beams they run,
Like stars returning to their fontal sun.
O parent of the world, immensely great!
Give me to rise to thy exalted seat;
With ravish'd eyes to view the beauteous store
Of sov'reign good, and trace its wonders o'er.
Give me through intellect's unclouded light,
In thee to fix the piercing mental sight;

To leave the sordid mass of earth behind,
And soar to thee with vigour unconfin'd;
To drink the waters of the life divine;
And with thy own immortal splendours shine.
For since no change thy perfect being knows,
The good alone in thee can find repose.
To view thy glories bursting on the sight,
The principle must be of true delight;
The goal to which, though ignorant, we tend,
And of each restless wish the secret end.
Supporter, ruler, father of mankind,
The path that leads to bliss, the light of mind;
Whose nature is the source whence order flows,
And though it bounds the world no limit knows.

1   This is an untitled work: the dedication to Jove is suggest by the Prometheus Trust.

2   Boethius composed this line -

Perfectasque jubens, *perfectum* absolvere parteis,

from the following passage in the *Timæus* of Plato: Των δε δη τετταρων εν ολον εκαστον ειληφεν η του κοσμου συστασις. εκ γαρ πυρος παντος υδατος τε και αερος και γης, συνεστησεν αυτον ο συνιστασ. τα δε διανοηθεις πρωτον μεν, ινα ολον οτι μαλιστα ζωον τελειον εκ τελειων των μερων ειη. That is, "The composition of the world therefore, received one *whole* of each of these four natures: for its composing artificer constituted it from *all* fire, water, air, and earth. For by a reasoning process he concluded in the first place, that it would thus be a *whole* animal, in the highest degree *perfect* from *perfect parts*."

The doctrine of these *perfect parts, or wholes* of the universe, is of the first importance in the philosophy of Plato, and forms one of the grand articles of belief in the creed of the Platonic philosopher.

Lord Bacon, as I have remarked in the Introduction to my translation of Plato's works, *sagely* observes, "that wings are not to be added to the human intellect, but rather lead and weights; that all its leaps and flights may be restrained. That this is not yet done, but, that when it is, we may entertain better hopes respecting the sciences." - "Itaque hominum intellectui non plumæ addendæ, sed plumbum potius, et pondera; ut cohibeant omnem saltum et volatum. Atque hoc adhuc factum non est; quum vero factum fuerit, melius de scientiis sperare licebit." See the 104th Aphorism of his *Novum Organum*.

Now this being the case, it may seem wonderful that no one of the numerous *viri summi*, who have written commentaries on this work of Boethius, should have any conception of the meaning of these perfect parts; for by inspecting their commentaries, it is obvious that they had not. And the wonder is greatly increased when we consider that all these *illustrious* men were *well grounded* at great Grammar Schools, than which no Institutions were ever better devised to *add lead and weights to human intellect, and restrain all its leaps and flights!*

3 This circle is called by Plato in the *Timæus*, the circle of *sameness*, and is the *dianoetic* part of the soul, or that part that reasons scientifically.

4 This circle Plato calls the circle of *difference*, and is that part of the soul that *opines*.

From the Oration

TO THE MOTHER OF GODS

By The Emperor Julian

A mother of gods and men! O assistant and partner in the throne of mighty Jupiter! O fountain of the intellectual gods! O thou whose nature concurs with the uncontaminated essences of intelligibles, and who, receiving a common cause from all intelligibles, dost impart it to intellectual natures! Vivific goddess, Counsel and Providence, and the fabricator of our souls! O thou who didst love the mighty Bacchus, who didst preserve the castrated Attis, and when he had fallen into the cavern of earth, didst again lead him upwards to his pristine abode! O thou who art the leader of every good to the intellectual gods, with which thou dost likewise fill this sensible world, and who dost impart to us all possible good in every thing belonging to our nature! Graciously bestow upon all men felicity, the summit of which is the knowledge of the gods: but especially grant to the Roman people in common, that they may wipe away the stains of their impiety; and that they may be blessed with prosperous fortune, which, in conjunction with them, may govern the empire for many thousands of years. But with respect to myself, may the fruit of my cultivation to thy divinity be the possession of truth in dogmata concerning the gods, perfection in Theurgy, in all the actions which I shall undertake, both political and military, virtue, in conjunction with good fortune; and lastly a departure from the present life without pain, and attended with glory, together with good hope of a progression to thy divinity.

Appendix I

Dissertation on

The Hymns of Orpheus

From the original 1787 edition of
The Mystical Initiations; or, Hymns of Orpheus.

Preface

There is doubtless a revolution in the literary, correspondent to that of the natural world. The face of things is continually changing; and the perfect and perpetual harmony of the universe subsists by the mutability of its parts. In consequence of this fluctuation, different arts and sciences have flourished at different periods of the world: but the complete circle of human knowledge has, I believe, never subsisted at once, in any nation or age. Where accurate and profound researches into the principles of things have advanced to perfection, there, by a natural consequence, men have neglected the disquisition of particulars: and where sensible particulars have been the general object of pursuit, the science of universals has languished, or sunk into oblivion and contempt.

Thus wisdom, the object of all true philosophy, considered as exploring the causes and principles of things, flourished in high perfection among the Egyptians first, and afterwards in Greece. Polite literature was the pursuit of the Romans; and experimental enquiries, increased without end, and accumulated without order, are the employment of modern philosophy. Hence we may justly conclude, that the age of true philosophy is no more. In consequence of very extended natural discoveries, trade and commerce have increased, while abstract investigations have necessarily declined: so that modern enquiries never rise above sense; and every thing is despised which does not in some respect or other contribute to the accumulation of wealth, the gratification of childish admiration, or the refinements of corporeal delight. The author of the following translation, therefore, cannot reasonably expect, that his labours will meet with the approbation of the many: since these Hymns are too ancient, and too full of the Greek philosophy, to please the ignorant and the sordid. However, he hopes they will be acceptable to the few, who have drawn wisdom from its source and who consider the science of universals as first in the nature of things, though last in the progressions of human understanding.

The translator has adopted rhyme, not because most agreeable to general taste, but because he believes it necessary to the poetry of the English language, which requires something as a substitute for the energetic cadence of the Greek and Latin Hexameters. Could this be obtained by any other means, he would immediately relinquish his partiality for rhyme, which is certainly when well executed, far more difficult than blank verse, as the following Hymns must evince, in an eminent degree.

And, here it is necessary to observe, with respect to translation, that nothing is more generally mistaken in its nature, or more faulty in its execution. The author of the Letters on Mythology gives it as his opinion, that it is impossible to translate an ancient author so as to do justice to his meaning. If he had confined this sentiment to the beauties of the composition, it would doubtless have been just; but to extend it to the meaning of an author is to make truth and opinion partial and incommunicable. Every person, indeed, acquainted with the learned languages, must be conscious how much the beauty of an ancient author generally suffers by translation, though undertaken by men who have devoted the greatest part of their lives to the study of words alone. This failure, which has more than any thing contributed to bring the ancients into contempt with the unlearned, can only be ascribed to the want of genius in the translators: for the sentiment of Pythagoras is peculiarly applicable to such as these, that many carry the Thyrsus, but few are inspired with the spirit of the God. But this observation is remarkably verified in the translators of the ancient philosophy, whose performances are for the most part without animation; and consequently retain nothing of the fire and spirit of the original. Perhaps, there is but one exception to this remark, and that is Mr. Sydenham: whose success in such an arduous undertaking can only be ascribed to his possessing the philosophical genius, and to his occasionally paraphrasing passages, which would otherwise be senseless and inanimate.

Indeed, where languages differ so much as the ancient and modern, the most perfect method, perhaps, of transferring the philosophy from the one language to the other is by a faithful and animated paraphrase: faithful, with regard to retaining the sense of the author, and animated, with respect to preserving the fire of the original; calling it forth when latent, and expanding it when condensed. Such a one will every where endeavour to improve the light, and fathom the depth of his author; to elucidate what is obscure, and to amplify what in modern language would be unintelligibly concise.

Thus most of the compound epithets of which the following Hymns chiefly consist, though very beautiful in the Greek language, yet, when literally translated into ours, lose all their propriety and force. In their native tongue, as in a prolific soil, they diffuse their sweets with full-blown elegance, but shrink like the sensitive plant at the touch of the verbal critic, or the close translator. He who would preserve their philosophical beauties, and exhibit them to others in a different language, must expand their elegance, by the supervening and enlivening rays of the philosophic fire; and, by the powerful breath of genius, scatter abroad their latent but copious sweets.

If some sparks of this celestial fire shall appear to have animated the bosom of the translator, he will consider himself as well rewarded, for his laborious undertaking. The ancient philosophy has been for many years the only study of his retired leisure; in which he has found an inexhaustible treasure of intellectual wealth, and a perpetual fountain of wisdom and delight. Presuming that such a pursuit must greatly advantage the present undertaking, and feeling the most sovereign contempt for the sordid drudgery of hired composition, he desires no other reward, if he has succeeded, than the praise of the liberal; and no other defence if he has failed, than the decision of the candid, and discerning few.

Section I

The great obscurity and uncertainty in which the history of Orpheus is involved affords very little matter for our information; and even renders that little, inaccurate and precarious. Upon surveying the annals of past ages, it seems that the greatest geniuses have been subject to this historical darkness; as is evident in those great lights of antiquity, Homer and Euclid, whose writings indeed enrich mankind with perpetual stores of knowledge and delight; but whose lives are for the most part concealed in impenetrable oblivion. But this historical uncertainty is no where so apparent as in the person of Orpheus, whose name is indeed acknowledged and celebrated by all antiquity (except perhaps Aristotle alone); while scarcely a vestige of his life is to be found amongst the immense ruins of time. For who has ever been able to affirm any thing with certainty, concerning his origin, his age, his parents, his country, and condition? This alone may be depended on, from general assent, that there formerly lived a person named Orpheus, whose father was Oeagrus, who lived in Thrace, and who was the son of a king, who was the founder of theology among the Greeks, the institutor of their life and morals, the first of prophets, and the prince of poets; himself the offspring of a Muse; who taught the Greeks their sacred rites and mysteries, and from whose wisdom, as from a perpetual and abundant fountain, the divine muse of Homer, and the philosophy of Pythagoras and Plato, flowed; and, lastly, who by the melody of his lyre, drew rocks, woods, and wild beasts, stopped rivers in their course, and even moved the inexorable king of hell; as every page, and all the writings of antiquity sufficiently evince. Since thus much then may be collected from universal testimony, let us pursue the matter a little farther, by investigating more accurately the history of the original Orpheus with that of the great men who have, at different periods, flourished under this venerable name.

The first and genuine Orpheus was a poet of Thrace, and, according to the opinion of many, the disciple of Linus; who flourished, says Suidas, at the time when the kingdom of the Athenians was dissolved. Some assert that he was prior to the Trojan wars, and that he lived eleven, or according to others, nine generations. But the Greek word γενεα, or generation, according to Gyraldus[†] signifies the space of seven years; for unless this is supposed, how is it possible that the period of his life can have any foundation in the nature of things? Plutarch indeed, Heraclitus, Suidas, and some grammarians, assert that this word signifies a space of thirty years: but omitting the discussion of this latter opinion, from its impossibility, we shall embrace the former, agreeable to which Orpheus lived sixty-three years; a period, if we may believe the astrologers, fatal to all, and especially to great men, as was the case with Cicero and Aristotle.

Our poet, according to fabulous tradition, was torn in pieces by Ciconian women: on which account, Plutarch affirms the Thracians were accustomed to beat their wives, that they might revenge the death of Orpheus. Hence, in the vision of Herus Pamphilius, in Plato, the soul of Orpheus, being destined to descend into another body, is reported to have chosen rather that of a swan than to be

---

[†] Syntag. Poet. p. 54.

born again of a woman; having conceived such hatred against the sex, on account of his violent death. The cause of his destruction is variously related by authors. Some report that it arose from his being engaged in puerile loves, after the death of Eurydice. Others, that he was destroyed by women intoxicated with wine, because he was the means of men relinquishing their connexion. Others affirm, according to the tradition of Pausanias, that upon the death of Eurydice, wandering to Aornus, a place in Threspotia, where it was customary to evocate the souls of the dead, having recalled Eurydice to life, and not being able to detain her, he destroyed himself; nightingales building their nests, and bringing forth their young upon his tomb; whose melody, according to report, exceeded every other of this species. Others again ascribe his laceration to his having celebrated every divinity except Bacchus, which is very improbable, as among the following hymns there are nine to that Deity, under different appellations. Others report that he was delivered by Venus herself into the hands of the Ciconian women, because his mother Calliope had not determined justly between Venus and Proserpine, concerning the young Adonis. Many affirm that he was struck by lightning, according to Pausanias; and Diogenes confirms this by the following verses composed, as he asserts, by the Muses upon his death:

> Here, by the Muses plac'd, with golden lyre,
> Great Orpheus rests; destroy'd by heav'nly fire.

Again, the sacred mysteries called Threscian derived their appellation from our Thracian bard, because he first introduced sacred rites and religion into Greece; and hence the authors of initiation in these mysteries were called Orpheotelestae. Besides, according to Lucian, our Orpheus brought astrology and the magical arts into Greece; and with respect to his drawing trees and wild beasts by the melody of his lyre, Palaephatus accounts for it as follows.[†] The mad Bacchanalian nymphs, says he, having violently taken away cattle and other necessaries of life, retired for some days into the mountains. When the citizens, having expected their return for a long time, and fearing the worst for their wives and daughters, called Orpheus, and entreated him to invent some method of drawing them from the mountains. But he tuning his lyre, agreeable to the orgies of Bacchus, drew the mad nymphs from their retreats; who descended from the mountains

---

† Opusc. Mythol. p. 45.

bearing at first ferulae and branches of every kind of trees. But to the men who were eye-witnesses of these wonders, they appeared at first to bring down the very woods; and from hence gave rise to the fable.

But so great was the reputation of Orpheus, that he was deified by the Greeks; and Philostratus relates, that his head gave oracles in Lesbos, which, when separated from his body by the Thracian women, was, together with his lyre, carried down the river Hebrus into the Sea. In this manner, says Lucian,[†] singing as it were his funeral oration, to which the chords of his lyre, impelled by the winds, gave a responsive harmony, it was brought to Lesbos and buried. But his lyre was suspended in the Temple of Apollo; where it remained for a considerable space of time. Afterwards, when Neanthus, the son of Pittacus the tyrant, found that the lyre drew trees and wild beasts with its harmony, he earnestly desired its possession; and having corrupted the priest privately with money, he took the Orphean lyre, and fixed another similar to it, in the temple. But Neanthus considering that he was not safe in the city in the day time, departed from it by night; having concealed the lyre in his bosom, on which he began to play. But as he was a rude and unlearned youth, he confounded the chords; yet pleasing himself with the sound, and fancying he produced a divine harmony, he considered himself as the blessed successor of Orpheus. However, in the midst of his transports, the neighbouring dogs, roused by the sound, fell upon the unhappy harper and tore him to pieces. The former part of this fable is thus excellently explained by Proclus in his commentaries (or rather fragments of commentaries) on Plato's *Republic*; a work I would earnestly recommend to the liberal, for the great light it affords to the recondite theology of the Greeks. Orpheus, says he, on account of his perfect erudition, is reported to have been destroyed in various ways; because, in my opinion, men of that age, participated partially of the Orphic harmony; for they could not receive a universal and perfect science. But the principal part of his melody was received by the Lesbians; and on this account, perhaps, the head of Orpheus, when separated from his body, is said to have been carried to Lesbos. Fables of this kind, therefore, are related of Orpheus, no otherwise than of Bacchus, of whose mysteries he was the priest. Thus far Proclus, and thus much concerning the first, or Thracian Orpheus. The second Orpheus was an Arcadian, or,

---

[†] In Oratione ad Indoctum.

according to others, a Ciconian, from Bisaltia of Thrace, and is reported to be more ancient than Homer, and the Trojan war. He composed figments of fables called (μυθοποιια) and epigrams; and is, according to Gyraldus, the author of the following hymns; though I rather choose to refer them, with the Fathers Vossius and Eschenbach, to Onomacritus, or the fourth Orpheus, of Crotonia. The third Orpheus was of Odrysius, a city of Thrace, near the river Hebrus; but Dionysius, in Suidas, denies his existence. The fourth Orpheus was of Crotonia, who flourished in the time of Pisistratus, about the fiftieth Olympiad; and is doubtless the same Onomacritus the author of these hymns. He wrote Decennalia, δεκαετηρια, and, in the opinion of Gyraldus, the Argonautics, which are now extant under the name of Orpheus, with other writings called Orphical, but which, according to Cicero,[†] some ascribe to Cecrops the Pythagorean. The last Orpheus was Camarinaeus, a most excellent versifier; and the same according to Gyraldus whose descent into hell is so universally known. And thus much for the life of Orpheus.

Section II

Let us now proceed to his theology; exchanging the obscurity of conjecture for the light of clear evidence; and the intricate labyrinths of fable for the delightful though solitary paths of truth. And here I must acquaint the reader, that I shall every where deduce my information from the writings of the latter Platonists, as the only sources of genuine knowledge, on this sublime and obsolete enquiry.[‡] The vulgar systems of mythology are here entirely useless; and he who should attempt to elucidate the theology, or hymns of Orpheus, by any modern hypothesis, would be as ridiculously employed, as he who should expect to find the origin of a copious stream, by pursuing it to its last and most intricate involutions. In conformity with modern prejudices, the author of the *Letters on Mythology* endeavours to prove, that the Orphic hymns deify the various parts of nature, not considered as animated by different intelligences but as various modifications of inert and lifeless matter. This hypothesis is no doubt readily embraced by the present philosophers, a great part of whom

---

[†] In I. De Nat. Deor.

[‡] In the latter part of this Dissertation, we shall discourse on the agreement between the doctrine of Orpheus and the Platonists.

deny the existence of any thing incorporeal; and the better sort, who acknowledge one supreme immaterial Being, exclude the agency of subordinate intelligences in the government of the world; though this doctrine is perfectly philosophical, and at the same time consistent with revelation. The belief indeed of the man who looks no higher than sense must be necessarily terminated by appearances. Such a one introduces a dreadful chasm in the universe; and diffuses the deity through the world like an extended substance; divided with every particle of matter, and changed into the infinite varieties of sensible forms. But with the ancient philosopher, the deity is an immense and perpetually exuberant fountain; whose streams originally filled and continually replenish the world with life. Hence the universe contains in its ample bosom all general natures, divinities visible and invisible; the illustrious race of dæmons; the noble army of exalted souls; and men rendered happy by wisdom and virtue. According to this theology, the power of universal soul does not alone diffuse itself to the sea, and become bounded by its circumfluent waters, while the wide expanse of air and aether is destitute of life and soul; but the celestial spaces are filled with souls, supplying life to the stars, and directing their revolutions in everlasting order. So that the celestial orbs in imitation of intellect, which seeks after nothing external, are wisely agitated in perpetual circuit round the central sun. While some things participate of being alone, others of life, and others are endued with sentient powers; some possess the still higher faculty of reason; and, lastly, others are all life and intelligence.

But let us rise a little higher, and contemplate the arguments by which the Platonists establish the Orphic doctrine of the existence and agency of subordinate intelligences. Thus then they reason.[†] Of all beings it is necessary that some should move only, that others should be entirely moved; and that the beings situated between these two should participate of the extremes, and both move and be moved. Among the first in dignity and order are those natures which move only; the second, those which move themselves; the third, those which move and are moved; and the fourth, those which are moved only. Now the second class of these, or the self-motive natures, since their perfection consists in transition and mutation of life, must depend upon a more ancient cause, which subsists perpetually the same; and whose life is not conversant with the circulations of time, but is constituted in the stable essence of eternity. But it is necessary

---

† Procl. lib. i. Theol. Plat.

that the third class, which both move and are moved, should depend on a self-motive nature. For a self-motive being is the cause of motion to those which are moved by another, in the same manner as that which is immovable inserts in all beings the power of moving. And again, that which is moved only must depend on those natures which are indeed moved by another, but which are themselves endued with a motive-power. For it is necessary that the chain of beings should be complete; every where connected by proper mediums, and deduced in an orderly and perpetual series, from the principle to the extremes. All bodies therefore belong to those natures which are moved only, and are naturally passive; since they are destitute of all inherent energy, on account of their sluggish nature, which participates of division, magnitude, and weight.

But of incorporeals some are divisible about bodies; while others are entirely free from such an affection about the lowest order of beings. Hence such things as are divided about the dead weight of bodies, whether they are material qualities or forms, belong to the orders of nature's moving and at the same time moved. For such as these because incorporeal, participate of a motive faculty; but because they are also divided about bodies, they are on this account exempt from incorporeal perfection, are filled with material inactivity, and require the energy of a self-motive nature. Where then shall we find this self-motive essence? For such things as are extended with magnitude, oppressed by material weight, and inseparably reside in bodies, must necessarily either move only, or be moved by others. But it is requisite, as we have before observed, that prior to this order, the self-motive essence should subsist. And hence we conclude that there is another certain nature exempt from the passivity and imperfection of bodies, existing not only in the heavens, but in the ever-changing elements, from which the motion of bodies is primarily derived. And this nature is no other than soul, from which animals derive their life and motive power; and which even affords an image of self-motion to the unstable order of bodies.

If then the self-motive essence is more ancient than that which is moved by another, but soul is primarily self-motive, hence soul must be more ancient than body; and all corporeal motion must be the progeny of soul, and of her inherent energy. It is necessary, therefore, that the heavens, with all their boundless contents, and their various natural motions (for a circular motion is natural to such bodies), should be endued with governing souls, essentially more ancient than their revolving bodies. According to the Platonic philosophers, therefore, these souls which orderly distinguish the universe and its contained parts, from their inherent cause of motion, give life and motion to every inanimate body. But it is necessary that every motive essence, should either move all things rationally, or irrationally; that is, either according to the uniform and unerring laws of reason, or according to the brutal impulse of an irrational nature. But the constant order observed in the periods of the celestial bodies, the convenience of their positions, and the admirable laws by which their revolutions are directed, plainly evince that their motions are governed by a rational nature. If therefore, an intellectual and rational soul governs the universe, and if every thing eternally moved is under the directing influence of such a soul, may we not enquire whether it possesses this intellectual, perfect, and beneficent power, by participation, or essentially? for if essentially, it is necessary that every soul should be intellectual, since every soul is naturally self-motive. But if by participation, there must be another nature more ancient than soul, which operates entirely from energy;. and whose essence is intelligence, on account of that uniform conception of universals, which it essentially contains. Because it is also necessary that the soul, essentially rational, should receive intellect by participation, and that intellectual energy should be of two kinds; one primarily subsisting in the divine intellect; but the other subsisting secondarily in its offspring soul. You may add too, the presence of intellectual illumination in body, which is received in as great perfection as its unstable and obscure nature will admit. For how is it possible that the celestial orbs should be for ever circularly moved in one definite order, preserving the same form, and the same immutable power, unless they participated of an intellectual nature. For soul is indeed the constant supplier of motion; but the cause of perpetual station, of identity and uniform life, reducing unstable motion to a circular revolution, and to a condition eternally the same, must be more ancient than soul.

Body, indeed, and whatever is the object of sense, belongs to the order of things moved by another. But soul is self-motive, embracing in itself, in a connected manner, all corporeal motions. And prior to this is immovable intellect. And here it is requisite to observe, that this immaterial nature must not be conceived as similar to any thing inert, destitute of life, and endued with no spirit, but as the principal cause of all motion, and the fountain of all life; as well of that whose streams perpetually return into itself, as of that which subsists in others, and has, on this account only, a secondary and imperfect existence.

All things, therefore, depend upon unity, through the medium of intellect and soul. And intellect is of an uniform essence; but soul of a mental form νοειδης, and the body of the world vivific, or vital ζωτικος. The first cause of all is indeed prior to intellect, but intellect is the first recipient of a divine nature; and soul is divine, so far as it requires an intellectual medium. But the body which participates a soul of this kind is divine, in as great a degree as the nature of body will admit. For the illustration of intellectual light pervades from the principle of things, to the extremes; and is not totally obscured, even when it enters the involutions of matter, and is profoundly merged in its dark and flowing receptacle.

Hence we may with reason conclude, that not only the universe, but each of its eternal parts is animated, and endued with intellect, and is in its capacity similar to the universe. For each of these parts is a universe if compared with the multitude it contains, and to which it is allied. There is, therefore, according to the Orphic and Platonic theology, one soul of the universe; and after this others, which from participating this general soul, dispose the entire parts of the universe into order; and one intellect which is participated by souls, and one supreme God, who comprehends the world in his infinite nature, and a multitude of other divinities, who distribute intellectual essences, together with their dependent souls, and all the parts of the world, and who are the perpetual sources of its order, union, and consent. For it is not reasonable to suppose that every production of nature should have the power of generating its similar, but that the universe and primary essences should not more abundantly possess an ability of such like procreation; since sterility can only belong to the most abject, and not to the most excellent, natures.

In consequence of this reasoning, Orpheus filled all things with Gods, subordinate to the demiurgus of the whole Δημιουργῳ, every one of which performs the office destined to his divinity, by his superior leader. Hence according to his theology there are two worlds, the intelligible and the sensible. Hence too his three demiurgic principles: Jovial, Dionysiacal, and Adonical, Διιος, Διονυσιακη, Ἀδωναϊκη, from whence many orders and differences of

Gods proceed, intelligible,[†] intellectual, supermundane, mundane, celestial, authors of generation. And among these some in the order of guardian, demiurgic, elevating and comprehending Gods; perfecters of works, vivific, immutable, absolute, judicial, purgative, &c.; and besides these to each particular divinity, he added a particular multitude of angels, dæmons, and heroes; for according to Proclus, relating the opinion of Orpheus, and the theologists:[‡] "About every God there is a kindred multitude of angels, heroes, and dæmons. For every God presides over the form of that multitude which receives the divinity." He likewise considered a difference of sex in these deities, calling some male, and others female; the reason of which distinction Proclus,[§] with his usual elegance and subtilty, thus explains.

"The division of male and female comprehends in itself, all the plenitude of divine orders. Since the cause of stable power and identity, and the leader χορηγος of being, and that which invests all things with the first principle of conversion, is comprehended in the masculine order. But that which generates from itself all various progressions and partitions, measures of life and prolific powers, is contained in the female division. And on this account Timæus also, converting himself to all the Gods, by this division of generated natures, embraces their universal orders. But a division of this kind is particularly accommodated and proper to the present Theory, because the universe is full of this two-fold kind of Gods. For that we may begin with the extremes, heaven corresponds with earth, in the order and proportion of male to female. Since the motion of the heavens imparts particular properties and powers to particular things. But on the other hand earth receiving the celestial defluxions, becomes pregnant, and produces plants and animals of every kind. And of the Gods existing in the heavens, some are distinguished by the male division, and others by the female: and the authors of generation, since they are themselves destitute of birth, are some of this order and others of that, for the demiurgic choir is abundant in the universe. There are also many canals as it were of life, some of which exhibit the male and others the female form. But why should I insist on this

---

[†] Θεοι Νοητοι, Νοεροι, Υπερκοσμιοι, Εγκοσμιοι Ουρανιοι, Γενεσιουργοι. Et inter hos, aliæ ταξεις φρουρητικων θεων, Δημιουργικων, Αναγωγων, Συνεκτικων, Τελεσιουργων. Ζωογονων, Ατρεπτων, Απολυτων Κριτικων, Καθαρτικων, etc. Eschenb. Epig. p. 58.

[‡] In Timaeum. p. 67.

[§] In Tim. p. 290.

particular? since from the absolute unities, whether endued with a masculine or a feminine form, various orders of beings flow into the universe." Thus far Proclus.

But that Orpheus was a monarchist, as well as a polytheist, is not only evident from the preceding arguments, originally derived from his Theology, but from the following verses quoted by Proclus.[†]

> Hence with the universe great Jove contains
> The aether bright, and heav'ns exalted plains;
> Th' extended restless sea, and earth renown'd
> Ocean immense, and Tartarus profound;
> Fountains and rivers, and the boundless main,
> With all that nature's ample realms contain,
> And Gods and Goddesses of each degree;
> All that is past and all that e'er shall be,
> Occultly, and in fair connection,[‡] lies
> In Jove's wide womb, the ruler of the skies.

And in the same place, Proclus has preserved to us another copy of Orphic verses, which are also found in the writer (de Mundo); previous to which he observes, that the demiurgus, or artificer of the world, being full of ideas, comprehended by these all things within himself, as that theologer (Orpheus) declares. With these verses we have connected others, agreeable to the order of Stephens, Eschenbach, and Gesner, as follows:

> Jove is the first and last, high thund'ring king,
> Middle and head, from Jove all beings spring;
> In Jove the male and female forms combine,
> For Jove's a man, and yet a maid divine;
> Jove the strong basis of the earth contains,
> And the deep splendour of the starry plains;
> Jove is the breath of all; Jove's wondrous frame
> Lives in the rage of ever restless flame;
> Jove is the sea's strong root, the solar light,
> And Jove's the moon, fair regent of the night;
> Jove is a king by no restraint confin'd,
> And all things flow from Jove's prolific mind;

[†] In Tim. p. 95.

[‡] I have here followed the correction of Eschenbach, who reads σειρα instead of συρρα, which is I think more expressive and philosophical.

One is the pow'r divine in all things known,
And one the ruler absolute alone.
For in Jove's royal body all things lie,
Fire, night and day, earth, water and the sky;
The first begetters pleasing love and mind;
These in his mighty body, Jove confin'd:
See, how his beauteous head and aspect bright
Illumine heav'n, and scatter boundless light!
Round which his pendant golden tresses shine
Form'd from the starry beams, with light divine;
On either side two radiant horns behold,
Shap'd like a bull's and bright with glittering gold;
And East and West in opposition lie,
The lucid paths of all the Gods on high;
His eyes, the sun, and moon with borrow'd ray;
His mind† is truth, unconscious of decay,
Royal, aetherial; and his ear refin'd
Hears ev'ry voice, and sounds of ev'ry kind.
Thus are his head and mind immortal, bright,
His body's boundless, stable, full of light;
Strong are his members, with a force endu'd
Pow'rful to tame, but ne'er to be subdu'd;
Th' extended region of surrounding air
Forms his broad shoulders, back, and bosom fair,
And thro' the world the ruler of the skies
Upborne on natal, rapid pinions flies;
His sacred belly earth with fertile plains,
And mountains swelling to the clouds, contains;
His middle zone's the spreading sea profound,
Whose roaring waves the solid globe surround;
The distant realms of Tartarus obscure
Within earth's roots, his holy feet secure;
For these earth's utmost bounds to Jove belong,
And form his basis permanent and strong.
Thus all things Jove within his breast conceal'd,
And into beauteous light from thence reveal'd.

---

† His mind is truth, and a little after, His body full of light; or, Νους δε αψευδης and Σωμα δε περιφεγγες, perfectly agree with what Pythagoras affirmed, concerning God; that in his soul he resembled truth, and in his body light.

These verses contain what Dr. Cudworth calls the grand arcanum of the Orphic theology, that God is all things; which is likewise an Egyptian doctrine, from whence it was derived through Orpheus into Greece: and this sublime truth Plotinus[†] himself proves with his usual sagacity and depth. But here it is necessary to observe, that Orpheus and the Platonists do not conceive the Deity to be all things, as if he were a divisible, corporeal nature; but that he is all things, because present every where, and to every being totally, though more or less intimately present, according to the various gradations and approximations of being. So that he is to be considered as containing all things, and yet as separate and apart from all; as the source of all multitude, yet himself perfect unity; and as immensely prolific, yet divinely solitary and ineffably good. Thus, according to Porphyry,[‡] explaining the properties of incorporeal natures, "God, intellect, and soul are each of them every where, because no where. But God is every where, and at the same time, in no place of any being posterior to his nature; but he is only such as he is, and such as he willed himself to be. But intellect is indeed in the Deity, yet every where and in no place of its subordinate essences. And soul is in intellect, and in the Deity, every where and no where with respect to body; but body exists in soul, and in intellect, and in God. And though all beings, and non-entities, proceed from, and subsist in the Deity, yet he is neither entities, or nonentities, nor has any subsistence in them. For if he was alone every where, he would indeed be all things, and in all: but because he is likewise no where, all things are produced by him; so that they subsist in him because he is every where, but are different from him because he is no where. Thus also intellect being every where and no where, is the cause of souls, and of natures subordinate to soul: at the same time it is neither soul, nor such things as are posterior to the soul, nor has it any subsistence in them; and this because it is not only every where in its subordinate natures, but at the same time no where. Thus too, soul is neither body, nor in body, but is the cause of body; because while it is every where diffused through body, it is no where. And this procession of the universe extends as far as to that nature[§] which is incapable of being at the same time every where and no where, but which partially

---

[†] Enn. 5. lib. vi. p 391 TTS III.

[‡] Vide Αφορμαι προς τα Νοητα, Aph. 31, p 179, TTS vol. II.

[§] Meaning material forms and qualities.

participates of each. And in another place of the same excellent fragment, he tells us that the ancients explaining the property of an incorporeal nature, as far as this can be effected by discourse, when they affirmed it to be one, at the same time add, that it is likewise all things; that it is every where, and no where, and that it is totally present in every whole. He adds, they express its nature entirely by contrary properties, that they may remove from it the fictitious and delusive conceptions of bodies which obscure those properties by which true being is known.†

We have before observed, that the Platonic philosophers, agreeable to the doctrine of Orpheus, considered fecundity as, in an eminent degree, the property of a divine nature; and from this principle filled the universe with Gods.‡ This opinion a modern philosopher, or a modern writer on mythology, will doubtless consider as too ridiculous to need a serious refutation: the one, because he believes the phenomena may be solved by mechanical causes; and the other, in consequence of a system originating from prejudice, and supported without proof. However, prejudice apart, let us hear what the philosophers can urge in defence of this doctrine, in addition to what we have already advanced. To begin then with Onatus§ the Pythagorean: "Those," says he, "who assert that there is but one God, and not many Gods, are deceived, as not considering that the supreme dignity of the divine transcendency consists in governing beings similar to itself, and in surpassing others. But the other Gods have the same relation to this first and intelligible God, as the dancers to the Coryphaeus, and as soldiers to their general, whose duty is to follow their leader. And although the same employment is common both to the ruler, and those who are ruled; yet the latter, if destitute of a leader, could no longer conspire together in one occupation; as the concord of the singers and dancers, and the expedition of the army, must fail, if the one is deprived of the Coryphaeus and the

---

† It is remarkable that in the Hymn to Nature, among the following, the Deity is celebrated as all things, yet the poet adds that he is alone incommunicable; which perfectly agrees with the preceding account of his subsisting in all things, and at the same time being separate and apart from all.

‡ If the word Gods offends the ear of the reader, he may substitute in its stead, thrones, dominions, etc. for I do not discourse concerning words.

§ Stob. Ecl. Phyf. p. 5.

other of the captain or commander." To the same purpose Plotinus shews† that it is perfectly philosophical to suppose a multitude of Gods subordinate to the One supreme. "It is necessary," says he, "that every man should endeavour to be as good as possible, but at the same time, he should not consider himself as the only thing that is good; but should be convinced that there are other good men, and good dæmons in the universe, but much more Gods: who though inhabiting this inferior region, yet look up to that higher world; and especially that most blessed Soul, the ruling Divinity of this universe. From whence a man ought to ascend still higher, and to celebrate the intelligible Gods, but above all their great King; declaring his majesty in a particular manner, by the multitude of Gods subordinate to his divinity. For it is not the province of those who know the power of God to contract all into one, but rather to exhibit all that divinity which he has displayed, who himself, remaining one, produces many, which proceed from him and by him. For the universe subsists by him, and perpetually speculates his divinity, together with each of the Gods it contains." Should it be objected, that if such Gods (or exalted beings) really existed, we should be able to demonstrate the reality of their existence, in the same manner as that of one supreme God; we cannot frame a better reply than in the words of Proclus.‡ "And perhaps," says he, "you may affirm that souls more swiftly forget things nearer to them; but have a stronger remembrance of superior principles. For these last operate on them more vigorously, through the sublimity of their power, and appear to be present with them by their energy. And this happens with respect to our corporeal sight; which does not perceive many things situated on the earth, yet observes the inerratic sphere, and the stars it contains; because these strongly irradiate our eyes with their light. So the eye of our soul is more forgetful, and sooner loses the sight of principles proximate to its nature, than of such as are more elevated and divine. In like manner all religions and sects confess that there is one highest principle, and men every where invoke God as their helper; but that there are Gods in subordination to this first cause, and that there is a providence proceeding from these to the universe, all men do not believe; and this because the one appears to them more perspicuously than the many."

---

† En. 2. lib ix. cap 9. (See pp 223 ff. of TTS vol. III).

‡ In Tim. p. 286.

Indeed in consequence of the Platonic doctrine of the pre-existence of the soul, it is not strange that we should know so little of those divine and exalted beings above us; since from our union with generation and material concerns, we are imbued with oblivion, ignorance, and error. "We are similar," as Porphyry[†] well observes, "to those who enter or depart from a foreign region, not only in casting aside our native manners and customs; but from the long use of a strange country we are imbued with affections, manners, and laws foreign from our natural and true religion, and with a strong propensity to these unnatural habits." As, therefore, it is not wonderful that the greatest part of those who inhabit a pestiferous region, should languish and decline, but that a very few should preserve their natural strength; so we ought not to wonder, that thus placed in generation, the multitude of mankind are obnoxious to passions and depraved habits; but we ought rather to be astonished if any souls, thus involved in the dark folds of the body, and surrounded with such great and unceasing mutations, are found sober, pure, and free from destructive perturbations. For it is surely astonishing that the soul should live immaterially, in material concerns; and preserve itself uncontaminated amidst such base defilements; that it should drink of the cup of oblivion, and not be laid asleep by the intoxicating draught; that it should elevate its eye above the sordid darkness with which it is surrounded; and be able to open the gates of truth, which, though contained in its essence, are guarded and shut by terrene and material species. But that it is possible to know more of such exalted natures than is generally believed, by the assistance of the ancient philosophy, accompanied with a suitable life, is, I am persuaded, true; and I would recommend the arduous and glorious investigation to every liberal mind. Let us now consider the nature of sacrifice according to Orpheus and the Platonists; previous to which, I must beg leave to inform the reader, that the Greek theologians and philosophers were not (as they are represented by modern writers on mythology) so stupid as to worship the creature instead of the Creator; and to neglect or confound that homage and veneration, which is due to the first cause of all. On the contrary, they considered the supreme Being as honoured by the reverence paid to his most illustrious offspring; and carefully distinguished between the worship proper to the Deity, and to the subordinate Gods, as the following discourse will abundantly evince.

[†] De Abstinentia, lib i, 30, (p 27 TTS vol. II).

How far, indeed, such opinions may be consistent with revelation, it is not my business to determine. It is sufficient for me, to give the most faithful account I am able of their sentiments on this subject; to free their opinions from misrepresentation; and to shew that God has not left himself without a witness among the wise and learned of the heathens. But as I cannot give a better account of the nature and antiquity of sacrifice than from the writings of Porphyry, I shall present the reader with the following paraphrase, on part of the second book of his excellent work on abstinence.[†]

"The period of time appears to have been immensely distant, from which, as Theophrastus says, a nation the most learned of all others, and inhabiting the sacred region formed by the Nile, began first of all, from the domestic fire, to sacrifice to the celestial divinities; not with myrrh or cassia, nor with the first fruits of frankincense mingled with saffron, (for these were applied many ages afterwards, from error increasing in certain degrees: I mean at the period when men having surmounted the difficulties of a life formerly oppressed with the cares of procuring necessaries, and from the beginning to the end attended with many labours and tears, sacrificed perhaps a few drops to the Gods). For at first they performed sacrifices, not with aromatics, but with the first fruits of the green herb; plucking it with their hands, as a certain soft down or moss of prolific nature. Indeed the earth produced trees before animals; but prior to trees, the annually rising grass, the leaves, and roots, and entire produce of which having collected, they sacrificed with fire: by this sacrifice, saluting the visible celestial Gods, and rendering them through the ministry of fire immortal honours. For we preserve as sacred to those divinities, a perpetual fire in our temples; since this element is most similar to their lucid frames. But with respect to fumigations from herbs produced by the earth, they called the censer or pan, in which the herbs were burnt, θυμιατηριος, and to perform sacrifice θυειν, and the sacrifices themselves θυσιαι; all which we have erroneously interpreted, as if these words were signatures of that error, which afterwards crept in among us; and hence it is that we call the worship consisting from the slaughter of animals θυσιαι.

"Indeed so great was the care of the ancients in retaining their primaeval customs, that they uttered imprecations against those who deserted the old manner, and introduced a new one: and therefore they called those herbs with which we now fumigate αρωματα,

---

[†] On Abstinence, II 5 - 7 (pp 46-48 TTS Vol II.)

aromatics. But the antiquity of the above mentioned fumigations will be perceived by him who considers that even now many odorous kinds of wood, cut into fragments, are employed in sacrifice. From whence it happened that the earth now bearing trees together with grass, its earliest production, men at first eating the fruits of oaks, burned only a few of these in sacrifices to the Gods, on account of the rarity of such sustenance; but sacrificed a multitude of the leaves. Afterwards human life passed to a gentle diet, and sacrifices were performed with nuts; from whence the proverb originated, αλις δρυος, enough of the oak.

"But among the fruits of Ceres, after the first appearance of leguminous barley, mankind were accustomed to sprinkle it, made into an entire mass, in their first sacrifices. Afterwards breaking the barley, and diminishing the nutriment into meal, having concealed the instruments of so great a work, which afford divine assistance to human life, they approached these as certain sacred concerns. But they cast the first fruits of the barley (when bruised into meal) and which was more esteemed than when whole, into the fire, in sacrifice to the Gods: from whence even now, at the conclusion of the sacrifice, we make use of meal mixed with wine and oil. By this custom indeed we indicate from whence, and from what beginnings sacrifices have increased to the present state: but, at the same time, we do not consider why such things are performed. Mankind proceeding from these small beginnings, and the earth yielding an abundant supply of corn and various fruits, they judged that the first produce of all the rest should be offered in sacrifices, with a view of pleasing the various orders of the Gods: selecting many things for this purpose, and mingling not a few others with these, if they possessed any thing beautiful, and on account of its odoriferous nature accommodated to divine sensation. With some of these, formed into garlands, they encircled the statues of the Gods; and others they sacrificed with fire. Likewise to the Gods as the proper causes, they poured forth the divine drops of wine, and honey, and oil, when their uses were first discovered.

"The truth of the preceding account appears to be confirmed by the procession celebrated even now at Athens, in honour of the sun and the hours. For in this solemnity grass is carried about, enwrapping the kernels of olives, attended with figs, all kinds of pulse, oaken boughs or acorns, the fruit of the strawberry, wheat, and barley, a mass of dried figs, cakes composed from the meal of wheat and barley, heaped in a pyramidal form, and last of all olives." Theophrastus then proceeds to shew the impropriety of animal sacrifices, after which he adds: "But the utility of fruits is the first and greatest of every production; the first fruits of which are to be sacrificed to the Gods alone, and to the Earth, the prolific parent of every herb. For Earth is the common Vesta of Gods and men, on whose fertile surface reclining, as on the soft bosom of a mother or a nurse, we ought to celebrate her divinity with hymns, and incline to her with filial affection, as to the source of our existence. For thus, when we approach to the conclusion of our mortal life, we shall be thought worthy of a reception into the celestial regions, and of an association with the race of immortal Gods, who now behold us venerating their divinities with those fruits, of which they are the authors, and sacrificing in their honour every herb of the all-bearing earth; at the same time not esteeming every thing worthy or proper to be offered as a testimony of our homage.

"For as every thing indiscriminately is not to be sacrificed to the Gods, so perhaps we cannot find any thing sufficiently worthy, with which we may worship them as they deserve." Thus far Theophrastus. Porphyry then proceeds to shew after what manner those ought to sacrifice who propose an intellectual life, as the ultimate object of their pursuit.

"Let us also," says he,[†] "sacrifice, but in a manner becoming the offspring of intellect, bringing with us the most exalted offerings, with our most exalted powers. To the Divinity indeed, who is above all things, as a wise man said, neither sacrificing nor dedicating any thing sensible or material; for there is nothing subsisting by material concretion, which must not be deemed impure by a nature entirely free from the contagion of body. Hence even the discourse, which is proffered by the voice is not proper to be addressed to a cause so sublime and ineffable; nor the internal speech of the soul, if contaminated with any perturbation, or mixed with any of the sensible phantasms of imagination. But we ought to worship the supreme God, in the most profound and pure silence; and with the purest thoughts concerning his exalted nature. It is requisite, therefore, that having conjoined and assimilated ourselves to him, we should approach this sublime principle with a pious sacrifice, which may redound to his praise, and to our safety. But such a sacrifice can only be performed by contemplating his divinity with a soul free from material affections, and with the rational eye filled with

---

[†] On Abstinence II, 34 - 39, (pp 64 - 68 TTS Vol. II.)

intellectual light. But to the offspring of this first God (I mean the intelligible divinities) we should present the sacrifice of hymns, composed by the rational principle. For it is customary to offer the first-fruits of such things as every God bestows upon us; by which he nourishes and supports our existence, and which are subservient to the purposes of sacrifice. As the husbandman, therefore, performs sacred rites, by presenting handfuls of pulse and fruits, so ought we to sacrifice our purest thoughts, and other goods of the soul, thanking the divinities for the sublime contemplations they afford us, and for truly seeding our intellectual part with the speculation of their essences; for, conversing with us, and appearing to our mental sight; for shining upon us with divine splendours, and by this means procuring for us true salvation.

"But an exercise of this kind is performed in an indolent manner, by many who apply themselves to philosophy, and who, more sedulously cultivating fame than honouring the divinity, are wholly employed about statues, taking no care to learn after what manner, or whether or not these intellectual beings are to be adored; nor by properly consulting divine concerns, are they anxious to know, in how great a degree, we ought to strive after an union with these exalted natures. With such as these we by no means contend; since our only endeavour is to obtain a knowledge of divinity, and to imitate pious and ancient men, by frequently sacrificing of that contemplation which the Gods have bestowed upon us, and by the use of which we are partakers of real salvation.

"The Pythagoreans indeed who were very studious of numbers and lines, for the most part sacrificed of these to the Gods; denominating this number Minerva,[†] another Apollo; and again, this Justice, and another Temperance. They proceeded also in a similar manner in geometrical figures. Hence they pleased the divinities by sacrifices of this kind, calling each of them by their proper names, for the purpose of obtaining their particular requests. They often besides made such invocations subservient to the purposes of divination; and if they required the investigation of any thing particular, they used the visible celestial Gods, also the wandering and fixed stars, of all which the sun ought to be placed as a leader, next to this the moon; and, as a theologian observes, we should make fire allied to these by a proximate conjunction. But the same person asserts that the

---

[†] In the latter part of this Dissertation, we shall shew the wonderful agreement of the following Hymns, with the names given by Pythagoras to numbers.

Pythagoreans sacrificed no animal, but offered the first fruits of flour and honey, and of the diversified productions of the earth; nor kindled fire on the bloody altar, says he, with other things of a similar nature: but why should I transcribe such relations~ For he who is truly studious of piety, knows why he ought not to sacrifice any thing animated to Gods; but alone to genii, and other powers superior to man, whether good or bad: he likewise knows to what kind of men it belongs to sacrifice these, and every circumstance respecting those beings, who require such sacrifices to be performed. With regard to other particulars I shall be silent. But what some Platonists have divulged will perspicuously illustrate the subject before us, which I shall relate as follows.

"The first God, since he is incorporeal, immoveable, and indivisible, neither existing in any being, place, or time, nor even circumscribed by, and as it were invested with himself, is in no respect indigent of any thing external to his nature, as we have already observed. But this last property of a divine essence is likewise true of the soul of the world, possessing a triple divisibility, and being naturally self-motive, yet so constituted that it chooses to move in an orderly and beautiful manner, and to agitate the corporeal fabric of the world according to the most excellent and harmonious reasons. But it associates to itself and is circularly invested with body, although incorporeal and entirely destitute of passion. But to the other Gods, to the world, and to the erratic and fixed stars, composed from body and soul, and to the visible divinities, testimonials of gratitude are to be offered by sacrificing with inanimate substances. After these there remains that multitude of invisible beings, which Plato indiscriminately calls dæmons. Some of these are allotted a peculiar name by mankind, from whom they obtain divine honours and other kinds of religious worship: but others of these are for the most part called by no peculiar name, but are obscurely worshipped by some men, and are denominated according to certain streets of cities. But the remaining multitude are called by the common name of dæmons. Concerning all these, a general persuasion obtains, that their influence is noxious and malignant if they are once angered because their accustomed worship is neglected; and that they are again beneficent if appeased by prayers and supplications, by sacrifices and convenient rites.

"But the confused opinion which subsists concerning these beings, and which has proceeded to great infamy, requires that we should distinguish their nature according to the decisions of reason. After this manner then they are distributed. As many souls as proceeding from the universal soul, administer considerable parts of those places contained under the lunar orb, who are indeed connected with an aerial part, but subject it to the dominion of reason, are to be esteemed good dæmons. We ought to believe that all their operations tend to the utility of the concerns subject to their dominion, whether they preside over certain animals, or over fruits assigned to their charge, or over things subservient to these particulars; such as prolific showers, moderate winds, serene weather, and whatever is calculated to promote these, as a good temperament of the seasons of the year, &c. They likewise administer to us the use of music, and of every discipline, together with the medicinal and gymnastic arts, and whatever else is allied to these. For it is impossible that such dæmons can supply what is convenient and proper, and at the same time be the authors of things destructive and improper. In this class the messengers, as Plato calls them, between Gods and men must be numbered, who convey our prayers and pious offerings to the Gods as judges of our conduct, and bring back to us in return divine warnings, exhortations, and oracles. But as many souls as do not properly govern the aerial part with which they are connected, but are for the most part subdued by its influence, and are agitated and hurried away by its brutal power in a rash and disorderly manner, whenever the wrathful irritations and desires of the pneumatic part grow strong; souls of this kind are properly denominated dæmons, but ought at the same time to be called malevolent and base.

"All these, together with those who obtain a contrary power, are invisible, and entirely imperceptible to human sensation; for they are not invested like terrene animals with a solid body; nor are they all endued with one shape; but they possess a diversity of forms. However, the forms impressed on their aerial part, are sometimes apparent, and at other times obscured. Sometimes too evil dæmons change their shapes. But this pneumatic part, so far as corporeal, is subject to passion and change; and although it is so confined by the coercive power of these demoniacal souls, that its form continues for a long time, yet it is not by this means eternal. For it is reasonable to believe, that something continually flows from this aerial part; and that it receives a nutriment accommodated to its nature. Indeed the πνευμα, or aerial part of the good dæmons, consists in a certain commensurate proportion, in the same manner as those bodies which are the objects of our present perception. But the bodies of the malevolent dæmons are of a discordant temperament, on which account they inhabit that aerial space proximate to the earth, with a passive affection; and for the most part govern things subject to their dominion with a turbulent malignity. Hence there is no evil which they do not endeavour to perpetrate. For their manners are entirely violent and fraudulent, and destitute of the guardian preservation of better dæmons; so that they machinate vehement and sudden snares with which they rush on the unwary; sometimes endeavouring to conceal their incursions, and sometimes acting with open violence against the subjects of their oppression." Thus far Porphyry: the length of which quotation needs no apology; both on account of its excellence, and because the unlearned reader will not find it elsewhere in English. I would also add that I wish (with a proper sense of the greatness of the undertaking) to offer this, together with the preceding and subsequent paraphrases, as specimens of that method mentioned in the Preface to this Work; and which I cannot but consider as the best means of exhibiting the Greek philosophy in modern languages.

Having then discoursed so largely from Porphyry concerning sacrifice, and as he particularly recommends the sacrifice performed by contemplation and divine hymns; let us hear his sentiments concerning the nature of prayer, as they are preserved to us by Proclus in his excellent Commentary on the *Timæus*, p. 64. "It is requisite (says Proclus) before all things, that we understand something perspicuously concerning the nature of prayer: I mean in what its essence consists, what its perfection is, and from whence it becomes natural to our souls." He then proceeds to relate the opinion of Porphyry as follows. "For Porphyry, discoursing concerning such of the ancients as either approved of or exploded prayer, leads us through various opinions, which I shall now summarily relate. Neither those who labour under the first kind of impiety, I mean denying the existence of the Gods, claim any advantage to themselves from prayer: nor yet those of the second class, who entirely subvert a providence; for though they acknowledge the existence of the Gods, yet they deny their provident concern for the affairs of the universe. Nor again those of a third order, who though they confess that there are Gods, and that their providence extends to the world, yet consider all things as produced by the divinities from necessity: for the utility of prayer is derived from such things as are contingent, and may have a different existence. But those who both acknowledge the being of the Gods, and their continual providence, and that some events are contingent, and may subsist in a different manner; these men indeed may be truly said to approve of prayer, and to confess that the Gods correct our life, and establish in it safety." Proclus then proceeds to relate the reasons by which Porphyry confirms its utility. "He adds that prayer in a particular manner pertains to worthy men, because it conjoins them with divinity; for similars love to be united together: but a worthy man is in an eminent degree similar to the divine natures. We may likewise add, that since good men are placed in custody, and confined by the dark bands of the body as in a prison, they ought to pray to the Gods, that it may be lawful for them to depart from hence. Besides, since we are as children torn from the bosom of our parent, we ought on this account to request by our prayers that we may return to the Gods, our true intellectual parents. If this is the case, do not they who deny that prayers are to be offered to the Gods, and who prevent their souls from being united with the divinities, that is with beings more excellent than themselves, appear similar to those who are deprived of their parents? Lastly, all nations who have flourished in the exercise of wisdom, have applied themselves to divine prayers: as the Brahmans among the Indians, the Magi among the Persians, and amongst the Greeks also, those who have excelled in the science of theology: for on this account they instituted mysteries and initiatory rites (τελεται). Besides, this consideration is not to be omitted, that since we are a part of this universe, it is consonant to reason that we should be dependent on it for support. For a conversion to the universe procures safety to every thing which it contains. If therefore you possess virtue, it is requisite you should invoke that divinity which previously comprehended in himself every virtue: for universal good is the cause of that good which belongs to you by participation. And if you seek after some corporeal good, the world is endued with a power which contains universal body. From hence therefore it is necessary that perfection should also extend to the parts." Thus far that most excellent philosopher Porphyry; in which quotation, as well as the preceding, the reader must doubtless confess, that Proclus did not without reason admire him, for what he calls his τα ιεροπρεπη νοηματα, or conceptions adapted to holy concerns; for surely no philosopher ever possessed them in a more eminent degree.

If it should be asked, in what the power of prayer consists, according to these philosophers? I answer, in a certain sympathy and similitude of natures to each other: just as in an extended chord, where when the lowest part is moved, the highest presently after gives a responsive motion. Or as in the strings of a musical instrument, attempered to the same harmony; one chord trembling from the pulsation of another, as if it were endued with sensation from symphony. So in the universe, there is one harmony though composed from contraries; since they are at the same time similar and allied to each other. For from the soul of the world, like an immortal self-motive lyre, life every where resounds, but in some things more inferior and remote from perfection than in others. And with respect to the super-mundane Gods, sympathy and similitude subsists in these as in their most perfect exemplars; from whence they are participated by sensible natures, their obscure and imperfect images. Hence (say they) we must not conceive, that our prayers cause any animadversion in the Gods, or, properly speaking, draw down their beneficence; but that they are rather the means of elevating the soul to these divinities, and disposing it for the reception of their supernal illumination. For the divine irradiation, which takes place in prayer, shines and energizes spontaneously, restoring unity to the soul, and causing our energy to become one with divine energy. For such, according to these philosophers, is the efficacy of prayer, that it unites all inferior with all superior beings. Since, as the great Theodorus says, all things pray except the first.

Indeed so great is the power of similitude, that through its unifying nature all things coalesce, and impart their particular properties to others. Whilst primary natures distribute their gifts to such as are secondary, by an abundant illumination, and effects are established in the causes from which they proceed. But the connection and indissoluble society of active universals, and of passive particulars, is every where beheld. For the generative causes of things are contained by similitude in their effects; and in causes themselves their progeny subsist, comprehended in perfect union and consent. Hence the celestial orbs impart a copious defluxion of good to this terrestrial region; while sublunary parts, assimilated in a certain respect to the heavens, participate a perfection convenient to their nature.

Hence too, from the progressions of similitude, there are various leaders in the universe. And many orders of angels dancing harmoniously round their ruling deities; together with a multitude of dæmons, heroes, and particular souls. There are besides multiform kinds of mortal animals, and various powers of plants. So that all things tend to their respective leaders, and are as it were stamped with one sign of domestic unity; which is in some more evident, and others more obscure. For indeed similitude in first productions subsists more apparently; but in those of the middle and extreme orders is obscured in consequence of the gradations of progression. Hence images and exemplars derive their hypostasis from conciliating similitude; and every thing through this is familiar to itself, and to its kindred natures.

But it is time to return from this digression to the business of sacrifice and prayer. That we may therefore have a clearer view of the nature and efficacy of each, let us hear the elegant and subtle Proclus,[†] upon sacrifice and magic, of which the following is a paraphrase.

"In the same manner as lovers gradually advance from that beauty which is apparent in sensible forms, to that which is divine; so the ancient priests, when they considered that there was a certain alliance and sympathy in natural things to each other, and of things manifest to occult powers, and by this means discovered that all things subsist in all, they fabricated a sacred science from this mutual sympathy and similarity. Thus they recognized things supreme, in such as are subordinate, and the subordinate in the supreme: in the celestial regions terrene properties subsisting in a causal and celestial manner; and in earth celestial properties, but according to a terrene condition. For how shall we account for those plants called heliotropes, that are attendants on the sun, moving in correspondence with the revolution of its orb; but selenitropes, or attendants on the moon, turning in exact conformity with her motion? it is because all things pray, and compose hymns to the leaders of their respective orders; but some intellectually, and others rationally; some in a natural, and others after a sensible manner. Hence the sunflower, as far as it is able, moves in a circular dance towards the sun; so that if any one could hear the pulsation made by its circuit in the air, he would perceive something composed by a sound of this kind, in honour of its king, such as a plant is capable of framing. Hence we may behold the sun and moon in the earth, but according to a terrene quality. But in the celestial regions, all plants, and stones, and animals, possess an intellectual life according to a celestial nature. Now the ancients having contemplated this mutual sympathy of things, applied for occult purposes both celestial and terrene natures, by means of which through a certain similitude they deduced divine virtues into this inferior abode. For indeed similitude itself is a sufficient cause of binding things together in union and consent. Thus if a piece of paper is heated, and afterwards placed near a lamp, though it does not

---

[†] As a Latin version only of this valuable work is published, the reader will please to make allowances for the Paraphrase, where it may be requisite.

touch the fire, the paper will be suddenly inflamed, and the flame will descend from the superior to the inferior parts. This heated paper we may compare to a certain relation of inferiors to superiors; and its approximation to the lamp, to the opportune use of things according to time, place, and matter. But the procession of fire in the paper aptly represents the presence of divine light, to that nature which is capable of its reception. Lastly, the inflammation of the paper may be compared to the deification of mortals, and to the illumination of material natures, which are afterwards carried upwards like the fire of the paper, from a certain participation of divine seed. Again, the lotus before the rising of the sun, folds its leaves into itself, but gradually expands them on its rising: unfolding them in proportion to the sun's ascent to the zenith; but as gradually contracting them as that luminary descends to the west. Hence this plant by the expansion and contraction of its leaves appears no less to honour the sun than men by the gesture of their eye-lids, and the motion of their lips. But this imitation and certain participation of supernal light is not only visible in plants, which possess but a vestige of life, but likewise in particular stones. Thus the sun-stone, by its golden rays, imitates those of the sun; but the stone called the eye of heaven, or of the sun, has a figure similar to the pupil of an eye, and a ray shines from the middle of the pupil. Thus too the lunar stone, which has a figure similar to the moon when horned, by a certain change of itself, follows the lunar motion. Lastly, the stone called Helioselenus, *i.e.* of the sun and moon, imitates after a manner the congress of those luminaries, which it images by its colour. So that all things are full of divine natures; terrestrial natures receiving the plenitude of such as are celestial, but celestial of supercelestial essences; while every order of things proceeds gradually in a beautiful descent, from the highest to the lowest. For whatever is collected into one above the order of things is afterwards dilated in descending, various souls being distributed under their various ruling divinities. In fine, some things turn round correspondent to the revolutions of the sun, and others after a manner imitate the solar rays, as the palm and the date: some the fiery nature of the sun, as the laurel, and others a different property. For indeed we may perceive the properties which are collected in the sun, every where distributed to subsequent natures constituted in a solar order; that is, to angels, dæmons, souls, animals, plants, and stones. Hence the authors of the ancient priesthood, discovered from things apparent, the worship of superior powers, while they mingled some things, and purified with others. They mingled many things indeed together, because they saw that some simple substances possessed a divine property (though not taken singly) sufficient to call down that particular power, of which they were participants. Hence by the mingling of many things together, they attracted upon us a supernal influx; and by the composition of one thing from many, they symbolised with that one, which is above many; and composed statues from the mixtures of various substances, conspiring in sympathy and consent. Besides this, they collected composite odours, by a divine art, into one, comprehending a multitude of powers, and symbolising with the unity of a divine essence. Considering besides, that division debilitates each of these, but that mingling them together restores them to the idea of their exemplar; hence the ancient priests, by the mutual relation and sympathy of things to one another, collected their virtues into one, but expelled them by repugnancy and antipathy; purifying, when it was requisite, with sulphur and bitumen, and the sprinkling of marine water. For sulphur purifies from the sharpness of its odour; but marine water on account of its fiery portion. Besides this, in the worship of the Gods, they offered animals, and other substances congruous to their nature; and received in the first place the powers of dæmons as proximate to natural substances and operations, by whose assistance they evocated these natural bodies to which they approached into their presence. Afterwards they proceeded from dæmons to the powers and energies of the Gods, partly indeed from dæmoniacal instruction, but partly by their own industry, aptly interpreting symbols, and ascending to a proper intelligence of the Gods. And lastly laying aside natural substances and their operations, they received themselves into the communion and fellowship of the Gods." Thus far Proclus, and thus much for the theological doctrine of Orpheus, as contained in the works of the latter Platonists. I persuade myself enough has been said in this Dissertation to convince every thinking and liberal mind, that the Greek theology as professed and understood by the Greek philosophers, is not that absurd and nonsensical system represented by modern prejudice and ignorance as the creed of the ancients. In consequence of a blind and mistaken zeal it is common to ridicule the opinions of the ancient philosophers, in order to establish the certainty of the Christian religion. But surely revelation does not require so unwarrantable and feeble a support, which in reality only betrays the cause it endeavours to defend, by giving infidels occasion to suspect, either weakness in its evidence, or obscurity in its fundamental doctrines. Besides, the generality of these uncandid opponents know nothing of the Platonical writers, from whom alone genuine information can be derived on this sublime and intricate subject; and from whose works the preceding Dissertation has been so abundantly enriched. Were these invaluable books more generally known and understood, if they did not refine our taste, at present so depraved, they would at least teach us to admire the strength which human reason is capable of exerting, and to be more modest in our pretensions to wisdom; they would silence ignorant declaimers, and stop the immense increase of books on modern philosophy, which are so rapidly hastening to the abyss of forgetfulness, like streams into the ocean from which they originally flowed.

Section III

But it is now time to speak of the following Hymns, of which, as we have before observed, Onomacritus is the reputed author. And first, with regard to the dialect of these Hymns, Gesner well observes it ought to be no objection to their antiquity. For though, according to Iamblichus,[†] the Thracian Orpheus, who is more ancient than those noble poets Homer and Hesiod, used the Doric dialect; yet the Athenian Onomacritus, who, agreeable to the general opinion of antiquity, is the author of all the works now extant, ascribed to Orpheus[‡] might either, preserving the sentences and a great part of the words, only change the dialect, and teach the ancient Orpheus to speak Homerically, or as I may say Solonically: or might arbitrarily add or take away what he thought proper, which Herodotus relates was his practice, with respect to the oracles. Gesner adds, that it does not appear probable to him that Onomacritus would dare to invent all he wrote, since Orpheus must necessarily, at that time, have been in great repute, and a variety of his verses in circulation: and he concludes with observing that the objection of the Doric dialect ought to be of no more weight against the antiquity of the present works, than the Pelasgic letters, which Orpheus used according to Diodorus Siculus.

The hymns of Orpheus are not only mentioned by Plato in his Eighth Book of *Laws*, but also by Pausanias,[§] whose words are

---

[†] De Vita Pythag. c. 34. p. 169. Kuft.

[‡] Philoponus observes, in his Commentary on Aristotle's books of the Soul, that Aristotle calls the Orphic verses reputed, because they appear not to have been written by Orpheus himself, as Aristotle affirms in his book concerning philosophy. For the Dogmata contained in them were indeed his, but Onomacritus is reported to have put them into verse.

[§] In Boeoticis p.770.

translated as follows by the author of the *Letters on Mythology*.[†] "The Thracian Orpheus (says Pausanias) was represented on mount Helicon, with ΤΕΛΕΤΗ (initiation or religion) by his side, and the wild beasts of the woods, some in marble, some in bronze, standing round him. His hymns are known by those who have studied the poets to be both short and few in number. The Lycomedes, an Athenian family dedicated to sacred music, have them all by heart, and sing them at their solemn mysteries. They are but of the second class for elegance, being far excelled by Homer's in that respect. But our religion has adopted the hymns of Orpheus, and has not done the same honour to the hymns of Homer." To the testimony of Pausanias may be added that of Suidas, who, among the writings of the Libethrian Orpheus mentions τελεται, or initiations, which he says are by some ascribed to Onomacritus.[‡] And Scaliger well observes, in his notes to these hymns, that they ought rather to be called initiations, because they contain only invocations of the Gods, such as the initiated in mysteries are accustomed to use; but they do not celebrate the nativities, actions, etc. of the divinities, as it is usual in hymns. It is on this account we have entitled them mystical initiations, which is doubtless their proper appellations. The author too of the Allegories in the Theogony of Hesiod,[§] relating the powers of the planets on things inferior, expressly mentions these hymns, or rather initiations, and many of the compound epithets with which they abound.[◦] From all which it is evident that the following Hymns were written by the Athenian Onomacritus, and are the same with those so much celebrated by antiquity. Indeed it is not probable they should be the invention of any writer more modern than the above period, as it must have been so easy to detect the forgery, from the original initiations which were even extant at the time in which Suidas lived.

In the former part of this Dissertation, we asserted that we should derive all our information concerning the Orphic theology from the writings of the Platonists; not indeed without reason. For this sublime theology descended from Orpheus to Pythagoras, and from

---

[†] Page 167.

[‡] It is remarkable that Sextus Empiricus more than once mentions Onomacritus in the Orphics. Ονομακριτος εν τοις Ορφικοις.

[§] Page 267.

[◦] Vide Fabric. Bib. p. 124.

Pythagoras to Plato; as the following testimonies evince. "Timæus (says Proclus)[†] being a Pythagorean, follows the Pythagoric principles, and these are the Orphic traditions; for what Orpheus delivered mystically in secret discourses, these Pythagoras learned when he was initiated by Aglaophemus in the Orphic mysteries." Syrianus too makes the Orphic and Pythagoric principles to be one and the same; and, according to Suidas, the same Syrianus composed a book, entitled the *Harmony of Orpheus, Pythagoras and Plato*.[‡] And again Proclus:[§] "it is Pythagorical to follow the Orphic genealogies; for from the Orphic tradition downward by Pythagoras, the science concerning the Gods was derived to the Greeks." And elsewhere,[°] "All the theology of the Greeks is the progeny of the sacred initiations ($\mu\nu\sigma\tau\alpha\gamma\omega\gamma\iota\alpha\iota$) of Orpheus. For Pythagoras first learned the orgies of the Gods from Aglaophemus; but Plato was the second who received a perfect science of these, both from the Pythagoric, and Orphic writings." Now in consequence of these testimonies, our hymns ought to agree with the doctrine of Pythagoras; especially since Onomacritus, their author, was of that school. And that they do so, the following discovery abundantly evinces.

Photius, in his *Bibliotheca*, has preserved to us part of a valuable work, written by Nicomachus the Pythagorean, entitled *Theological Arithmetic*; in which he ascribes particular epithets, and the names of various divinities to numbers, as far as to ten. There is likewise a curious work of the same title, by an anonymous writer, which is extant only in manuscript. From these two, and from occasional passages respecting numbers according to Pythagoras, found in the Platonic writers, Meursius has composed a book, which he calls *Denarius Pythagoricus*; and which is an invaluable treasure to such as are studious of the ancient philosophy. On perusing this learned book, it seemed to me necessary, that as the divinities, ascribed to each number, had a particular relation to one another, they should also have a mutual agreement in the following hymns. And on the comparison I found the most perfect similitude: a few instances of which I shall select, leaving a more accurate investigation of this matter to the learned and philosophical reader.

[†] In Timæum. p. 291.

[‡] Συμφωνια Ορφεως, Πυθαγορου, και Πλατονος.

[§] In Tim. p. 289.

[°] In Theol. Plat. p. 13.

In the first place then, among the various names ascribed to the monad or unity, are those of the following Gods; *viz.* the Sun, Jupiter, Love, Proteus, Vesta. Now in the hymn to the Sun we find the epithet αθανατε Ζευ, O immortal Jove. In that to Love πυριδρομος, or wandering fire, which is likewise found in the hymn to the Sun. In the hymn to Love, that deity is celebrated as having the keys of all of things;[†] *viz.* of aether, heaven, the deep, the earth, etc. And Proteus is invoked as possessing the keys of the deep.[‡] Again, Vesta, in the Orphic Hymns, is the same with the mother of the Gods; and the mother of the Gods is celebrated as "always governing rivers, and every sea";[§] which perfectly agrees with the appellations given both to Love and Proteus. Again, among the various epithets ascribed to the duad, or number two, are, Phanes, Nature, Justice, Rhea, Diana, Cupid, Venus, Fate, Death, etc. Now Phanes, in the Orphic hymns, is the same with Protogonus; and Nature is called πρωτογενια, or first-born, and δικη, or Justice, as also πεπρωμενη, or Fate. Likewise Rhea is denominated, θυγατερ πολυμορφου Πωτογονοιο, or daughter, of much formed Protogonus; and in the same hymn the reader will find other epithets, which agree with the appellation given to Nature. Again, both Nature and Diana are called ωκυλοχεια, or swiftly bringing forth; and Love as well as Nature is called διφυη, or two-fold. In like manner Rhea and Venus agree, for he says of Venus παντα γαρ εκ σεθεν εστιν, for all things are from thee; and of Rhea, Μητηρ μεν τε θεων ηδε θνητων ανθρωτων, or mother of Gods and mortal men. After which he expressly says that earth and heaven, the sea and the air, proceed from her divinity. Besides this, he celebrates Venus as governing the three Fates; και ηρατεεις τρισσων μοιρων. And lastly he says of Love, after representing that Deity as invested with the keys of all things; thou alone rulest the governments of all these;[°] which he likewise affirms of Death in the same words. And thus much for the duad. The triad, or number three, they denominated Juno, Latona, Thetis, Hecate or Diana, Pluto, Tritogenia or Minerva, &c. Now Latona and Thetis, are each of them called in these initiations, κυανοπεπλος, or

---

[†] - παντων κληιδα εχοντας,
    Αιθερος, ουρανιου, κ.λ.

[‡] - ποντου κληιδας εχοντα.

[§] Σοι ποταμοι κρατεονται αει πασα θαλασσα.

[°] In the hymn to Love Μουνος γαρ τουτων παντων οιηκα κρατυνεις. And in that to death οι παντων θνητων οιηκα κρατυνεις.

dark-veiled; and Minerva and the Moon, who is the same with Diana, θηλυς και αρσην, female and male. The tetrad or number four, they denominated Hercules, Vulcan, Mercury, Bacchus, two-mothered, Bassarius, key-keeper of nature, Masculine, Feminine, the World, (which in these initiations is the same with Pan) Harmony, Justice. Now Onomacritus calls Hercules and Vulcan, Καρτεροχειρ, or strong-handed; and he celebrates Hercules and Mercury as "having an almighty heart." παγκρατες ητορ εχων. And so of the rest. The pentad or number five they called Nature, Pallas, Immortal, Providence, Nemesis, Venus, Justice, etc. Now Nature is called in these hymns, or rather initiations πολυμηχανε μητερ, or much-mechanic Mother, and παντοτεχνης, or universal Artist; and Minerva is denominated μητερ τεχνων, or Mother of Arts. Likewise Nature is expressly called αθανατη τε προνοια, or Immortal, and Providence. The hexad or number six, they denominated, Venus, Health, the World, Εκατηβελετις, or far-darting, (because compounded of the triad, which is called Hecate), Persaea, triform, Amphitrite, etc. Now Venus, as we have already observed in the names of the duad, is said to be the source of all things; and Health is expressly called μητερ απαντων, or Mother of all things. Again the heptad, or number seven they called Fortune, Minerva, Mars, etc. And Fortune, in these initiations, is the same with Diana or the Moon, who is called male and female as well as Minerva; and Minerva and Mars are each of them denominated οπλοχαρης or armipotent, and Minerva πολεμοκλονε, or full of warlike tumult. The ogdoad, or number eight, they called Rhea, Love, Neptune, Law. And the Mother of the Gods, who is the same with Rhea, is represented as we have observed on the monad, as governing rivers and every sea; and Love is said to have the keys of all things; of heaven, the deep, etc. The ennead, or number nine, they denominate Ocean, Prometheus, Vulcan, Poean (*i.e.* Apollo or the Sun), Juno, Proserpine, etc. Now Saturn (who is called in these initiations Prometheus) and Ocean, are each of them celebrated as the source of Gods and men: and Vulcan is expressly called ηλιος or the Sun. And lastly they denominated the decad, Heaven, the Sun, Unwearied, Fate, Phanes, Necessity, &c. Hence Heaven is called in these initiations φυλαξ παντων, or Guardian of all things; and the Sun πιστοφυλαξ, or faithful Guardian; and ακαμα or Unwearied, is an appellation of the Sun, in the hymn to that Deity. The reader too will find many epithets in the hymn to Protogonus or Phanes, corresponding with those of the Sun. And thus much for the agreement of these hymns, with the Pythagoric names of numbers. The limits of the present work will not permit me to be more explicit on this particular; but he who wishes to understand the meaning of many of the preceding appellations, may consult the valuable book of Meursius, already cited, where he will meet with abundant matter for deep speculation. But before I conclude this Dissertation, I must beg leave to acquaint the reader with another discovery which I have made respecting these hymns, equally curious with the former.

Ficinus, on Plato's Theology,[†] has the following remarkable passage, translated, most likely from some manuscript work of Proclus, as I conjecture from its conclusion; for, unfortunately, he does not acquaint us with the author. "Those who profess," says he, "the Orphic theology, consider a two-fold power in souls and in the celestial orbs: the one consisting in knowledge, the other in vivifying and governing the orb with which that power is connected. Thus in the orb of the earth, they call the nostic power Pluto, the other Proserpine.[‡] In water, the former power Ocean, and the latter Thetis. In air, that thundering Jove, and this Juno. In fire, that Phanes, and this Aurora. In the soul of the lunar sphere, they call the nostic power Licnitan Bacchus, the other Thalia. In the sphere of Mercury, that Bacchus Silenus, this Euterpe. In the orb of Venus, that Lysius Bacchus, this Erato. In the sphere of the sun, that Trietericus Bacchus, this Melpomene. In the orb of Mars, that Bassareus Bacchus, this Clio. In the sphere of Jove, that Sebazius, this Terpsichore. In the orb of Saturn, that Amphietus, this Polymnia. In the eighth sphere, that Pericionius, this Urania. But in the soul of the world, the nostic power, Bacchus Eribromus, but the animating power Calliope. From all which the Orphic theologers infer, that the particular epithets of Bacchus are compared with those of the Muses on this account, that we may understand the powers of the Muses, as intoxicated with the nectar of divine knowledge; and may consider the nine Muses, and nine Bacchuses, as revolving round one Apollo, that is about the splendour of one invisible Sun." The greater part of this fine passage is preserved by Gyraldus, in his *Syntagma de Musis*, and by Natales Comes, in his *Mythology*, but without mentioning the original author. Now if the Hymn to the Earth, is compared with the Hymns to Pluto and Proserpine; the one to Ocean, with that to Thetis; and so of the other elements agreeable to the preceding account, we shall discover a wonderful similitude. And with respect to the celestial spheres, Silenus Bacchus, who, according to the

---

[†] Lib. iv. p. 128.

[‡] The reader may observe that this two-fold power is divided into male and female; the reason of which distribution we have already assigned from Proclus.

preceding account, should agree with Mercury, is called in these initiations τροφη, or Nourishment, and Mercury, τροφιουχε, or Nourisher. Venus, who should agree with Lysius Bacchus, is called κρυφια or Occult, and ερατοπλοκαμος, or lovely-haired, and σεμνη Βακχοιο παρεδρε, or venerable attendant of Bacchus; and Lysius is denominated κρυψιγονος, or an occult offspring and καλλιεθειρα, or fair-haired. In like manner Trietericus Bacchus is called παιαν χρησεγχης, or Apollo pouring golden light, which evidently agrees with the sun. Again, Bassarius Bacchus is celebrated as rejoicing in swords and blood, ος ξιφεσιν χαιρεις, ηδ' αιμασι, κ.λ. which plainly corresponds with Mars, as the hymn to that Deity evinces in a particular manner. Sebazius and Jupiter evidently agree, for Sebazius is expressly called υιος Κρονου, son of Saturn. And Amphietus is celebrated as moving in concert with the circling hours, Ευαζων κινων τε χορους ενι κυκλασιν ωραις, which corresponds with Saturn, who is called in these Hymns Τιταν, or the Sun.† And lastly, Dionysius who is called in these Initiations Eribromus, is denominated δικερωτα, or two-horned, which is also an epithet of Pan, or the soul of the world. And thus much for the doctrine of these Hymns, so far as is requisite to an introductory Dissertation. What farther light we have been able to throw on these mysterious remains of antiquity, will appear in our following Notes. If the valuable Commentary of Proclus on the *Cratylus* of Plato was once published, I am persuaded we should find them full of the most recondite antiquity:‡ but as this

---

† I have omitted a comparison between the eighth sphere and Pericionius from necessity, because there is no hymn among the following to that orb. And I have not contrasted Licnitan Bacchus with the lunar Sphere, because the resemblance is not apparent; though doubtless there is a concealed similitude.

‡ This is evident from the following epistle of Lucas Holstenius to P. Lambecius, preserved by Fabricius in that excellent work, his Bibliotheca Graeca. tom. i. p. 117: "Habeo et Orphei exemplar non contemnendum, ex quo Argonautica plurimis locis emendavi. Auctor ille huc usque a Criticorum et Correctorum vulgo derelictus tuam exposcere videtur operam. Hymni autem reconditae antiquitatis plenissimi justum commentarium me entur, quem vel unius Procli scripta ανεκδοτα tibi instruent, ut ex notis meis ad Sallustium Philosophum prospicies: ne quid de caeteris, quos apud me habeo, Platonicis nunc dicam, in quibus της μυθικης θεολογιας thesaurus latet."
[Tr.: I have also a copy of Orpheus which is not to be despised and from which I have emended the Argonautica in several passages. This author, who has so far been neglected by the body of Critics and Emendators, seems to demand your attention. Moreover, the hymns are steeped in remote antiquity, and deserve an adequate commentary which even the unedited writings of Proclus alone will provide for you, as you will see from my notes on Sallust the Philosopher - to say nothing at the moment of the other writers on Plato I have with me, in whom there is a great wealth of mystical theology.]

is not to be expected in the present age, the lovers of ancient wisdom will, I doubt not, gratefully accept the preceding and subsequent elucidations. For on a subject so full of obscurity as the present, a glimmering light is as conspicuous, and as agreeable to the eye of the mind, as a small spark in profound darkness is to the corporeal sight.

Appendix II

A simplified guide to the Greek Theogony

By The Prometheus Trust[†]

This simple framework by which the choirs of the Gods may be considered is offered to those who are coming anew to the doctrine of the Gods: *it is by no means comprehensive or final (if such could be devised) but may be a help during the initial phases of study.*

At the outset it should be realised that the Gods, in themselves, are beyond all thought - even the very highest intuition - because they are super-essential, super-vital and super-intellectual. In other words they are beyond *being* which is that which the mind perceives. As Proclus says:[‡] "For we assume all things in the Gods except *The One*, as suspended from them and secondary, *viz.* essence, life and intellect. *For the Gods do not subsist in, but prior to these, and they produce and contain these in themselves, but are not defined in them.* But it is necessary not to be ignorant that these are in reality thus distinguished from each other." In other words, our intellect may perceive the differences between the gods by the natures which are produced by them; for the Gods produce Being, Life, Intellect, Soul, Nature and Matter from themselves as monads suspended from the unities. We know the Gods by their effects but we can never know them in themselves alone. Strictly speaking the names by which men address the gods are nothing but titles (or descriptions of their operations and processions).

Having understood this first point the aspiring philosopher should now be armed against the danger of imagining that he can rise above the Gods merely because he knows their descriptions. The human soul, noble and profound as she is, may - by exercising her whole self and discovering her own pure unity -*follow* the procession of the Gods.

Paradoxically, however, we can know nothing which is not of the gods, for "the gods fill all things" - and it is they who unfold into light that which is held by *The One* as utterly unknown. And so it is that those who aspire to understand both themselves and the universe must, with due reverence, look up to the Gods who are all good and all wisdom.

[†] The Trust would like to acknowledge the help of the Platonic Guild in the preparation of this appendix.

[‡] In *The Theology of Plato* Book i, 26 (TTS volume VIII.)

Proclus, in his Commentary on the *Parmenides* of Plato, writes that "all the processions of the Gods may be comprehended in six orders -

The Intelligible, [Noëtic]

The Intelligible-Intellectual, [Noëtic-noëric]

The Intellectual, [Noëric]

The Supermundane, [Supercosmic]

The Liberated and

The Mundane [Cosmic]."

He continues: "For the *intelligible*, as we have already observed, must hold the first rank, and must consist of *being, life,* and *intellect,* i.e. must *abide, proceed* and *return*, and this super-essentially; at the same time that it is characterized, or subsists principally according to *being*. But, in the next place, that which is both *intelligible* and *intellectual* succeeds, which must likewise be triple, but must principally subsist according to *life*, or *intelligence*. And, in the third place, the *intellectual* order must succeed, which is *triply convertive*. But as, in consequence of the existence of the sensible world, it is necessary that there should be some demiurgic cause of its existence, this cause can only be found in *intellect*, and in the last hypostasis of the *intellectual triad*. For all forms in this hypostasis subsist according to all-various and perfect divisions; and forms can only fabricate when they have a perfect intellectual separation from each other. But since *fabrication* is nothing more than *procession*, the demiurgus will be to the posterior order of the Gods what *The One* is to the orders prior to the *demiurgus*; and consequently he will be that secondarily which the first cause is primarily. Hence, his first production will be an order of Gods analogous to the *intelligible* order, and which is denominated *supermundane*. After this he must produce an order of Gods similar to the *intelligible-intellectual* order, and which are denominated *liberated* Gods. And in the last place, a procession correspondent to the *intellectual* order, and which can be no other than the *mundane* Gods. For the demiurgus is chiefly characterized according to diversity, and is allotted the boundary of all universal hypostases."

This six-fold division of the choirs of Gods, according to effect, underlies not only the work of Proclus, who can be considered as the last great philosopher of ancient Greece, but also Orpheus who was the first of her wise men. We reproduce here, with one emendation, G R S Mead's chart of the Orphic Theogony which appeared in his *Orpheus* (1896). The one change to the original is the repositioning of the *Abiding, Proceeding* and *Returning* from the Noëtic-noëric triad to the Noëtic triad: this is in conformity with the writings of Proclus who says: "All these likewise are uniform and *intelligible*, viz. the abiding, the proceeding and the returning."[†]

[†] *Theology of Plato*, iii, 14.

```
                    ╱─────────────╲
                   ╱ The Ineffable ╲
                  │                  │
                   ╲ Thrice-unknown ╱
                    ╲───Darkness───╱

                         Unaging Time

      The          The                      ⎧ Universal Good
      Primordial   One-Many-      △         ⎨ Universal Soul
      Triad        All                      ⎩ Universal Mind
```

Super-sensible World	Noëtic Triad	Being [Vestibule of the Good]	Bound (Hyparxis—Father) [One] 'The Abiding'	⎧ Æther ⎨ Chaos ⎩ Egg
			Infinity (Power—Mother) [Many] 'The Proceeding'	⎧ Egg [Night] containing the Triple God [The 'Dragon of Wisdom']
			Mixed (Mind—Son) [All] 'The Returning' [Beauty] [Truth] [Symmetry]	⎧ Phanes [Gt. Grandfather—Manifestor—Animal Itself] ⎨ Ericapæus ⎩ Metis
	Noëtic-noëric Triad	⎧ Essence ⎨ Life ⎩ Intellect,	Supercelestial Place [Plain of Truth; Kingdom of Adrastia]	
		Life ⎧ Infinite Power ⎩ Intelligible Life	Celestial Arch [Heaven]	Uranus [Grandfather]
		⎧ Intelligible Intellect	Subcelestial Arch	
	Noëric Triad [Hebdomadic]	Intellect	Cronus—Saturn [Father] [and a septenary hierarchy] Rhea [and a septenary hierarchy] Zeus—Jupiter (Demiurgus) [and a septenary hierarchy]	Curetic or Unpolluted Triad [each a septenary hierarchy]
			The Seventh Monad [The Separative Deity] Oceanus	
Sensible World	Super-cosmic Order	Demiurgic Triad	Jupiter—Celestial Jupiter Neptune—Marine Jupiter Pluto—Subterranean Jupiter	(Ruler of Inerratic Sphere) (Ruler of Planetary Spheres) (Ruler of Sublunary Region)
		Zoogonic Triad	⎧ Coric Diana ⎨ Coric Proserpine ⎩ Coric Minerva	The Corybantic Triad
		Apollinia-cal Triad	⎰ Apollo, the Triple Sun	Superessential Light Intellectual Light Sensible Light
	Liberated Order [Dodecad]	⎧ Jovian Monad ⎩ Vestan Monad	The Decad [completed by]	⎧ Apollo or the Prophetic Life ⎨ Mars or the Divisive Life ⎩ Venus or the Amatory Life
	Cosmic Order [Dodecad]	⎧ Fabricative Triad ⎨ Defensive Triad ⎨ Vivific Triad ⎩ Harmonic Triad	⎰ Jupiter ⎱ Vesta ⎰ Ceres ⎱ Mercury	Neptune Vulcan Minerva Mars Juno Diana Venus Apollo

Index to hymns by title

Adonis, To 118	Ippa, To 108
Amphietus Bacchus, To 114	Isis, To 256
Apollo, To 216	Jove, To 271
Apollo and the Sun, To ... 218	Juno, To 59
Apollo, To 83	Jupiter, Lightning, To 64
Artificer of the Universe ... 210	Jupiter, To 227
Aurora, To 146	Jupiter, To 56
Bacchus Pericionius, To ... 105	Justice, To 127
Bacchus, To 76	Latona, To 89
Being Itself, To 197	Latona, To 254
Boreas, To 148	Law, To 129
Ceralian Mother, To the ... 98	Leucothea, To 142
Ceres, To 240	Liberated Gods, To the 214
Ceres, To 96	Licknitus Bacchus, To 104
Clouds, To the 65	Life, To 199
Common Hymn, A 270	Love, To 245
Corybas, To 95	Love, To 120
Curetes, To the 93	Lysius Lenæus, To 109
Curetes, To the 77	Mars, To 130
Dæmon, To the 141	Melinoe, To 138
Death, To 158	Mercury, To 72
Diana, To 90	Mercury, To 238
Dionysius Bassareus, To ... 103	Mercury, To 251
Dreams, To Divinity of 157	Minerva, To 230
Earth, To 70	Minerva, To 232
Equity, To 128	Minerva, To 234
Esculapius, To 132	Minerva, To 268
Ether, To 35	Misa, To 99
Fates, To the 123	Mnemosyne, To 145
Fortune, To 139	Moon, To the 41
Furies, To the 136	Mother of Gods, To the ... 71
Furies, To the 134	Mother of Gods, To the ... 275
Graces, To the 125	Musæus, To 25
Health, To 133	Muses, To the 263
Heaven, To 34	Muses, To the 144
Hecate, To 28	Nature, To 44
Hercules, To 49	Nemesis, To 126
Intellect, To 201	Neptune, To 60
Intelligible, To the 195	Neptune, To 248
Intelligible-Intellectual Order	Nereids, To the 68
of Gods, To the 204	Nereus, To 67

Night, To 30	South Wind, To the 150
Nymphs, To the 110	Stars, To the 38
Ocean, To 151	Sun, To the 242
Osiris, To 255	Sun, To the 39
Palæmon, To 143	Sun and attendants, To the .. 259
Pallas, To 78	Terrestrial Hermes, To the . 119
Pan, To 47	Tethys, To 66
Pluto, To 61	Themis, To 147
Proserpine, To 74	Thundering Jupiter, To 63
Proteus, To 69	Titans, To the 91
Prothyræ, To the Goddess .. 29	Trietericus, To 112
Protogonus, To 36	Venus, To 116
Rhea, To 52	Venus, To 242
Rising Sun, To the 222	Venus, To 267
Sabazius, To 106	Venus, To 266
Saturn, To 51	Vesta, To 236
Seasons, To the 100	Vesta, To 153
Semele, To 102	Victory, To 82
Silenus, &c. To 115	Vulcan, To 131
Sleep, To 156	Zephyrus, To 149

Index to hymns by first line

A celebrated royal fount I sing	266
A fertile god, intelligible life	199
A lucid, royal, foam-begotten fount	242
A mother of gods and men	275
A sacred light I sing, which leads on high	263
Aerial Clouds, thro' heav'ns resplendent plains	65
Approach, queen Fortune, with propitious mind	139
Bacchus I call loud-sounding and divine	76
Bacchus Pericionius, hear my pray'r	105
Bacchus phrenetic, much nam'd, blest, divine	112
Blest Pæan, come, propitious to my pray'r	83
Boreas, whose wintry blasts, terrific, tear	148
Bounteous Ceres, thee I sing	240
Brass-beating Salians, ministers of Mars	93
Cadmean Goddess, universal queen	102
Ceralian queen, of celebrated name	98
Come, blessed Dionysius, various-nam'd	103
Dark-veil'd Latona, much invoked queen	89
Daughter of ægis-bearing Jove, divine	268
Daughter of Jove, Persephone divine	74
Daughter of Saturn, venerable dame	153
Daughters of darkling Night, much nam'd, draw near	123
Daughters of Jove and Themis, Seasons bright	100
Daughters of Jove, loud-sounding, and divine	144
Daughters of Nereus, resident in caves	68
Einodian Hecate, Trivia, lovely dame	28
Etherial father, mighty Titan, hear	51
Great Esculapius, skill'd to heal mankind	132
Great Heav'n, whose mighty frame no respite knows	34
Great nurse of Bacchus, to my pray'r incline (To Ippa)	108
Great nurse of Bacchus, to my pray'r incline (To Silenus)	115
Great progeny of Jove, divinely bright	230
Great zoogonic monad, thee I sing	232
Hail, mother goddess! beauteous offspring fam'd	270
Hear golden Titan! king of mental fire	259
Hear me, illustrious father, dæmon fam'd	106
Hear me, illustrious Furies, mighty nam'd	136
Hear me, illustrious Graces, mighty nam'd	125
Hear me, Jove's daughter, celebrated queen	90
Hear me, Jove's son, blest Bacchus, God of wine	109

Hear me, O Death, whose empire unconfin'd 158
Hear me, O Goddess, whose emerging ray 146
Hear, blessed Hermes, Maia's beauteous son 251
Hear, Goddess queen, diffusing silver light 41
Hear, golden Titan, whose eternal eye 39
Hear, Neptune, ruler of the sea profound 60
Hear, strenuous Hercules, untam'd and strong 49
Heav'nly, illustrious, laughter-loving queen 116
Hermes I sing, a god supremely bright 238
Hermes, draw near, and to my pray'r incline 72
Hermes, I call, whom Fate decrees to dwell 119
I call the mighty, holy, splendid, light 64
I call Thesmophorus, spermatic God 99
I call, great Love, the source of sweet delight 120
I call, Leucothea, of great Cadmus born 142
I call, Melinoe, saffron-veil'd, terrene 138
Illustrious Rhea, to my pray'r incline 52
Illustrious Themis, of celestial birth 147
Leaping Curetes, who with dancing feet 77
Learn, O Musæus, from my sacred song 25
Licknitan Bacchus, bearer of the vine 104
Magnanimous, unconquer'd, boist'rous Mars 130
Mother of Gods, great nurse of all, draw near 71
Much nam'd, and best of dæmons, hear my pray'r 118
Nature, all-parent, ancient and divine 44
Night, parent Goddess, source of sweet repose 30
Nymphs, who from Ocean fam'd derive your birth 110
O all-bountiful, all-powerful, and all-merciful Isis 256
O all-bountiful, all-powerful, and all-merciful Osiris 255
O blessed Equity, mankind's delight 128
O ever untam'd Ether, rais'd on high 35
O Fairest Offspring of a fire unknown 195
O Father Jove, who shak'st with fiery light 63
O Jove, much-honour'd, Jove supremely great 56
O Mighty first-begotten, hear my pray'r 36
O mighty Titans, who from Heav'n and Earth 91
O Mother Earth, of Gods and men the source 70
O much desir'd, prolific, gen'ral queen 133
O Nurs'd with Dionysius, doom'd to keep 143
O Powerful Victory, by men desir'd 82
O royal Juno, of majestic mien 59
O thou who are the mother of all vivific light 254
O Thou who dost the roots of Ocean keep 67
O universal mother, Ceres fam'd 96
O venerable Goddess, hear my pray'r 29
Ocean I call, whose nature ever flows 151

Of the mundane gods the king	227
Only-begotten, noble race of Jove	78
Parent of nature, venerable mind	271
Pluto, magnanimous, whose realms profound	61
Proteus I call, whom Fate decrees to keep	69
Saturn's daughter, ancient dame	236
Sea-born, aerial, blowing from the west	149
See! how with thund'ring fiery feet	222
Sleep, king of Gods, and men of mortal birth	156
Strong past'ral Pan, with suppliant voice I call	47
Strong, mighty Vulcan, bearing splendid light	131
Terrestrial Dionysius, hear my pray'r	114
Tethys from hoary Ocean's deeps	224
Tethys I call, with eyes cerulean bright	66
The consort I invoke of Jove divine	145
The highest order of the gods I sing	197
The holy king of Gods and men I call	129
The middle triad of the Gods I sing	204
The mighty liberated Gods I call	214
The mighty ruler of this earthly ball	95
The piercing eye of Justice bright I sing	127
The second monad of the ruling kings	248
The Sun's resplendent deity I sing	218
The third bright offspring of the thrice-unknown	201
The untam'd deity sublimely pure	234
Thee I invoke, blest pow'r of dreams divine	157
Thee, mighty Daemon, anagogic Love	245
Thee, mighty ruler of the world, I sing	216
Thee, mighty ruling Dæmon dread, I call	141
Thee, Nemesis, I call, almighty queen	126
Thee, Venus, royal Lycian queen, I sing	267
To thee great Demiurgus of the world	210
Vociferous Bacchanalian Furies hear	134
Wide-coursing gales, whose lightly leaping feet	150
With holy voice I call the stars on high	38